EMBODYING THE REVOLUTION

EMBODYING THE REVOLUTION

The Hebrew Experience and the Globalization of Modern Sports in Interwar Palestine

OFER IDELS

RUTGERS UNIVERSITY PRESS
New Brunswick, Camden, and Newark, New Jersey
London and Oxford

Rutgers University Press is a department of Rutgers, The State University of New Jersey, one of the leading public research universities in the nation. By publishing worldwide, it furthers the University's mission of dedication to excellence in teaching, scholarship, research, and clinical care.

Library of Congress Cataloging-in-Publication Data

Names: Idels, Ofer, author.
Title: Embodying the revolution : the Hebrew experience and the globalization of modern sports in interwar Palestine / Ofer Idels.
Description: New Brunswick, New Jersey : Rutgers University Press, [2025] | Includes bibliographical references and index.
Identifiers: LCCN 2025000818 (print) | LCCN 2025000819 (ebook) | ISBN 9781978844452 (paperback) | ISBN 9781978844469 (hardcover) | ISBN 9781978844476 (epub)
Subjects: LCSH: Sports—Palestine—History—20th century. | Jewish athletes—Palestine—History—20th century. | Zionism—Influence.
Classification: LCC GV663.I8 I34 2025 (print) | LCC GV663.I8 (ebook) | DDC 796.095694/09041—dc23/eng/20250210
LC record available at https://lccn.loc.gov/2025000818
LC ebook record available at https://lccn.loc.gov/2025000819

A British Cataloging-in-Publication record for this book is available from the British Library.

∞ The paper used in this publication meets the requirements of the American National Standard for Information Sciences—Permanence of Paper for Printed Library Materials, ANSI Z39.48-1992.

rutgersuniversitypress.org

For my family

The dead can be studied scientifically, but science cannot tell us what we desire to know about the dead. Or rather, those aspects of the past that can be studied scientifically do not yield the kinds of information or knowledge that drives us to the study of the past in the first place.

—Hayden White, 2005

In a Revolutionary ideology meant to channel the "sublime enthusiasm" of the people toward a sublime religion, that of the Supreme Being, and to make the people favor public over private interests, the "sublime project" suffered from a double threat: the moral law it proclaimed defied all representation, and the political structure it relied upon, by virtue of its representative principle, could only betray the sublime principles it meant to translate.

—Marie-Heléné Huet, 1994

We have not yet found a better way than that.

—Yehoshua Alouf, 1938

CONTENTS

	Preface	ix
	Introduction	1
1	Teaching Nordau to Play Football: Gymnastics and Sports Before and After World War I	11
2	Competing in Hebrew: Revolutionary Language and the Sporting Presence	25
3	"Keep away from the Prima Donnas": Hebrew Purpose and the Athletic Body	43
4	"The Whole World Will Know Our Answer": Sports, Internationalism, and the Jewish Return to History	61
5	"We Have to Learn to Sacrifice Everything": Militarism and the Zionist Desire for a Useful Experience	77
	Epilogue	93
	Acknowledgments	101
	Notes	103
	Bibliography	127
	Index	137

PREFACE

Many moons ago, when I was still an undergraduate student in the history department at Tel Aviv University, I found myself sitting among the crowd attending one of those "preparation for PhD" workshops. Everything was unfolding predictably, with each faculty member offering the usual clichés and advice you'd expect at such events, until one of the department's most respected professors entered the room, quickly stood up, and took the floor. "Writing a PhD," she said, "is dedicating your life to history." At the time, I thought she might be slightly exaggerating. Yet, now, many moons later, I realize she was right in more ways than I could have imagined. I don't mean it in the Romantic sense of the brooding intellectual devoting their life to art, but in a more practical sense—the sheer amount of time it took to bring this book to print. Though it was not an exceptionally long or tedious process, for several years working on this project consumed most of my days and nights. In simple terms, writing history was what I did.

With that, I embraced this task with earnestness, pondering not only history and historiography but also theory—particularly the "how" and "why" we today turn to the past. In our polarized and technologically fluid world, straightforward answers to these crucial questions remain elusive, and what seems like common knowledge one day can swiftly be upended the next. Thus, this book does not seek to present something entirely original or champion a new dogma or paradigm but rather aspires to spark curiosity, reflection, and rethinking in the spirit of humanism.

At its heart, this book is about Hebrew culture and modern sports; specifically, it explores the intersection of Jewish life in Mandatory Palestine with the global rise of the sporting spectacle during the interwar period. The young Hebrew athletes on the cover—standing on the field of the London stadium at the 1934 Women's World Games—embody much of this tension between the global and the local. At first glance, the image seems to capture a moment of triumph: teenage girls raising their national flag in the capital of the British Empire. But a second look reveals half-empty stands, with even the onlookers on the field—the so-called world—seemingly indifferent to the Jewish athletes' "return" to the international stage.

Yet the picture also hints at something more abstract and perhaps unexpected. We are accustomed to Zionist representations that, like its ideological rhetoric, idealize strong, muscular, and healthy Jewish figures. Yet, the athletes in this image are neither particularly strong nor exceptionally athletic. And notably, they are not men. Against this contrast, it might be tempting to view "muscular

Judaism" and Zionism as mere elitist ideological constructs, detached from the realities of daily life, identity, and experience. However, in what follows, I take a more nuanced approach, considering how the gap between these young, "ordinary-looking" women and the celebrated global athletic body is not a contradiction of Zionist ideology but rather an outcome of it.

Thus, although scholars of sport and Zionism may be its primary audience, this work is anchored by a third essential theme: revolution. Not revolution in the traditional political sense of a coup d'état, where the people overthrow a king to establish a new regime, but rather a more intimate process, in which people attempt to transform themselves; Specifically, the Zionist Revolution—with its ideological quest to reshape selfhood and experience through linguistic control, bodily transformation, and the creation of safe spaces—could resonate with a broader audience fascinated by these themes and open to engaging with the triumphs and tribulations of past revolutions. In methodological terms, this book contributes to ongoing conversations around the "emotional turn." Scholars engaged with phenomenology, presence, and postcritique—as well as historians exploring emotions and lived experience—will likely find its approach both relevant and thought-provoking.

Yet, regardless of your background, my suggestion is to approach the text slowly. Although it is a scholarly work, complete with its share of endnotes and primary sources, the not-so-long narrative is preferably meant to be read from start to finish. Those who are inclined to skim and summarize can still, of course, do so, but my friendly recommendation is to engage with it patiently and with curiosity, resisting the temptation to rush to abstract elevator-pitch conclusions. Instead, take the time to linger with the voices of the past, embracing the challenge of listening and thinking with "the other," along with the intellectual impasse it often presents.

EMBODYING THE REVOLUTION

INTRODUCTION

Israeli men and women have often been portrayed in popular culture as embodiments of physical strength and resilience. From the 1960s character Ari Ben Canaan, the intrepid captain of the *Exodus* played by Paul Newman, to Adam Sandler's *You Don't Mess with the Zohan,* Israelis are often depicted as determined individuals who can shape reality to their will.[1] Yet, a classic Israeli television skit from the 1990s offers a contrasting image of the Jewish body: a frail Hebrew athlete at the World Athletics Championships in Munich desperately relies on a brash Israeli bureaucrat pleading with the German referee for a better starting position.[2] This biting parody of Zionist hyper-exploitation of Holocaust memory is based on an acidic brand of parochial humor that may not "translate" well into other languages. However, the crux of the joke relies on the assumption that Israeli viewers instinctively grasp the image of their athletes as klutzes who require assistance.

This self-deprecating humor is rooted in cultural self-awareness, as Israelis rarely deny the accusation of lacking athletic skills.[3] On the contrary, they often accept it calmly and are more than satisfied by offering the intuitive, non sequitur, response: "We're just not good at it."[4] The empirical truth of this popular confession is another matter, but why, on the athletic field, do Israelis, so often, no longer see themselves as muscular "doers" but as weaklings who, as in the skit, can only scold the world once again: "Haven't the Jewish people suffered enough?" Why does a culture characterized by a firm adherence to physical cultivation have such a conflicted attitude toward what may be the most dominant global symbol of "strength," "health," and "manliness" in the twentieth century? This unexplained tension invites a new historical discussion about the "Hebrew experience" and the essence of Zionism that goes beyond academic and cultural clichés.

To that end, this study revisits what is arguably the most significant period in the history of modern sports—the interwar years (1918–1939)—and explores the origins of the gulf between modern sports and the Hebrew experience. Departing from the linguistic turn paradigm, in which "subjects are constituted discursively, and experience is a linguistic event," this study does not view human experience primarily as a performative and representational process of social constructs and hegemonic power.[5] Instead, it demonstrates that Hebrew culture's primary concern was the modern sporting spectacle's inherently emotional and autotelic experience.[6] The result sheds light on a rather unconventional case of an interwar society in which athletes did *not* attain a dominant position of national pride and distinction.

Drawing on newspaper articles, visual materials, archival sources, letters, and journals, this study navigates the transformative impact of the interwar years and the distinctions between gymnastics and modern sports (chapter 1), the modernization of Hebrew and origins of sports media (chapter 2), the dynamics of professionalism versus amateurism and the interwar juncture of gender and boxing (chapter 3), the emergence of international sports (chapter 4), and sports militarization (chapter 5). Through these topics and more, it contextualizes the emergence of Jewish sports in Palestine within broader historical frameworks, illustrating how Zionist ideology was not mere "white noise" but also was a decisive and enduring element of Jewish life in interwar Palestine. Thus, providing a renewed perspective on the appeal and rise of modern sports while reconstructing a fresh discussion on Zionist aesthetics and meaning.

WRITING ON ZIONISM AGAINST THE END OF HISTORY

Zionism was born out of chaos and suffering, a consequence of the upheaval of modernity that thrust European Jewish existence into crisis with profound epistemological and ontological implications. As radicalized politics intensified and financial and demographic troubles deepened, the escalation of antisemitism into brutal pogroms shattered the progressive promises of emancipation. This turbulence gave rise to a deep preoccupation with Jewish culture and identity,[7] and to a wide range of proposals for resolving the "modern Jewish question."[8] Some chose to remain in Europe, others sought refuge in the "New World," but a small number turned toward a different path: a "return" to the "Old World," to what they understood as their ancestral land—Eretz Israel.

In retrospect, the success of Zionism is nearly indisputable. From a small group of a few thousand settlers in the early twentieth century, who lacked a unified culture and language, the Jewish community in Palestine (the Yishuv) grew with remarkable speed during the interwar years. It established a vast array of institutions and saw its population swell to nearly a half-million. This trajectory of growth continued after the Holocaust, culminating in the founding of the State of Israel in 1948 as a central hub of Jewish life.

Yet, despite these undeniable achievements, Zionism was not always regarded at the time as an obvious, popular, or rational solution. The movement's ambitions transcended the mere pursuit of statehood and political autonomy, offering its followers a bold, revolutionary vision. Defying an era perceived as bereft of prospects, Zionists embraced hope and action while casting aside the religious and diasporic experiences that had seemingly consigned Jews to a perpetual state of passivity and degeneration. Instead, they envisioned the emergence of an active, sovereign "New Jew," or Hebrew, reclaiming a rightful place in history by living in Zion, speaking Hebrew, and cultivating both physical and mental vitality. Zionist aspirations therefore extended far beyond the establishment of society and culture, aiming to "build" and "revive" the very essence of human experience—language, body, and space.[9]

These revolutionary notions, however, are often foreign to the prevailing globalized liberal worldview, which tends to view agency and selfhood in different, ideological terms. Thus, while living in what is sometimes considered the "end of history," the desires of people in the past to radically shape themselves and the future are frequently perceived as tired metaphors or deceptive statements that obscure "true" experience, which is either resisting or being manipulated by ideology. As Sophie Wahnich, for example, argued regarding the historiography of the French Revolution, "We are no longer in an age in which different standpoints argue over an event that resists interpretation, but rather one of unquestioned detestation of the event."[10] This monolithic view may be waning, yet it is unsurprising that, in recent decades, the study of revolution has reached a "interpretive cul-de-sac," where—as David A. Bell and Yair Mintzker describes—much research continues to focus on familiar themes such as human rights and global influences.[11]

This tendency to "fit revolutions into different transnational historical frameworks" also characterizes current scholarship on Jewish life in twentieth-century Palestine.[12] Downplaying past political and intellectual historiography for its Zionist sentiments and emphasis on the dominant revolutionary pioneers (*halutzim*), recent studies tend to interpret Zionist ideology as a façade and its primary goal—the "New Jew"—as myth.[13] Consequently, the once-prevailing themes of revolution and selfhood have been overshadowed by discussions of colonialism and materialistic-nostalgic "daily life" anecdotes, which contemporary rationale categorizes as "historical truths."[14] As the historian Gur Alroey noted, he wishes to focus on "'simple' people . . . whose work and deeds in Jewish Palestine were driven not from purely ideological terms but from pragmatic economic considerations."[15]

Accordingly, advocates of this globalized approach frequently highlight the significant urban, non-pioneer, Jewish sectors in Palestine, alongside the diverse pragmatic reasons that drew Jews to the region and shaped their lives. Certainly, without events such as the US Immigration Act of 1924 and the rise of Nazism in 1933, which triggered waves of "bourgeois migrations," the size and character of the young and dynamic Yishuv would have been markedly different. However, does this attest to ideological diversion, suggesting that Jewish urban dwellers in Palestine were indifferent to Zionist Revolutionary aspirations for a new selfhood? Although it is undeniable that the experience of the small Jewish minority in interwar Palestine—like that of any community—was continuously shaped by a complex tapestry of political, social, and cultural circumstances, it seems unlikely that the mere 3 percent of the global Jewish population who *chose*, for whatever reason, to emigrate to the Middle East, were entirely unaffected by the existential and ideological promises of the Zionist Revolution for a new Jewish experience. Thus, perhaps in response to our current dichotomous scholarly notions, we should heed historian Jochen Hellbeck's suggestion to think of ideology not as a binary phenomenon but as "a ferment working in individuals and producing a great deal of variation as it interacts with the subjective life of a particular person."[16]

Modern sports provide a compelling lens through which to explore these key issues. Fueled by the rise of nationalism, internationalism, and mass culture, sports quickly expanded in the interwar years beyond its British roots to become a global phenomenon.[17] Jews, in particular, eagerly embraced the athletic body, with Jewish champions thriving in both the United States and Central Europe, where the standardized rules of competition appeared to transcend social and ethnic divides.[18] However, in Tel Aviv and Haifa, there was no "golden age" of Jewish sports, because local Hebrew culture mostly considered modern competitions a form of foreign mimicry "with no reason or honor."[19] Consequently, the fundamental perspective of all political and cultural factions, including many of the athletes themselves, openly rejected this new form of physical competition. As the prominent athlete Walter Frankel ruefully complained, "We Hebrews have been removed from sports. One can hear open derision from our people toward our movement of physical improvement. Our true attitude toward sports is yet to be determined."[20]

But why was Hebrew culture hesitant to embrace sports? From a globalized perspective, one might argue that the chronology of sports in the Yishuv reflects a disjunction between the vigorous public criticism of Zionism and the capacity of elitist revolutionary ideology to influence the lives of the masses. In this view, the absence of an athletic "golden age" in Palestine could be attributed to the relatively small population and limited resources. However, although demographic and material factors played a role, the primary protagonists of this book—the men and women responsible for the development of Jewish sports in Palestine, whom I refer to as "Hebrew Athletes"—tell a different story.

Comprising some 15,000 physical culturists, most of whom were born around the turn of the twentieth century and arrived in Palestine during their youth or early adulthood, the Hebrew Athletes were a diverse tapestry of athletes, coaches, journalists, and association members, primarily residing in the major cities of Jerusalem, Haifa, and Tel Aviv.[21] Representing a range of political affiliations, organizations, and roles, they typically belonged to an affluent, well-connected urban class that wielded a pervasive cosmopolitan influence and established and organized numerous clubs and events, including sending delegations to international competitions and matches during the interwar years.[22]

And yet, despite their prolific work and their urban-bourgeois characteristics, the main theme in their writings was not pride in their numerous accomplishments but an unfulfilled desire to contribute to the revolutionary undertaking.[23] In other words, rather than rejecting prevailing mores, according to which sport "will not be our salvation and will give us neither a healthy body nor a healthy soul,"[24] these Hebrew Athletes actually often sided with them. Hence, in their frequently melancholy writings, they repeatedly ask how they may overcome the "purposelessness" of modern sport and contribute to creation of a "a new Hebrew type, healthy of mind and body and of an honest and generous soul."[25]

Such a statement coming from individuals who were generally not part of the hegemonic pioneer elite, but rather were "simple" urban people, implies that ideology is not a binary zero-sum game, resulting in either fantasy or history. Accordingly, as this book demonstrates, the Hebrew Athletes consistently viewed sport through a revolutionary mindset aimed at forming a new selfhood, experience, and meaning. Their perspective on sport, therefore, was rarely confined to its physical benefits but extended to its impact on their desire to "learn to know ourselves, the problems of our nation, the path we follow—the path of salvation."[26]

POSTCRITICAL READING AND RECEPTIVITY TO THE PEOPLE OF THE PAST

It remains unclear, however, how we, as contemporary readers, can engage with and derive meaning from such historical statements when they seem so foreign to our current worldview. One way is to treat language as a nominalist conception, thus viewing ideological phrases like "salvation" as no more than empty words that conceal the supposedly "real" human yearnings that lurk behind the text. Yet, like many revolutionaries, Zionists rarely desired to deconstruct language but to reconstruct through it a new experience (chapter 2).[27] In that spirit, and akin to a diverse range of contemporary theories in the humanities, it may be more useful to try and listen to the Zionist ideological language.[28]

This "naive" attempt to listen to the people of the past resonates strongly with the principles and approaches found in the ongoing scholarly attempt to form new reading and interpretation via postcritique.[29] Revisiting the writing of renowned French philosopher Paul Ricoeur, advocates of postcritique like contemporary literary scholar Rita Felski remind us that the common "hermeneutics of suspicion" is not a default but rather a simple genre choice and that Ricoeur himself suggested an additional non-imposing possibility: reading in a desire to learn about the text and the world from the text itself.[30]

Rejecting both conspiracy theories that claim to expose the true "power mechanisms" and the postmodern critical theory "decoder," scholars of postcritique emphasize that "critics who think they are uncovering hidden truths don't read any differently from critics who don't share this picture of reading."[31] Hence, although they categorically oppose the notions of "deep" or "close" reading, they encourage a return to text and language "with respect, care, and attention, emphasizing the visible rather than the concealed, in a spirit of dialogue and constructiveness rather than dissection and diagnosis."[32]

Postcritical insights therefore, allow us to return to the sources of the Zionist Revolution free from Marxian or Freudian suspicions and from the familiar grand narratives of colonialism, nationalism, or "globalization" that repeatedly emphasize materialist interests, power, and well-being as the primary agents of history.[33] Consequently, The following text, , is often less concerned with uncovering "what really happened" through the deconstruction or aggregation of data than with confronting the sources "nakedly," echoing Hayden White's assertion that history "could hardly be more complete or more compelling in regard to its 'facticity'; what we need are imagination and poetic insight to help us divine its meaning."[34] Dispelling the false hope of achieving a "scientific" feel, it, thus, embraces the notion that language carries an essence of "truth," fostering a *decelerated reading experience* that, as Ricoeur claimed, posits that the essential first step toward meaningful interpretation is faith.[35]

THE AESTHETICS OF SPORTS AND THE VOICE OF THIS TEXT

Such postcritical faith, deliberately distancing itself from both cynicism and nostalgia, acquires special significance when reflecting on the ambivalent history of modern sports. Since their inception in eighteenth-century Britain, modern athletic competitions have been intertwined with various conceptualizations that portray them as "pure" and "holy" phenomena existing for their own sake.[36] This notion, most famously encapsulated by the belief that sports stand apart from politics, has long puzzled scholars, who have often sought to interpret sports as symbols of "something else."[37] Framing modern sports within broader contexts such as nationalism, globalization, or class struggle, to name just a few, has its advantages, yet it also neglects the visceral aesthetic experience at the heart of the modern spectacle. Thus, inspired by postcritique and the phenomenological work of Hans Ulrich Gumbrecht, I attempt to follow and reposition this autotelic aesthetic experience at the core of the modern historical sporting spectacle, as well as its tension with the Zionist Revolution.[38]

And indeed, more than its social characteristics, Hebrew athletes were continually anxious about the aesthetic experience of the modern sporting spectacle. Thus, they continuously refused to reconcile the autotelic nature of modern sports with their distinctive visceral revolutionary desires and aspired to infuse the seemingly "purposeless" and soulless athletic act with an existential essence that transcended the playing field or the arena through action. Such a paradigm, however, also dictates that the Zionist meaning must be conferred from the "outside," the world of sports. Hence, the Hebrew Athletes were not celebrated as incarnations of extraordinary professional, physical, and moral attributes but were shaped to *be* and *behave* like "normal people." In simpler terms, for Hebrew Athletes to become symbols of the nation, they had to *embody the revolution*.

This does not mean that Zionist criticism regarding sports was always unique.[39] If we isolate and contextualize many of their arguments, we can identify a tapestry of global connections and influences. Certainly, as the popularity of sporting spectacles increased during the interwar years, they sparked numerous lively, global social and cultural debates surrounding the young sensation, addressing issues such as gender, colonialism, nationalism, and eventually modernity itself. For instance, we can note that, somewhat paradoxically, the attitude of the members of Morgenshtern—the Bund's physical-culture organization—may have been the closest to that of the Hebrew Athletes.[40] The Yiddishist athletes may have openly reviled Zionism, but like their Jewish siblings in Palestine, they also loathed competitive sports and professionalism, often boycotting popular sports such as football and boxing. Such parallels highlight the difficulties of understanding the pre–World War II Yishuv without its Eastern European context and demonstrate that, in various parts of the globe, sports mirrored modernity, eliciting similar reactions and counteractions.

Nonetheless, like all cultures, Zionists often interpreted this "athletic discourse" in a way that aligned with their own desires. For example, during the interwar years, a dual phenomenon emerged: On the one hand, "extreme" sporting activity was deemed hazardous to the female body and its reproductive capacities, whereas, on the other hand, the rising tide of feminist advocacy ensured that female athletes gained increased visibility and presence in traditionally male-dominated arenas like the Olympic Games.[41] Hebrew female athletes were active participants in this dynamic. However, interwoven with this struggle was a distinct local narrative, shared by the athletes themselves, that viewed the female athletic body as central to the Zionist Revolution—not only for its heredity potential but also for its ability to showcase the new Hebrew self internationally, thereby "returning the Jews to history."[42]

This text, therefore, situates Hebrew Athletes within the expansive global context of the interwar sports boom yet focuses primarily on a key Zionist revolutionary voice. Accordingly, as with any historical account, the following narrative is neither exhaustive nor comprehensive but rather an exploration of a dominant and often overlooked perspective in the annals of Zionism. Thus, the viewpoints of female and rank-and-file athletes, as well as their interactions with Arab athletes, are woven into the narrative, predominantly guided by the Yishuv's two main sports organizations: Maccabi, founded in 1906 and later associated with the Jewish liberal demographic, and Hapoel (the worker), aligned with the dominant socialist-pioneer-labor movement.

Engaging with this crucial voice, as Felski suggests, "with respect, care, and attention," does not require us to empathize or identify with it.[43] On the contrary, accentuating the revolutionary zeal of the Hebrew Athletes repeatedly reveals their distinctiveness from contemporary sensibilities. It asks us to remain open to the possibility that people meant what they wrote, even when their language was "steeped in ideology."[44]

WHAT'S AHEAD

The following five chapters, therefore, illuminate how the Hebrew Athletes imbued their world with meaning. Chapter 1 propels the narrative by exploring the origins of the Zionist–sporting tension during the interwar years. In contrast to traditional historiography, which often traces the beginnings of Zionist sports to Max Nordau's 1898 "Muscular Judaism" (*Muskeljudentum*) speech or the 1906 establishment of the first Maccabi club in Jaffa, I argue that modern competitive sports reached Palestine only after World War I. The chapter, therefore, establishes a novel global historical framework for discussing Hebrew sports in Palestine. By differentiating between modern sports and gymnastics (*Turnen*), it underscores the moment when the Hebrew physical-culturist revolutionary flag weakened and the disconnect between modern sports and Jewish life in Palestine emerged.

After presenting the historical background and the interwar period as a transformative era for modern sports, chapters 2 and 3 elucidate the gaps and tensions between Zionism and the autotelic elements of sports. Chapter 2 describes the limited capacity of the Hebrew language and the occasional reluctance of Hebrew speakers to use that language to articulate the sportive experience, whereas chapter 3 points out the Zionist hesitation to ascribe revolutionary meaning to the "purposeless" athletic body.

The next two chapters present the varied efforts of Hebrew Athletes to bridge the gap between sports and the Hebrew experience. Chapter 4 focuses on Zionist attempts to integrate into the international sports community, notably through the Fédération Internationale de Football Association (FIFA) and the International Olympic Committee (IOC). Seen as avenues through which the Zionists could contribute to their revolutionary cause, these global platforms' foundational principles quickly led to conflict with the Hebrew Athletes. By highlighting this tension, particularly the separation of participation from ethnic identity, the chapter adds a missing emotional dimension to the growing study of Jews and internationalism, demonstrating how, paradoxically, the longing to "return to history" led to the continued alienation of the Hebrew body.

The fifth and final chapter concludes the exploration of body and language themes with a discussion on the amalgamation of sports and military training during the latter half of the 1930s. Focusing on the period of the Arab Revolt of 1936, the chapter highlights the emergence of the soldier-figure as a central symbol in the Zionist national ethos and describes how Hebrew athletes perceived the escalation of the Jewish-Arab conflict as a particular opportunity to engage in the revolutionary struggle by transforming their "purposeless" athletic bodies into soldiers. Thus, by embracing paramilitary training, which they referred to as "useful sport" (*sport shimushi*), the Hebrew Athletes, albeit temporarily, tragically fulfill the revolutionary experience they had sought amid overt and violent upheaval.

The epilogue concludes the narrative by summarizing the themes, processes, and events explored in the previous chapters and extending the discussion on Zionist/Israeli sports from 1939 to the present. Emphasis is placed on the global moment of the 1990s and early decades of the 2000s and the enduring, though often obscure, traces of the Zionist Revolution. Indeed, in retrospect, one can say that the Zionist revolutionary language had a distinct shelf life. However, although the revolutionary vocabulary has dulled somewhat with the passage of time, the absurdist skit with which I began this introduction points to the fact that the specific experience created by the Zionist Revolution in the early twentieth century has not fully disappeared in today's globalized Israel. Thus, "returning" to the past without deconstructing it through contemporary conventions of nostalgia and cynicism is not merely a historical-methodological desideratum but a démarche that carries profound consequences for the exploration of contemporary Israel and the hope for a better and more peaceful future.

1 • TEACHING NORDAU TO PLAY FOOTBALL

Gymnastics and Sports Before and After World War I

In late 1932, an entry appeared in the Hebrew journal of Maccabi, the Jewish physical-culture movement: "The idea of the muscleman has conquered almost the whole world. Many must have mocked the idea of sports as they habitually mock any new phenomenon . . . but what many failed to comprehend just a short time ago they now see as fact." Illuminating the novelty of the "new phenomenon," this statement succinctly reflects on the interwar transformation of modern sports, from being scorned to becoming an idea that "conquered almost the whole world."[1] It emphasizes that the emergence of sports in the small Jewish Yishuv was not an isolated local event but part of a global process that developed between the world wars. As contemporary historian Barbara Keys has told us, during the 1930s, sports contests underwent rapid globalization during which they "attained a level of popularity and worldwide significance that set them apart from what came before and that crystallized the attributes that would shape the enormous sport extravaganzas of the second half of the twentieth century."[2]

This contextualization and periodization are particularly significant for the historiography of modern sports in the Yishuv. The literature tends to examine Jewish sports development in Palestine as a local-national historical phenomenon, consequently, it frequently recounts an internal Jewish–Zionist narrative that begins with Zionist leader Max Nordau's 1898 "invention" of "Muscular Judaism" (*Muskeljudentum*) and continues directly to the establishment of the first Maccabi club in Palestine in 1906.[3] Countering this conventional narrative, this chapter presents an alternative chronology for the origins of sports in the Yishuv by arguing that, like many places around the globe, the development of

Jewish sports in Palestine should be examined with a focus on the second and third decades of the twentieth century.

Such an exploration, however, beckons contemporary readers to reimagine the familiar sporting spectacle through the lens of its historical context, encouraging us to view this invented tradition as a specific historical process that was once far from self-evident. As Keys notes, "Sport occupies center stage in today's conceptions of 'physical culture' to such an extent that we now find it difficult to grasp just how historically conditioned and narrowly framed it is."[4] Recognizing sports' evolving meaning invites comparison with other modern physical cultures, notably gymnastics.[5] Specifically, highlighting, the often-overlooked history of gymnastics underscores that Nordau and the early Maccabi members ardently supported it while frequently opposing modern sports. Thus, illuminating that, contrary to existing scholarship, the early pre–World War I Maccabi activities in Palestine should not merely be seen as the modest beginnings of the organization's rich sports legacy but also as an earlier chapter overshadowed by a dramatic shift with significant implications.

A CONCISE HISTORY OF THE ORIGINS OF GYMNASTICS AND MODERN SPORTS

Despite the crucial significance of the interwar years, modern sports did not begin with the 1918 Armistice or the Treaty of Versailles. In fact, the word "sport" is not new; some of its manifestations date back to fourteenth-century England. Nonetheless, the *Oxford English Dictionary* for example, defines sport as "an activity involving physical exertion and skill, esp[ecially] (particularly in modern use) one regulated by set rules or customs in which an individual or team competes against another or others."[6] Thus, according to this definition, sports are a historical act primarily associated with the period known as modernity, which are distinguished from other physical activities and skills that do not involve competition.[7] This conceptualization is reinforced by scholars in various disciplines who point out that, unlike "traditional games," modern sports are not a parochial custom demarcated by the bounds of a specific community but are based on fixed rules that impose discipline on violence as an expression of the modern separation of the public and the private domains and of work and leisure.[8]

This perspective is also reflected in prevailing historical research, which customarily positions the onset of modern sports in eighteenth-century England, as marked by the writing of rules meant to determine an explicit winner. In the course of the nineteenth century, this measurable change, which also allowed gambling and economic gains to occur, was given an added dimension of values when the elitist schools of the burgeoning British "middle class" mated the discourse of sport with markedly anti-aristocratic values such as courage, selflessness, teamwork, toughness, discipline, and fair play.[9] Hence, in the eyes of the new British bourgeoisie, the rugby pitch served as a platform for transforming the youth into the "new man," fit to serve across the empire.[10]

As the nineteenth century proceeded, sports began to seep into American culture and the British working class as well.[11] Although still almost totally male, this process expedited the popularization of sports and enabled the number of sports settings, events, and clubs to grow significantly within twenty-five years.[12] Concurrently, the sporting phenomenon began to overstep the boundaries of the Britain and America world.[13] And indeed, by the turn of the twentieth century, clubs devoted to football, rugby, track and field, and other sports were already established across Europe and beyond. However, they still commanded the interest of mostly small and elitist population groups and did not translate into a phenomenon of perceptible global cultural importance.[14]

The limited interest in sports competition outside the United Stats and the British world does not mean that European men and women had no interest in their bodies: Indeed, while men in Britain played cricket and various versions of football, those in Central Europe embraced gymnastics to nurture both body and soul. Like British sports, the formation of gymnastics was closely tied to modernity and the German middle class's need to educate itself in new standards of masculinity, aesthetics, and health.[15] The first gymnastics club was established in 1811 in Berlin by educator Friedrich Ludwig Jahn. Originally its activities were strongly influenced by German patriotic tendencies that followed Prussia's fall to Napoleon.[16] Nonetheless, the German gymnasts did not engage intensively in competition. Instead, their aim was to nurture the nexus of body and nation through the medium of physical activity. For this purpose, they invented and perfected individual-strength equipment such as the pommel horse, parallel bars, gymnastics rings, and a welter of devices that ostensibly promoted harmony and solidarity between the individual and the national body.[17]

This worldview of gymnastics resonated strongly, yet its rise in popularity occurred primarily at the turn of the century when it became associated with the *Lebensreform* ("life reform") movement. Its linking with the struggle against degeneration and the ills of modernity infused gymnastics with widespread practices such as nudism, hiking, and vegetarianism.[18] Accordingly, while sports remained chiefly an elitist and limited phenomenon outside the United States and the British Empire, gymnastics clubs established a transnational presence.[19]

THE SHORT HEYDAY OF (JEWISH) GYMNASTICS

Gymnastics was warmly embraced within the Jewish world.[20] The first Jewish gymnastics club was established in Istanbul in 1895, and in the ensuing years institutions that sought, to varying extents, to transform Nordau's idea of "muscular Judaism" into physical reality began to sprout throughout Europe.[21] This proliferation of gymnastics resonated profoundly with the aspirations of Zionism. The intertwining of gymnastics with nationalistic rhetoric and the ideals of *Lebensreform* proved a natural fit for a movement dedicated to transcending the entrenched notions of degeneration, neuroticism, and deformity that had long stigmatized Jews in the Western world. Consequently, in the eyes of many turn-of-the-century Zionists, the experience of the "revival" of the Jewish body and mind was intricately tied to the pervasive language of gymnastics. Thus, it was an expression of the zeitgeist, when, Nordau concluded his article by stating his hope that "the Jewish gymnastics association [would] blossom and flourish and set an example for all centers of Jewish life!"[22]

The cultural presence of "Jewish gymnastics" was also evident in Palestine. Initial signs of gymnastics in the region can be found already in the mid-nineteenth-century curricula of the Evelina de Rothschild and Lemel schools in Jerusalem.[23] Yet, it was only in 1905, as part of the revolutionary momentum of the Second Aliya (1904–1914), which witnessed the growth of Tel Aviv and the establishment of the Hebrew Gymnasium in Jaffa, that a new stage of Hebrew gymnastics was ushered in: No longer an amateurish activity taught by uncertified instructors merely to improve the health of the pupils, it became a vital platform for national "revival."

Thus, in 1906, the Hebrew Gymnasium's doctor, Leo Cohen, founded the Rishon Lezion-Jaffa Jewish Gymnastics Association and started, de facto, the Maccabi movement in the region.[24] Although the new club soon fizzled because of Cohen's unexpected death, it reopened in 1908 and ushered in the development of organized Hebrew gymnastics in Palestine. Likewise, in 1911, the sons of the Hebrew educator David Yellin and students at his teachers' college established a separate association that they called Maccabi Jerusalem.[25] Aided by an itinerant teacher named Ernst Hermann, Maccabi associations were established in Petah Tikva, Haifa, Zikhron Ya'akov, Rehovot, and other villages.[26] These local developments gained national cachet in 1912, when the citywide associations in Jerusalem and Tel Aviv merged with that in Petah Tikva to form a national organization called the Maccabi Eretz Israel Federation.[27]

Even though the flourishing of Hebrew gymnastics was culturally supported by the aftermath of the Young Turks Revolution, as with Nordau, the nexus of gymnastics and Zionism was a conservative choice. This transfer of "familiar" knowledge is perhaps why Maccabi's membership was so diverse, representing a broad swath of the Jewish political map: immigrants, pioneers, the native-born, women, and even haredim for a short time. Given gymnastics' reputation, Maccabi's political aspirations were also high, seeking vigorously to disseminate gymnastics among all "walks of the nation" and to "unify and organize for the work of revival on the basis of gymnastics."[28] In other words, Maccabi leaders envisioned the gymnastics association as the focal point of Hebrew life in Palestine. "Esteemed audience!" proclaimed one of the movement's spokespeople in a speech in Jerusalem, "you have come to see gymnastics, the gymnastics that develops the body, the *gymnastics, solely by means of which we Sons of Israel will be able to raise a generation healthy in body and in mind*."[29]

Maccabi, however, never fulfilled its political and cultural ambitions. The movement's initial activities were heavily tainted by sloppiness and poor organization.[30] Disorder often originated from ongoing deficiencies in professional knowledge that bedeviled and sometimes totally stymied routine training. Such troubles were not unique in the young and impoverished Yishuv. However, after World War I, it was the pioneers who became the hegemonic ethos and engine of the Zionist Revolution. Thus, while Maccabi gymnasts were still struggling to organize a Saturday trip, the more radical pioneers quickly established the Histadrut (the General Federation of Jewish Labor in Palestine) in 1920, putting an end to Maccabi's political aspirations to serve as the organizer of Hebrew life in Palestine. In the mid-1920s, the Histadrut even founded its own body-culture organization, Hapoel, which broke Maccabi's monopoly on its own physical "home court." From then on, organized Hebrew physical activity would have an overarching class dimension that rendered the basic "Maccabian" aspiration to represent all "walks of the nation" irrelevant.[31]

THE ASCENDANCY OF SPORTS AND THE DECLINE OF GYMNASTICS

The decline of Hebrew gymnastics was closely tied to the global interwar rise of modern sports and the emergence of new perspectives on play and the human body, succinctly captured by a Maccabi member: "In the game, there is one purpose: to win."[32] But the embrace of this competitive view had to be learned, as it marked a major departure from the pre-war gymnastics perspective. As Zvi Nishri, the first professional gymnastics teacher in the Yishuv and the unofficial intellectual of Hebrew body culture in Palestine, explained,

> Of all enlightened peoples, the British were distinct in their physical education in our times. With them, everything takes place by competition. . . . A fierce war between the sports devotees and the gymnasts went on for some time. . . . In England and in America, too, sports of all types have developed in the past century . . . but these sports have a great drawback: they do not offer complete development that encompasses the entire body. While gymnastics tries to develop the weak limbs of the body and harmonize all bodily strengths, sport always chooses areas of activity in which one can excel and develop the stronger parts of the body at the expense of the other weak ones.[33]

Simply put, gymnastics and competitive sports were regarded as distinct and often opposing phenomena.[34]

And indeed, body culture in the Yishuv before World War I was mostly associated with enjoyment and relaxation, not competition and winning. In May 1908, for example, the local *Hashkafa* newspaper ran an article titled "A Little Sport,"[35] in what seems to have been the first use of the word *sport* in the Hebrew press. Here, however, as in other articles from the turn of the century, the concept does not denote competition but serves as a synonym for amusement and friendly play while hunting and going on outings in carts and automobiles.[36] In that manner, the sporting games that took place in the 1912 "Rehovot Festivities" (*Hagigat Rehovot*) included, alongside wrestling and football, tug-of-war, leapfrog (*chikhrada, чихарда,*) and horse races, accompanied by "cheering and gunfire."[37]

In this spirit of gymnastics, the objective of sporting games before the Great War was to provide a liberating and "natural" experience that promoted happiness, cooperation, and national solidarity.[38] "Games are especially valuable for moral education," wrote a member of Maccabi in his explanation of the fundamentals of gymnastics: "No matter how well we play the game, we cannot manifest ourselves and our personal traits in it. The individual is subsumed into the collective of his comrades at play and submits to the general game and its ideas." The author continued, "By playing games, we learn that we do not exist for ourselves and that only by collaborating with everyone can we attain the goal that humanity has set for itself. It demands of us self-sacrifice, defeat of self-pride, and setting aside our personal qualities. In this manner, game-playing serves as an educational medium."[39]

This national gymnastics outlook was reflected in how the people of the Yishuv understood "competitive sports." Thus, the new game called *kaduregel* (football), for instance, was defined in the Hebrew press as "something like gymnastics," and like most "sportive games" that took place in the prewar Yishuv, it was not customary to count time, keep scores, or play by clear and fixed rules.[40] "The game of football was played very primitively back then," the Maccabi member Yosef Yekutieli recalled in 1936: "Players would climb onto one of the sandy fields near Tel Aviv, split into two camps, take off their jackets and hats, and each camp built a goal for itself from its comrades' jackets and coats. They did not adhere to the rules of the game because they did not know them."[41] It was not only a lack of funds that forced the games to be played this way but also the "gymnastics worldview" that believed in health, enjoyment, and natural happiness, according to which the game was played not to determine a winner but for "Sabbath pleasure, family pleasure, and comradely pleasure."[42]

The worldview of gymnastics rapidly lost purchase after the war. As the Yishuv expanded during the interwar years—from a small and somewhat marginal society of several tens of thousands into a small but mass society numbering nearly a half-million people and equipped with multiple forms of infrastructure—the rise of sports was locally described as "indubitable." As early as 1929, for example, a commentator in the Hebrew press wrote, "It is creating new values even among peoples that had no basis for this vision."[43] It appears there was no escape for members of Maccabi but to concede that "the sports frenzy that gripped the entire world after the world war has gripped us, too."[44]

The new British rulers of Palestine likely facilitated this development because they viewed sports as a vehicle for modernization. The Mandate, however, had arrived at a time when, as the prominent sports historian Tony Collins wrote, sports stopped "being a minority middle-class interest outside the anglophone and anglophile nations" and became a commercial, cultural, and political phenomenon that captured the imaginations of tens of millions of people in Europe, Latin America, and Asia, commanding the attention of governments and politicians."[45] In that context, it is less surprising that games like cricket and rugby became integral to the national cultures of India and Australia while never taking root in Palestine.

In the Yishuv, as in many other places, the interwar ascendancy of sports was often understood not as a strictly colonial phenomenon but as parallel to the decline of gymnastics. Only two years after the end of the world war, the following appeared in the Hebrew press: "Artificial and dry gymnastics is ceding its place to various sports games, particularly football."[46] Once widely celebrated as a delightful and splendid pastime, gymnastics was then instead treated with indifference because it "promises neither medals nor prizes."[47] By 1922, a member of Maccabi lamented, "Among the entire public of ours, [now] flowing en masse to watch the football contests, we do not find, to our great sorrow, the same willingness to help and support the gymnastics association."[48]

This decline in the appeal of gymnastics had an obvious economic dimension. As the indigent body-culture organizations struggled to survive on scanty budgets, the economic gains of organizing contests and selling tickets made for a definitive impact.[49] "Arranging contests is our only means of existence," the Hapoel journal reported candidly.[50] Yehoshua Alouf, a senior member of Maccabi, also admitted at one of the organization's meetings, for lack of choice that "we all understand the scourge of football and we know that gymnastics stand higher, but the associations are in such a condition that we have to give consideration to football first."[51]

Despite the economic "facts on the ground," prominent body-culture devotees continued to believe that the tide could be reversed and gymnastics restored.[52] Thus, despite the organizations' class and partisan tensions, the heads of Maccabi and Hapoel stood together in supporting gymnastics and resisting modern sports. From their standpoint, gymnastics reflected an orderly worldview that should not be relinquished in favor of a young and passing fad "that has captured all hearts."[53] In 1926, for example, the following was stated at a Maccabi meeting: "Maccabi is not just a football group. First and foremost, it should give room to gymnastics, broad popular gymnastics in all walks of the nation, a national cultural movement. . . . Maccabi will not find succor in football because the typical policy of football is its individuality and that of Maccabi—its collectivity."[54] With economic necessity in the background, some even sought a pragmatic solution that would allow gymnastics to make a comeback. "Football should stop being the breadwinner of our sports associations," claimed a member of Hapoel; he called for the nationalization of body culture by the Zionist organization so that

> football will lose its hegemony by ceasing to serve the sports associations as a source of income; in turn, it will not be cultivated with excessive firmness and admission charges to sports grounds will be abolished. Association members should engage in gymnastics, outings, swimming, and other activities that are healthier, and in games that do not aggravate the urge to provocation and disputation in the crowd, making it possible to reduce the number of spectators.[55]

This optimistic attempt to restore gymnastics' centrality failed. Most books on gymnastics written as early as the Mandate era already began with apologetics that limited the activity, as the title of one of the instruction manuals expressed it, to "fifteen minutes [of exercise] per day for health."[56] Thus, gymnastics had not totally vanished but rather, as in many other places, had begun to be reincarnated as a scientific discipline called "physical education."[57] In the course of the twentieth century (particularly in its second half), it appeared in the gym, on television, and over the radio—but mainly in schools.[58] In 1926, for instance, the principal of the Hebrew Gymnasium, Benzion Mossinson, threatened the teacher Zvi Nishri with dire consequences unless he stopped giving gymnastics lessons on the Sabbath: "We wish to inform you officially that if such a thing happens again, we will close the gymnasium . . . and give you [in the plural] no access to the yard."[59]

Concurrently, gymnastics was reinterpreted in a competitive vein. "Can gymnastics possibly be called a sport?" a member of Maccabee asked in late 1929.[60] Although he admitted that "of course, the gymnastics that take place in the schools and in our sports federations cannot be called a sport," he also pointed out "there is another gymnastics, a unique [activity] that the opponents of the lovely sport call 'acrobatics' or, in its more dignified name, artistic gymnastics. These gymnastics should be treated like a sport that can be arranged in competitions."[61] This point of view also resonated with one of the members of Hapoel: "Thus far," he wrote "we have not put the competitive fundament of gymnastics to adequate use."[62] Accordingly, to appeal to "members who are gymnasts, particularly the young ones, [who] are looking for a point of attraction in bodily exercises" he recommended "inserting the competitive moment in gymnastics and establishing contests in various branches . . . may reinvigorate the exercises and make the activity attractive to the members."[63] In other words, gymnastics might survive outside the school only in one incredibly narrow way—as a sport.

SPORTS AS A NOVELTY

Despite its popularity in the interwar era, sports competition was still a new phenomenon that needed time to attain cultural assimilation. During the 1930s, for example, the Austrian Jewish writer Stefan Zweig wrote about the phenomenon of sports in his Viennese milieu: "In the last century the sport wave had not yet reached our continent from England. There were yet no stadiums where a hundred thousand people went wild with joy when one boxer hit another on the chin. The newspapers did not yet send reporters to fill columns with Homeric rapture about a hockey game."[64] Aligned with Zweig, a diverse array of intellectuals—from the American Christopher Isherwood to the Central Europeans Robert Musil and Bertolt Brecht—delved into discussions concerning the emerging phenomenon of physical competition. In Palestine, key Zionist intellectuals, such as the poet Chaim Nahman Bialik, reflected on the "world of yesterday," where sports were absent.[65] "Have you already heard the new word, 'sport'?" wrote Hebrew author Avigdor Hameiri, ironically. "It's the new flag, the new ideal, the new way."[66]

In Hebrew culture, the "new ideal" was primarily distilled into a singular concept: competition. Thus, when Hebrew journalists referred to various sports events, they normally avoided the "old" word *mis'haq* (game), preferring *taharut* (competition or contest).[67] In this context, sports journalist and Hapoel member Meir Benayahu, for instance, mocked the new custom of quantifying everything from drinking coffee to chewing gum to sailing in a washtub for measurable competition.[68] "Factually, someone who's running cannot be thought of as [engaging in] an act of sport," a commentator in the Maccabi journal wrote. "The crux of sport is the aspiration to place the maximum focus on action. This [other] running, called 'running for the sake of health,' is a sport to the same extent that chasing a streetcar to catch a train may be called a "sport."[69]

Simultaneously, to counter the lack of a tradition in the new phenomenon, the engineers of Hebrew body culture labored feverishly to translate, write, and continually disseminate the rules of competition.[70] The rules of football alone—the most popular sport in Palestine—were published at least four different times.[71] At the beginning of his 1927 book on the rules of football, for example, Yosef Yekutieli expressed his hope of "enabling the crowd of observers to understand [more easily] everything that takes place on the playing field, an understanding that will reveal to one and all the immense beauty of this appealing popular game."[72] Despite his hopes, however, incomplete knowledge of the rules of competition remained typical of the Hebrew culture in Palestine. The author Moshe Smilanski, for instance, realized at the age of fifty that "my ears have not yet accommodated all the new 'terms.'"[73] Thus, even in 1939, men and women in the Yishuv needed a quick lesson to understand what is a penalty kick (*fendel*) and the nuances of the offside rule.[74]

The new "extreme" competitive phenomenon, no longer focusing on "harmonizing all bodily strengths," also aroused fears about its ill effects on participants' health. Visitors to a physical-health exhibition in Tel Aviv were apprised of "the damage associated with overexertion in sports and with specialization in one eminent sport, particularly by a person whose body is not fit for strenuous effort. In such a case," the exhibition concluded, "a sport that is meant to create health and add strength becomes an impediment, of course."[75]

The effects of sports on the female body were of special concern.[76] Embracing the scientific stance of a medical system whose physicians had been educated largely in turn-of-the-century Europe, a Viennese doctor wrote in the local Hebrew press, "Competitive light athletics may diminish a woman's grace and beauty and give her a masculine form." As a remedy for this "extreme athletic development," the physician recommended that "a woman's body needs multilateral development" that should be attained "not by specializing in a particular sport but by participating in different sports concurrently. Only then," he concluded, "will this trove of strength and health be exploited appropriately for the benefit of woman and her calling as the mother of all life" [cf. Gen. 3:20].[77]

Just as competition was thought to impair women's fertility, so it was also considered harmful to children's sound development. The doctor of the Reali School in Haifa, for example, claimed that "sports are associated with extremism" and "there is a difference between gymnastics and competition passionate urge." In this physician's "scientific" eyes, sport was a radical and dangerous element that may damage pupils' heart muscles and subject the young to mental trauma: Sports "affect the child's psyche more than anything. The paths of competition . . . develop and accustom him to extremism and also to crudity." Against this threat of degeneracy to the child's body and soul, he argued, "The school should object to this sport from an educational standpoint" and he recommended a turn to gymnastics: "The football craze has breached all limits such that it endangers our children's health. . . . Gymnastics ought to deliver the hoped-for utility for the physical and spiritual development of the young generation."[78]

The fear of harm to athletes' health may sound a little far-fetched to today's ears, but at that time, violence was indeed one of the most conspicuous features of the new competitive playing field. The football pitch suddenly turned into a "killing field," a reporter for one Yishuv newspaper noted in his account of a brawl that erupted during a match.[79] Such altercations among the players, fans, and even referees were common in Palestine.[80] "Week in and week out," the sports journalist Shimon Samet complained, "In almost every contest that takes place between Hebrew groups, one encounters the same savage hatred and provocation of the rival that may endanger people's lives and generate hatred of sports even among its fans."[81] Violence occurred so commonly that it sometimes took on a comic complexion, thus,: handball, for example, was parodically described in a 1931 Maccabi journal as "a game much like football except in this game it is not the legs but the hands that are fractured."[82]

SPORTS TAKING ROOT

The various concerns regarding the rise of sports began to wane by the latter half of the 1930s, as Hebrew culture in Palestine started to embrace the once-controversial but now increasingly familiar competitive phenomenon with a more sympathetic view.[83] We will return to this shift in the subsequent chapters, but it was not unique to the Yishuv. Comparable processes were observed, for example, in the Soviet Union, the Bund's Morgenshtern body-culture association, and in other collectives in which initial resistance to modern sports gradually subsided.[84] Thus, in Palestine, only four years after criticizing "games that are unable to stir provocation and polemic passion," journalist Meir Benayahu wrote, "Competition is an organic part of human nature . . . because it is the motive force for progress, ascent, and personal growth. Without it, the game lacks its essence and purpose."[85] Similarly, Emanuel Gill of Hapoel claimed, "[As against] the opponents of sports (competition) and devotees of gymnastics who find competition inimical to the development of the human body," it deserves emphasis that sports "impose ethical virtues and personal and social traits of the highest order."[86] This kind of moral significance was echoed by Maccabi members as well, such as Yosef Yekutieli, who praised sports for "never asking who the person is but rather what he can achieve. Sports abound with appreciation and respect for the rival's ability. Therefore, let there be no doubt, the sportive idea is an invincible force that always knows how to deflect any extraneous factor."[87]

Competitive sports also began to seep into the Jewish education system in Palestine. In the early 1920s, gymnastics teachers and parents still decried the concept of a school-level championship as an abomination. Only a decade later, however, championship competitions and measurement of athletic records had become integral parts of physical-education classes in urban schools.[88] Even the principal of the Reali School in Haifa, Arthur Biram, a man of German origin who, under the influence of gymnastics, favored physical education as a paramilitary activity, neither opposed nor totally repudiated the virtues of competition: "We do not wish to prevent this competition, which will undoubtedly be one of the factors that will take popular physical education to a higher step."[89] Concerns within the medical establishment, also, began to diminish, giving way to a focus on harnessing scientific biological knowledge to enhance performance and results.[90] As a commentator in the Hapoel journal argued, "The doctor should carry out examinations during the contest and create suitable conditions, so that [the athletes] can improve their scores."[91]

In early 1935, the Rishon Lezion branch of Hapoel delivered an announcement: "The members' gymnastics department has discontinued its activity due to lack of interest and participation on the members' part."[92] The indifference of Rishon's townspeople was not exceptional: During the interwar years, gymnastics rapidly and drastically lost its place in body culture both in the Yishuv and around the world. The dominant place of gymnastics as a worldwide medium for coping with the challenges of modernity had ended. The era of competitive sports had begun.

An understanding of this process provides the foundation for three pivotal insights about the onset of Hebrew sports in Palestine. First, it allows us to set local developments within a broad transnational context. For instance, the decision of several members of Maccabi to secede from the organization during the 1920s and establish a separate association named Hapoel—a key event in the history of Hebrew sports—represents more than an isolated case of a struggle within the Histadrut for primacy among the Yishuv middle class.[93] Instead, it was influenced by the establishment of the Socialist Workers' Sport International (Sozialistische Arbeitersport Internationale, SASI) several years earlier.[94] Indeed, the heads of Hapoel joined the SASI and accepted its authority as one of their first moves.[95]

Second, the elucidation of the principled difference between gymnastics and sports enhances our understanding of the key influence of gymnastics on the development of Hebrew and Israeli sports. Unlike many cultures, in the Yishuv the transition from gymnastics to sports nestled de facto under the same organizational umbrella. Thus, the management of sports by gymnastics enthusiasts did not thwart the rise of sports but rather resulted in an artificial fusion of the two.[96] For example, at some unknown time the heads of the Maccabi movement added the word "sport" to the name of their organization, making it the Maccabi Palestine Federation for Gymnastics and Sports. Several years later, they deleted "gymnastics" and left themselves, at least officially, with "sports" alone.

The Hebrew translation of Nordau's *Muskeljudentum* speech underwent a similar process of sportification. In the new 1923 version, Nordau's original hope that "the Jewish gymnastics association will blossom and flourish and set an example for all centers of Jewish life" was replaced with the exclamation, "Long live Hebrew sports! May the branches of Hebrew sports spread and flourish!"[97] The new interpretation under Nordau's imperative, "Thus spoke Nordau," hangs today at the entrance to the Maccabi offices in Ramat Gan and, no less importantly, appears on the Hebrew Wikipedia page on "Muscular Judaism" (*Yahadut ha-sharerim*).[98]

Similarly, the current edition of the *Even-Shoshan Hebrew Dictionary* gives the word "sport" a general and broad definition: "physical exercises, chiefly in the form of various games or competitions meant to develop and strengthen the body and enhance courage and psychological alertness."[99] Following this definition, which, unlike the English one, does not limit sport to modern competition, "sport" in contemporary spoken Hebrew is used as a noun for a broad range of physical activities. To this day physical education classes in Israeli schools are known colloquially as sports lessons (*shi'ure sport*), and Israeli doctors warmly encourage patients to "do a little sport" (*Ta'ase ktzat sport*). This common coinage, amusingly echoing the first occurrence of the concept in the Yishuv in 1908, attests that many indicators of gymnastics did not totally disappear in the first half of the twentieth century but sank their roots in language and daily life.

Third, the exploration of the decline of gymnastics and the rise of sports shows that the transition from the former to the latter was not just a footnote but a material and weighty process in contemporaries' eyes. Thus, throughout the interwar years the Hebrew Athletes perceived—and expressed—their self-imposed distancing from gymnastics as a tipping point that dealt a fatal blow to their ability to attain their original goal of contributing, if not leading, the Zionist Revolution and the formation of a new Jewish experience in Palestine. About a year before World War II, one of the heads of Maccabi conceded during an internal meeting of the organization, "After the inner soul-searching that this serious hour deserves, I must admit that Maccabi has not even partly fulfilled its national roles and callings. . . . The idea of 'kelal Yisrael' [the Jewish commonwealth] and 'national unity' that Maccabi espoused and continues to espouse remains an idea only, with no chance of fulfillment and inculcation in Yishuv life . . . to the disadvantage of the Yishuv itself and before its living eyes as it strives for building and redemption."[100]

The gap between modern sports, Zionism, and Hebrew Athletes is the central theme of the chapters ahead. In this exploration of revolutionary meanings and desires, the evocative nexus of experience and language serves as a resonant starting point.

2 • COMPETING IN HEBREW

Revolutionary Language and the Sporting Presence

In the 1942 short story "The Sermon" by Haim Hazaz, a man named Yudke addresses a gathering of Haganah members: "Comrades! We have no history! From the day we were exiled from our land we've been a people without a history. You're absolved. Go play football."[1] But why should a people without history play football? About three years before "The Sermon" came out, a brief comment appeared in an article in the liberal newspaper *Haaretz*: "No urging to this day has helped to shake the public out of its 'traditional' attitude toward Maccabi. What does the public really know . . . about goings-on in the ranks of that movement? Nothing or next to nothing. 'Playing at football'—that's the 'famous' [response] that many express."[2] This indifference toward sports competition appeared also in the socialist newspaper *Davar*. In a 1936 joke, for example, a man asks his friend, who has no interest in sports, why he is attending a football game. "I heard that my boss would be the referee there," the friend replies, "and when would I have a better opportunity to curse him out as a bum if not here?"[3] Sephardi author Shoshana Shababo also expressed a similarly dismissive attitude toward a football game in Tel Aviv: "And there from way up in the high heavens," she wrote, "the sun chuckles as it taunts the nullity of human beings."[4] Namely, the apathy, distinctiveness, and condescending that appear in the three texts suggest that Hazaz sent the "people without a history" to play football not to make a future for themselves but because, he saw Jewish life in Palestine, like modern sports, as a rootless experience existing "outside history."[5]

This sentiment found resonance among many western interwar writers, who likewise critiqued and celebrated the autotelic nature of sports which seemed to exist outside history. Often seen with ambivalence, they were described as both kitschy circuses of amusement and as vessels of praise for the "authentic" passion they unveiled during the spectacle.[6] The German playwright Bertolt Brecht, for example, wrote that he favored sports competition as long as it is "dangerous (unhealthy), uncultured (socially unaccepted), and an aim unto itself."[7]

This particular characteristic of modern sports is also a prevailing theme in contemporary scholarship.[8] The anthropologist Victor Turner, sees sports, like multiple modern leisure phenomena, as a "liminoid" experience, a moment beyond time that creates disengagement from society but does not lead to a change of status.[9] Likewise, the noted sociologist Norbert Elias explores modern sports as a space where industrialized society still allows excitement to occur.[10] Taking a more aesthetic stance, contemporary scholar Hans Ulrich Gumbrecht defies the Western separation of body and mind, holding that sport derives its allure from its ability to exist in itself. According to Gumbrecht's phenomenological view, therefore, sport needs no external cultural-linguistic interpretation; rather, like art or literature, it successfully creates an ontological connection that allows people "to immerse themselves in the realm of presence"—an intense emotional aesthetic bodily experience that plants them in the here and now.[11]

This tangible nexus between the individual and the world, which Gumbrecht terms "presence," however, has relevance not only in relation to modern sports but also weaves an ambivalent thread through the fabric of the Zionist Revolution. On the one hand, Zionism aimed to return to history itself. Whether through breathing the air of the homeland, savoring its produce, or speaking the secularized holy tongue, the Hebrew experience persistently celebrated the emotional and sensory richness of life in the Land of Israel. Pioneer philosopher A. D. Gordon even coined the term the Hebrew term for experience, *Ḥavaya,* to capture the moment when life is grasped not through cultural interpretation but through pure existence.[12] This Hebrew portmanteau of *ḥavaya* (being) and *ḥayyim* (life) might resonate with contemporary Dutch historian Eelco Runia's definition of presence as a moment where "life breathes into what has become routine and clichéd—it is fully realizing things instead of just taking them for granted."[13] On the other hand, however, in this raw Hebrew culture, the sporting presence—embodying fleeting beauty existing outside history—was seen as a threat to the Zionist Revolution's quest for immediacy.[14] Consequently, it was habitually rejected for its autonomous essence, which might undermine the Zionist visceral desires, and was perceived not as a place of inherent "pure" meaning but merely as a futile object one might "curse out as a bum."[15]

Maccabi member Selig Rosecki, for instance, described a boxing event in Tel Aviv this way: "An atmosphere cold as ice reigned in the hall and the onlookers sat as though drowsy. The psychological contact between the crowd of onlookers and the stage was lacking. The thousands of hidden strands that connect the warring boxer with his fans were lacking."[16] Similarly, in 1939, a Hebrew sports journalist compared European youth with the children of the Yishuv. In contrast to the former, "who are totally enchanted by the dramatic démarche of the sports spectacle, our youth are chilly and indifferent to what happens on the sporting grounds." They obtained, the writer claimed, "greater pleasure from playing tag among the crowd, exchanging blows, bothering the adults, and embittering the ushers' lives. These brats don't visit the pitch to see, to be moved, and to imbibe what is beautiful and aesthetic of human movements and to learn from it."[17]

HEBREW REVIVAL'S DISPASSIONATE SPORTING GRAMMAR

This tension between the emotional presence of modern sports and the Zionist Revolution was perhaps most vividly reflected in the most cherished element of modern Hebrew culture—the Hebrew language itself. Beginning slowly at the turn of the century, the revival of Hebrew—from a written language rooted in canonical texts to a living, vernacular tongue—gained significant momentum in the early twentieth century. The origins of this transformative journey were in Eastern Europe, where the Jewish Renaissance was taking shape and new syntax, grammar, and vocabulary were emerging. Yet, it was only in Palestine that Jews could fully immerse themselves in this reborn language, transforming it into a vibrant *spoken* medium capable of encompassing every facet of life.[18] The result, as prominent literary scholar Benjamin Harshav wrote, "was not an ancient language of a great ancient civilization, stagnant for hundreds of years (as Arabic or Indian cultures were), that is now gradually growing into the twentieth century; but rather a new language, re-created in the very heart of the transitions of modernity."[19]

Such a dramatic creation demands a revolutionary faith in the future, where men and women bequeath to their children a language not yet fully formed, without the assurance that there would be a supporting social or cultural framework during their adolescence. Moreover, such circumstances call for the creation not only of a grammar but also of a lived experience. Thus, Zionists perceived Hebrew not merely as a language but as an identity: The modernization of the tongue was intimately intertwined with the revival of the body in the Land of Israel. As Gordon wrote shortly before his death, "One should speak of what I wrote only if and insofar as it retains living value, that is, neither literary nor publicistic value but vital value for self-renewing life."[20] Similar sentiments echoed among the Hebrew Athletes who, even in the early days of gymnastics, crafted lexicons, inventing and translating terms into Hebrew with the conviction that training in "the language of rebirth" was essential for "living healthy and natural lives."[21] This process continued with the transition to competitive sports, where scoring a goal became a "conquest" (*kibush*) and the "forward" and "striker" on the football pitch were transformed in Hebrew into "pioneers" (*ḥaluẓim*).

Hebrew's modernization, however, had an additional element: The revered Hebrew language was not to be used frivolously but only in service of the revival itself.[22] As Gordon insisted, "One should speak of what I wrote only if and insofar as it retains living value."[23] This fear of the nonvital use of language manifested in various aspects of Hebrew culture and identity. For instance, common terms like *dugri* and *tachles*, borrowed from Arabic and Yiddish, were embraced to encourage direct and practical speech, free from unnecessary linguistic embellishments—a reminder that, in its secular form, language—as Bialik wrote in his seminal essay "Revealment and Concealment" (*Gilui ve-kisui ba-lashon*)—"does not introduce us at all into the inner being of things but rather stands between us and them."[24] This ambivalent aspect, in which the severing of Hebrew from its religious roots left it secondary to the purpose of action, was also evident in the realm of sports. Thus, in the face of the perceived meaninglessness of the sporting experience, key concepts such as "professionalism," "football," "boxing," and "champion" were often transliterated from English. Even the word "sport" itself has never been widely translated, and the attempt by the "reviver" of the language, Eliezer Ben-Yehuda, to translate "sport" into *mil'av* failed to gain traction.[25]

Much of the apprehension stemmed from the belief that the fervent enthusiasm for sports was closely linked to the potential risks of foreign influences on language and identity within the Hebrew experience. "Sport is also a means of national education," an unknown journalist claimed, "and it is unacceptable that foreign languages should be spoken at the [boxing] event."[26] Likewise, Shababo describes her literary protagonist, a sports fan named Grisha, as follows: "Cigar after cigar, hands trembling, yellowish mustache twitching irritably. His body twists right and left . . . another moment he shouts with all his might about the injustice . . . : 'Out! Out! Mr. Referee, he was out!' . . . When no one's looking at him, he grumbles, blurts words in Russian, and smokes uninterruptedly." Shababo continues her condescending narrative before taking the matter to its conclusion. "Ah, these Hungarians are so nice. . . . What a language they speak! Now, *that* was foot-ball!"[27]

In response to this fear, Hebrew Athletes persistently discussed when and how one could *speak* about competitive sports. Meir Benayahu, for example, declared it the role of the spectators "to appreciate and even to express its opinion, its feeling, but only after the spectacle or the contest, and not in the middle."[28] Shimon Samet also expressed the wish to silence the totality of the "sports moment," which exists "outside history" per se: "One may speak of sports affectionately and even passionately but should not make it into an absolute monarch as extreme sports zealots do."[29] Correspondingly, another writer contended, "The public clamor that many of our experts see as an inseparable part of a successful boxing event, one or two respectful cheers could not do any harm, but . . . wild jeering and shouting must be stopped immediately and forcefully."[30] In that vein, Hebrew Athletes even occasionally referred to impassioned rooting as "doping," using the English word in its denotation of being drugged, as a sign that underscored the undifferentiated nature of the uncontrolled experience akin to the goading and destruction of the physical body itself.[31]

This Hebrew anxiety that uncontrolled language might possess the body was intertwined with the reluctance to describe the "sporting moment." In contrast to the detailed pioneer illustrations of the "reviving" act of cultivating the Land of Israel, the Hebrew Athletes rarely provided descriptions of their craft. Thus, for instance, a comprehensive account of a special Maccabi delegation to London in the diary of the trip's manager, Meira Belkind, abruptly ends before the competitions began.[32] Moreover, even when attempting to provide a literal narrativization of the "sporting moment," Hebrew writers were often disinclined to endow it with meaning. Shababo, for example, decided to focus on the ball and not on the ballplayer: "First one kick is made, up it goes, dips a little, and down it comes. Right away, it's pushed into its place by the foot of an agile player, hits the ground, and bounces back to an opposing player's head. For a while it twists and turns among heads and feet, brushing hands and bodies lightly and knocking heads angrily as it makes its way."[33]

Similar to Shababo's meaningless portrayal, in which the game is reduced to mere "feet, feet, feet . . . kicking, repelling, retreating, shoving," young footballer Ben-Ami Machlis from Maccabi Petah Tikva also described his playing experience as a mere bundle of nouns and verbs: "I lift my foot and send [the ball] back without letting it fall. The opposing goalie kicks the ball and it falls between two of my opponents. I run and jump between them and I fail to get the ball. The fielder passes at my extreme. I chase him, steal the ball from him, and pass it on." However, this verb-intensive style is abandoned shortly after the game ends, when Machlis describes his post-match fatigue: "My knees buckle and my legs seemed like stones."[34] In other words, when the match is over and the player leaves the field, the writer needs a simile to describe his body's experience and life itself. This literary style, characterized by a minimal use of adjectives, has parallels in both biblical and modern Hebrew literature.[35] However, it is distinct from standard practices in writing about modern sports.

THE HEBREW SPORTS PRESS AND ITS GLOBAL CONTEXT

Before the visual age of television, language played a key role in shaping the sports spectacle. [36] Accordingly and not by chance, one thread in the beginning of modern sports literature is the Romantic writing of the famous British essayist William Hazlitt in the early nineteenth century. Seeking to transcend the dry and formal reportage of his time, Hazlitt aimed to convey to the reader the emotions that unfolded during the "sporting moment."[37] This style, also found in the writing of the British sports journalist Pierce Egan, swiftly became influential.[38] About fifty years later, with the development of the tabloid press in the late nineteenth century, this emotional writing style had established a definitive presence in the burgeoning sporting press in Britain and the United States.[39] After the post–World War I global popularization of sports, the penetration of "American concepts" in news reportage led to the creation of a model of sporting press coverage that aimed not only to describe and convey information but also, and mainly, to shape the experience.[40]

Diverging from these patterns, Hebrew sports journalists in the Yishuv consciously steered clear of emotional flourishes. A member of Maccabi, for example, claimed that the movement's journal should express not emotion but rather "order and precision as worthy of a vehicle of the [Maccabi] organization, which stands for both of these qualities."[41] Similarly, the sports editor of *Davar* promised to avoid spectacle, "which blinds the eyes with its fake wealth of colors," and "to turn out a healthy and well-shaped body, strengthen character, and invest the sportsman with freshness, nobility, and dignified virtues."[42] Hebrew sports journalists, thus, intended their writing "not only to convey information about contests held here and there but rather, and foremost, to teach the youth and the ignorant a lesson about the rules of physical culture and to help make sports part of the public's portion."[43] This Zionist outlook on the creative use of language was captured with simplicity by the sports journalist Meir Benayahu in his call for "the avoidance of cheap sensationalism in favor of the concrete."[44]

The goal of spurning cheap sensation had a perceptible impact on Hebrew sports texts. In 1933, the bout between former world champion Max Schmeling and the rising star Max Baer attracted much interest in the international boxing community.[45] Nevertheless, the Yishuv press largely ignored the event. Even the tabloid-like newspaper *Do'ar HaYom* gave it only dry, factual coverage, and like Shababo and Machlis earlier, described it as a sequence of actions and episodes:

> The American wrestler [*sic*] Max Baer defeated Max Schmeling by technical knockout in the tenth of the fifteen rounds that had been determined. Schmeling surmounted his rival until the ninth round, when Baer launched a spirited attack on Schmeling's head and body. One punch made [Schmeling] dizzy, and the next one dropped [him] to the ground. In the tenth round, Schmeling fell again and did not get up until the referee counted to nine. But because Schmeling wobbled as he walked, the referee stopped the contest.[46]

In contrast to the terse Hebrew reportage, the Yiddish press in Poland told a different story.[47] "Jewish Boxer Max Baer Defeats Hitlerite World Champion Max Schmeling" shouted the *Der Moment* headline.[48] Although Schmeling was not a fervent supporter of the Nazi Party, the sporting competition between "a German" and "a Jew" was sufficient for the two largest Yiddish daily newspapers *Haynt* and *Der Moment* to provide lavish coverage of the match. Thus, despite many differences between the Eastern European and US press, Yiddish journalists mobilized language to describe what transpired in the ring and the arena. "But now, after his brilliant triumph—the crowd was overtaken by indescribable excitement. . . . Tens of thousands of people suddenly went mad with delight that a young Jew of Semitic stock defeated a contender of the German race," *Der Moment* wrote.[49] The account in *Haynt*, devoted to the moment of the knockout itself, was even more detailed: "Suddenly a powerful thud is heard and Schmeling lays on the mat. Baer gave Schmeling such a blow with his right that the German lost consciousness. For a moment, silence reigned. All eyes turned to the referee, who counted calmly one . . . two . . . three. . . . When he got to seven, Schmeling began to move. When he got to nine, Schmeling stood up but could not hold himself up for long."[50] This Yiddish account, unlike the Hebrew text, does more than string actions together. It pauses and pays attention not only to occurrences in the ring but also to the crowd and the atmosphere in the arena. Simply put, it describes not a physical event but an experience.[51]

Indeed, in comparison to Yiddish and various other languages, the Hebrew writing style was shaped partly by its being a young vernacular, where even its speakers sometimes fell short of complete proficiency.[52] Shababo, for example, related how, in the stands, "a woman pioneer not fluent in the language" misspoke when asked about how the bout would end ("it will end with 'scores'!").[53] Thus, even when a Hebrew newspaper did intend to describe a sports moment in depth—usually in rare cases of large international sporting events held abroad—it encountered serious difficulties.

The scanty vocabulary of Hebrew was especially conspicuous in contrast to the rich reportage in the Western press. Again, in the coverage of boxing, Hebrew lacked lexemes for concepts such as "clinching" and" knockout," which became "body-to-body struggle" and "striking him to the ground," respectively.[54] Furthermore, where English or German, with their rich vocabularies, presented readers with a varied, colorful text, the Hebrew journalist, straining to communicate what was going on, usually turned out repetitive articles with an excessive use of quotation marks.

Still, perhaps the most blatant difference between Hebrew reportage and its English counterpart was not in vocabulary but in the expression of time. In October 1926, a month after Jack Dempsey and Gene Tunney fought for the heavyweight championship, *Do'ar HaYom* published a direct translation of a piece that had appeared on the front page of *The New York Times* the morning after the event.[55] The Hebrew newspaper did not indicate that the text was a translation and presented it as a letter posted from Philadelphia. Whether this was deliberate or unintentional, the Hebrew version clearly strays from the source. "Dempsey attacks Tunney with feverish speed," *Do'ar Ha-Yom* wrote in its account of the first round:

> Dempsey sends a heavy left to Tunney's chin, Dempsey approaches and takes a heavy right on the chin and managed to extricate himself from a second blow. Again, in the middle of the ring, Tunney sends two heavy blows to Dempsey's body. Dempsey pushes him aside and tried to punch him, but Tunney is careful,

> and Dempsey falls on the rope. Tunney approaches quickly and sent a heavy right fist into the champion's chin, and in the exchange of blows he struck his opponent's chin left and right. Dempsey was in a state of confusion and blood flowed from Tunney's mouth.[56]

Apart from the repeated use of "heavy" to describe the boxers' blows and the abundance of mistranslations, among other characteristics, the Hebrew text describes a series of discrete actions. The US reportage, in contrast, generates a narrative that has a beginning and an end. It tells a story:

> As the round started Dempsey, with a scowl on his face, rushed out and drove Tunney to his own corner. Dempsey again rushed. Jack sent a terrific left to the jaw. Dempsey kept rushing in and drove Tunney into his own corner. Dempsey went in and Dempsey swung a hard right to Dempsey chin. Dempsey weaved in again and Tunney was short with a right. They boxed in the center of the ring for a moment, then Tunney missed a right for the head, but ripped two rights to the body. Dempsey jabbed Tunney away, and then lunged over the ropes after missing a left swing. Tunney rushed in again and sent a heavy right to the chin. In a terrific exchange Tunney showered left and right swings to Dempsey's jaw and Dempsey was groggy. Gene's only mark in the exchange was a bleeding mouth. Between rounds Dempsey appeared very tired, and his seconds worked hard over him.[57]

Like the Yiddish correspondent who emphasizes "suddenly a powerful thud is heard" and "for a moment, silence reigned," the American journalist makes sure to note that these events took place at the beginning or the end of the round or only for a moment. The translator in the Yishuv must have known the word *Bereshit* ("in the beginning," the first word in the Torah) but did not use that biblical term or any other linguistic device that defines time.

This aspect of the sporting time and experience stands out even more when one considers the monopoly of the written word in the Hebrew media in Mandatory Palestine. Unlike sports fans in Europe or the United States, those in the Yishuv relied solely on their newspaper until 1937, when radio stations went on the air. Yet, even then, they experienced the sports event after a delay, rather than through a live broadcast. This technical difference also had a more subtle effect. Broadcasters aim to produce continual reportage that captures the events and shapes an experience with a tempo; they strive to reduce any "dead time." The morning after the Dempsey–Tunney fight, for example, *The New York Times* published a transcript of the radio broadcast that allowed the reader to return to the lost "sports moment." The description of the end of the first round reads as follows:

> Tunney puts a right glancing blow to Jack's jaw, but it doesn't bother Jack at all. They are in the center of the ring. Jack backs away from Tunney's lead and takes a

> light right on the face. He backs away to the ropes. Jack does not show the speed he is accustomed to showing. It is not the Jack we are accustomed to at all. They immediately go into the clinch as Tunney puts over a light right to the face. Tunney slips over a good left. He retaliates with two little light taps to the neck of Tunney. They mean nothing at all. Tunney is short with a jab to Jack face; he is short with another one. Now Tunney is driven to the ropes. Jack overshoots him and backs up against the ropes. Tunney gets in twice with a left to the face and right to the face. Everybody is howling, "Dempsey is groggy!", but he does not look [it] to me. This is not the Jack Dempsey we are accustomed to see. He has just taken two clips on the jaw from Tunney, both rights one glancing blow, the other flush. Jack is buried in close; he is putting up no defense at all. He bears into the clinch. Tunney hit him at least six times with rights and lefts to the face, and Jack gets another on the eye as the bell rings. The first round: Tunney's round by a mile.[58]

When talking is written down and read, something of the experience is inevitably left behind. Yet this account, produced by the legendary American broadcaster Graham McNamee, was built atop a description of a series of actions. He consistently adds commentary that gives the action meaning and produces a narrative, thus also making it accessible to the lay listener. His pronouncement, "This is not the Jack Dempsey we are accustomed to see," stands out: It adds historical weight to the description based on the sportscaster's expertise, giving the sports moment substance that transcends fleeting action.[59]

Sportscasting came to the Yishuv a decade later in 1937.[60] Like the American iteration, it demanded that the sports journalist educate the "viewing public" about how to become a "listening public." As one Hebrew sports journalist wrote: "It's obvious that listeners lose much of their pleasure—the very act of viewing of the game—but one should not forget that not everyone can attend the game. Beside this, it will take the listener only a few moments to get used to this kind of coverage and imagine the game as it is." [61] In other words, the journalist had to try to convince his audience that speaking and hearing could generate a reliable experience—that the language could in fact "tell it like it is."[62]

THE HEBREW SPORTING PRESS AND THE YISHUV

From many standpoints, it is unfair to compare US sports coverage with that in the Yishuv. For one thing, the dire economic situation of the Hebrew press should be borne in mind. Certainly, in the 1920s and the early 1930s, Hebrew newspapers were relatively small and had to leave a good deal of room for advertising, limiting the Hebrew sporting press to a few intermittent reports.[63] Against this background, much of the public sports discourse took place in the journals of the physical culture associations: *HaMaccabi* (founded in 1913) and *Uzenu*, introduced at roughly the time of the establishment of Hapoel in the second half of the 1920s. Reflecting the prevailing worldview, these publications allotted much space to discussion of calisthenics and physical education, management of the associations, and current events from a sociopolitical perspective. Furthermore, these journals came out sporadically, in small print runs, and did not have a wide exposure.

The limited media coverage of sports did not change materially but did increased somewhat in the second half of the 1920s. Amid the general evolution of the Hebrew press, special sports sections began to appear, but the reportage remained terse, was usually on the back page, and was not accompanied by photos. As Benayahu remarks, "The press in the Eretz Israel attributed no great value to sports and did not acknowledge their power and influence; thus, they did not reserve space for questions of that kind. . . . A few writings and reports, usually descriptions of football games, were published. Of regular information and explanation—there was not a trace."[64]

This state of affairs made the Hebrew sports journalist a lonely voice in the newspapers' editorial constellation. Benayahu describes how he began work at the newspaper *Haaretz* in the late 1920s: "At first, I had the impression that not all members of the editorial board looked smilingly on the new creature [the sports section]. The traditional view, nestling in many of our writers and educators, saw physical culture as kids' stuff, unworthy of a decent individual and a respectable reader." Writing for the Hebrew sports section became a solitary pursuit for devoted individual journalists. Benayahu recalls, "When the editor went abroad in the summer months—it left its imprints on the [sports] section."[65] Given the marginalizing cultural and journalistic attitude toward modern sports, the Hebrew sports journalist often arrived "from the ranks of sport" and spent much of his life "defending the sports department, and convincing the public that sports were not an afterthought to the rest of the paper."[66] To wit: The Hebrew sports journalist not only reported about Hebrew Athletes but also *was one as well.*

This allegiance to the purpose of sport, however, merely emphasizes how much the language was perceived as an empty vessel that formed a barrier to delving into what Bialik called "the inner being of things."[67] "Functionary B isn't one of those quill-pullers," a writer remarked in the sports column of *Davar*. "Thus he attests about himself. Only orally does he fume about the criticism that's leveled at the group that he manages. . . . It's obvious that many functionaries are not enthusiastic about the writing. In contrast, nearly all of them are infected with 'insultitis.' Every critical word . . . offends them to the bottom of their heart."[68] That is to say, journalistic criticism was regarded not as a necessary professional tool for public discussion and development but as verbal falsification of actual events.[69]

Therefore, even though the journalists avoided the spectacular and sought to educate by means of "regular information and explanation," many Hebrew Athletes still treated the "language-athlete" contemptuously.[70] "The sportswriters," several football players charged, "either understand little or are subjective. They ballyhoo one of us and hound the other, and that's before one gets to the writer's personal attitude toward the player."[71] Accordingly, sportswriters were often sent to the far end of the stadium, where they could hardly see and report on the game in progress.[72] "I should not have come at all," wrote a Hebrew sports journalist after spectators interfered with his work.[73] Similarly, a staff member of *Sport Haaretz* complained about "big disruptions" of his work after a Maccabi footballer deliberately sat down in his chair.[74]

THE NEW AND OLD LANGUAGE OF THE LATE 1930S

The marginalizing cultural attitude toward sports journalists saw little change in the interwar era. However, in the 1930s (mainly in the second half of the decade), some Hebrew Athletes did begin to call for disengagement from the "informative" approach in favor of more emotional reportage. Meir Shkedi, a member of Maccabi and an immigrant from Lithuania, pronounced the movement's journal "heavy and dry." Even though it contains "interesting and important intellectual and scientific material," he continued, "it does not express what the Maccabi organization in Eretz Israel does, instead serving as a supplement for matters of physical education," in which the sports chronicle

> is an afterthought of sorts, and a boring one at that. Instead of conveying important content in a few words, we are often presented with boring and superfluous stenography. I always have the impression that instead of pushing the button—let there be light—we behold a mass of glowing embers. The fire of youth that our young people demand, rightly, is lacking. And these young people are the very core of our movement; they are the living, vibrant, and pliable material . . . and outwardly there is much demand: Give us a sports newspaper.[75]

Shkedi, it is true, still preferred "a few words" over "boring and superfluous stenography," but what he wanted Hebrew to do was to describe and capture the "fire of youth" and the emotions accompanying the sporting experience. Shkedi was not alone in insisting on this. In the Yishuv in the 1930s, as in Germany and the Middle East, magazines, newspaper sections, and periodicals that proposed to cover and interpret the new sports phenomenon had begun to appear across the entire political spectrum.[76]

The popular press that evolved in the Yishuv during the 1930s gave this development its first entrée. The editors of this journalistic genre, first attested in the biweekly *Kolnoa* and afterward in the magazine *Tesha ba-'Erev* (an early iteration of the famous tabloid *Haolam Hazeh*), made it their explicit goal to distance themselves from the "quality" press. As Daniel Persky, the American Jewish editor of *Kolnoa,* proclaimed in his periodical, "There is no place [here] for lengthy articles, weighty questions, and bitter topics. For all of them, thank God, we have boring newspapers that sag with 'serious material.' Here everything's alive and kicking; everything flies and flutters."[77] In this spirit, *Kolnoa* devoted much discussion to matters of literature, theater, and music in the Yishuv and abroad. The wish to focus on light, non-obligatory consumer culture that was ostensibly unrelated to the national endeavor also typified the paper's attitude toward competitive sports.

Although *Kolnoa* had little to say about sporting events themselves, its content, packed with photos and cartoons, often featured interviews with athletes, along with light-hearted discussion of movie stars from Germany and Hollywood. Despite being somewhat of an anomaly in the Hebrew press of the time, the journal, with a circulation of around two thousand copies, made notable inroads into the Yishuv's sports circles and featured regular contributions from prominent sports personalities such as Yosef Yekutieli and Lipa Levitan.[78]

However, on the few occasions when it described a game itself—as opposed to light gossip off the field—the popular press also made do with concise and informative summations. "The game ended in a tie," we read about a derby match in Tel Aviv. "Each group made one goal. Neither team played very well this time. Maccabi's defense was better, but Hapoel prevailed on offense."[79] In the four-year lifetime of *Kolnoa,* discussions of sports in the magazine (which suffered from a surfeit of editors) remained largely eclectic and made no explicit statement about the journalist style and essence of sports competition. Therefore, it seems that its sports coverage squared with the assessment of the sociologist Deborah Bernstein regarding *Kolnoa* : Despite its attempt to integrate cosmopolitan content and patterns into its product, the popular press was unable to disengage from the national discourse. Its vehicles continued to deal with domestic affairs, promotion of original Hebrew works, and dissemination of the Hebrew language.[80]

Despite *Kolnoa*'s limited "sporting" success, its coverage style continued to some extent in the late 1930s when the "new sporting press" of the Yishuv consciously aimed to integrate sports and sports reportage into the national revolutionary enterprise. Champions of this "new" approach were not interested in tabloid journalism but considered the "informative" tendency of the Hebrew sporting press a "primitive approach" that originated in "total misunderstanding about the role of the press and its writers."[81] Prominent contributors to this emerging journalistic trend included magazines like *Sport, HaSport,* and *Hed haSport,* each with a short-lived existence. However, the Sunday sports supplements of the daily newspapers *HaBoker* (1936), *Haaretz* (1938), and *Davar* made the most notable and significant contributions.[82]

The most prominent journalistic champion of this view was the editor of *HaBoker*'s sports section, thirty-year-old Alexander Alexandrovich. After working in the sports press in his native Poland, he launched his own sports section in

1936, *HaBoker Sport,* about a year and a half after arriving in the Yishuv—only to find a press environment that, as he described it, was plagued by "conceptual confusion about thoughts that have long since gone out of style." Thus, the young immigrant and member of Maccabi was stunned when one of the "veteran" functionaries of the organization proclaimed it "totally unnecessary to publish the outcomes of games in the sports chronicle." To confront the conviction that "the sporting press should acquire a scientific-academic nature"—an outlook that he called "a conservative and unrealistic concept of sporting life"—Alexandrovich stated that he and his colleagues "become unboundedly passionate when we see the sportsman at war—sublime war—on the field of competition." Accordingly, he felt it his duty to "[give] the reader an idea about the game so that he, too, will *sense what is important and beautiful* . . . because that's how we understand the role of the sporting press and our role as well."[83] Alexandrovich, therefore, saw the journalist as an emissary of the passion of sports, tasked with conveying this enthusiasm to the readers. In simpler terms, Alexandrovich sought to design an aesthetic experience by means of words.

This new outlook on the role of the sporting press was part of the growing role of competitive sports in Hebrew culture in the second half of the 1930s. What is more, the new sports periodicals did not claim that the passions of sports were for entertainment purposes only; on the contrary, they considered them a material part of the revolutionary project at large. The editors of *Sport* magazine, for example, launched their debut edition by explaining "the role of sports in its national sense,"[84] and Alexandrovich declared his wish "to give broader room to all the problems of sports in our country, the foundation of the nation's healthy physical education."[85] The editors of *Haaretz*'s sports supplement went so far as to claim that sports are important not only physically but also mentally: "Bodily development has the additional aspect of convenient distraction from the continual despondency that besets us at the present time. Sports banish political contrasts and make the individual freer, whether he be the performer or the spectator."[86] The editors of the sports supplement of *Haaretz* seemed to shine in crafting the overarching message of the "new sporting press": "It's not too late to develop the idea of sports and help to shape a new type of Jew."[87]

The fresh revolutionary mission of sports also invested the sporting press with a national purpose. "Within our forest of newspapers," Alexandrovich stated, "only a few treat sports understandingly; this causes damage to sports, which cannot grow anywhere in the world without support from the press. . . . Very few people develop writing about sporting affairs solely for the benefit and utility of *sport itself*."[88] The editors of *Sport Haaretz* argued similarly: "We should demand that the leaders of our sports movement understand the role of the press and treat its representatives properly."[89] Furthermore, "new sports journalists" regarded the press and the public discussion of sports as real political tools. Thus, they asserted, "The press should be critical of all sports events and should insist that the leaders of sports take this duty of theirs seriously, because it is the newspapers that propagandize for serious work in sports and support the aspirations of the movement."[90] In addition, the editors of the weekly journal *HaSport*, for example, stated that their magazine acted "in belief in the need for, if not the utter necessity of, the creation of a free forum for the sports movement to that it may advance and grow in strength."[91]

Nonetheless even the "new sports journalists" continued to scorn the nonpurposive use of language. "We would never be enchanted by the loveliest speech of a sports functionary," Alexandrovich stated. Concurrently talking and writing about sports were perceived, in their eyes, as an inseparable part of the sports act itself. Accordingly, Alexandrovich argued he would "always [discuss] any problem that might elevate and ennoble sports. We will never stray," he continued, "from the path of discussing vital current questions, particularly those that fall within the general frame of sporting life."[92]

This inclusion of the "sporting moment" also had a visual aspect. In their debut edition, the editors of *Sport Haaretz* promised to include in every issue "several current photographs that will breathe living spirit into matters."[93] This was done on a modest scale, limited to a few photos that augmented the text without trying to replace it. Compared with the American, German, or Yiddish press, it was a first step only. Just the same, when *HaSport* covered the Yishuv championship in track and field, it added several "atmosphere" photographs in the middle of the page that created an impression of vigorous and impressive surroundings. The photos themselves documented mundane events: an announcer introducing the participants, referees consulting with each other, journalists going about their work. The ground-up angle of the camera, however, lent the aesthetics of these banalities the dramatic aspect of fatefulness and cruciality.[94]

This change in style had textual manifestations as well. The game reports in *Sport Haaretz,* for example—especially those written by German immigrant Kurt Benjamin (see chapter 3)—were lengthy and detailed and included a running temporal dimension that created an ongoing narrative.[95] Additionally, several professional terms such as *nok-auut* (knockout) and *nivdal* (offside) entered the lexicon, making goings-on easier to understand.

However, even in these texts, the reportage of the sports act itself remained scanty.[96] Commenting on a 1938 football match, Benjamin wrote, "The game still shows no sign of being decided; no one yet knows who's going to win. But only in the thirty-fifth minute did Hakoah manage to score the second goal due to a mistake by Herzliya's goalie, nicely exploited."[97] However, Benjamin neither identifies the goalkeeper nor describes the occurrences that led to the goal being scored. Accordingly, the sports act that reaches the reader adds up to a goalkeeping error and a laconic remark about the mistake being "nicely exploited."[98]

Hence, much of the Hebrew sporting press continued to use the "informative" writing style.[99] In its account of a season-opening game in 1931, for example, a writer for *HaSport* mentioned the names of the players but still described the sporting experience as a chain of actions expressed with verbs: "The striker, Zelibanski, exploits two opportunities and scores two goals in succession. How often do they [Petah Tikva] seriously threaten Tel Aviv's goal. The ball hits Beck's leg from a kick toward the Tel Aviv goal and bounces over the goalkeeper's head and enters the goal. Petah Tikva continues its offensive and after it's already dark, Jielowicki kicks from twenty-five meters away and the ball goes in."[100]

The limitations of Hebrew in describing a sports moment are especially evident in comparison with coverage in the English-language Zionist newspaper *The Palestine Post.*[101] The sporting events in Tel Aviv, unlike the heavyweight *battles royales* on the other side of the Atlantic, were observed by English and Hebrew journalists together. Their reports, however, were significantly different. For instance, *The Palestine Post* launched its report on a local boxing evening in 1936 by presenting what it called the climax of the event—the triumph of "the best boxer in Palestine," Sigge Stadlaender:

> Sigge Stadlaender celebrated the occasion of his hundredth ring appearance with a smashing victory over Walter Hass, star Hapoel welterweight. Haas had a considerable advantage in reach so the crafty Atid boxer abandoned his usual body attack and concentrated on a two-fisted attack to the head. Hass's eye was opened by a stinging jab in the first round, and he was badly battered at the conclusion of the bout. In disposing of the Hapoel flash so handily Stadlaender fortified his claim as Palestine's foremost exponent of the art of pugilism.[102]

The identity of the *Post's* sports correspondent, "Secundus," who wrote this article, is not known. Yet, like the authors of texts in *The New York Times,* Secundus creates a narrative that takes place entirely in the ring; that is, within the bounds of the sports moment. This narrative, written in vivid English and possibly alluding to the anonymized writer's origin, generates drama and professional commentary that make the boxer, Stadlaender, into a person who has history and skills—as one who should be followed. Unlike the freighted English text, Alexandrovich's account in *HaBoker Sport* deliberately skirts the "sporting space" and refrains from making a clear statement. Accordingly, his description of Stadlaender's match appears only in the middle of the report and follows the chronological sequence of the evening: "Despite the fact that Stadlaender won the match by rights, we had hoped to see more from him than he showed this time." The writer argued, "We cannot say that he was in his finest form in this contest. It is a fact that both athletes showed us an excellent fight. Hass did not fear his opponent. The bout proceeded spiritedly but this time too, as usual, there was a loss of wind in the last round."[103]

Thus, instead of making a professional journalistic statement, Alexandrovich offers mainly commentary and external criticism that flows from his wish to see "more from him." Moreover, he gives only a general account of what happened in the ring itself. This detached tone of voice recurs in the Hebrew coverage of the climactic moment of the match, the knockout:

> It's hard to speak of Sasson as a boxer because he does not project that kind of personality. Therefore, it amazes us somewhat that the Hapoel management isn't using Bacchi A., the young pugilist who's a member of the group, and is holding him in reserve. Plainly, Bacchi would have been a better fit for the role than Sasson was. Davidowitz had a very easy time of it because the referee stopped the fight right away and proclaimed D. the winner by technical knockout.[104]

Alexandrovich invests little rhetoric in what happened in the ring apart from the minimum needed to get the information across; he devotes most of his account to commentary about decisions made before the fight. Thus, even though the Hebrew text is longer than the *Post's*, the non-Hebrew paper takes only two sentences to describe the "sporting moment": "Jonny Davidowitz made quick work of Sasson, the Hapoel lightweight, stunning with him with hard blows to the head. The seconds threw in the towel in the first round to save Sasson from further punishment."[105]

The interwar rise of modern sports ushered a new era of athletic competition and aesthetic experience. Yet, as late as the eve of World War II, Hebrew culture still grappled with fully appreciating this emerging spectacle. In 1939, for example, Alexandrovich lamented that, in contrast to their European counterparts, the youth of the Yishuv did not exhibit the same "trembling enthusiasm" necessary to "follow the contests and overlook no movement that the players make." Consequently, the Hebrew journalist argued, they were not "totally entranced by the dramatic unfolding of the sports spectacle."[106]

As Alexandrovich noted, this aesthetic gap was intertwined with Hebrew culture's failure to cultivate national role-model athletes. The significance of exceptional bodies that children wish to have to "imitate their paragons" is the focus of the next chapter.[107] However, the physical aspects of the Zionist Revolution were also closely intertwined with its cultural and linguistic elements. Thus, the emotional intensity of sports, focused on the here and now, was often regarded by Hebrew eyes and ears as forms of excessive visceral expression, which could lead individuals like Grisha, Shababo's literary hero, to express their "diasporic" excitement in a foreign tongue. In this context, even reading about sports could be seen as somewhat taboo. Reflecting on the "veterans" of the early twentieth century who had driven the Zionist Revolution (the Second Aliyah), *Davar*'s sports correspondent noted in 1938, "They read the sports section of the newspaper but are too embarrassed to admit it. They merely glance at it and enjoy it."[108]

Accordingly, the Hebrew Athlete, akin to Hazaz's protagonist Yudke, was often characterized as "not one to waste words," reflecting a broader reluctance to use language unnecessarily. As *Davar*'s sports journalist ironically noted, "Athletes and grammar don't share the same house."[109] Even today, few Israeli athletes are recognized for their rhetorical abilities. This characteristic of modern sports was even given an official dictionary definition. In the *Even-Shoshan Hebrew Dictionary*, written several decades later, the inclusive and simplistic definition of "Sports" (see chapter 1) is accompanied by another critical definition that explicitly connects it to the meaningless of the sporting act: "engaging in acts that have neither importance nor utility per se and that take place, in essence, merely to set a record or to outperform others."[110]

This worldview frequently melded with a journalistic style that avoided imbuing sports with intrinsic meaning, instead celebrating a style of expository and "factual" prose as the epitome of national educational purpose.[111] In 1938, a writer in *Davar* critiqued his rival in *HaBoker Sport* who wished, ostensibly and only ostensibly, to develop a sports language that was not meant to inform and educate: "This time—the pinnacle of the journalistic art! To fill up a hundred lines about sports . . . and to say nothing. Indeed, that kind of writing is the most convenient type for young writers who repeat themselves and never risk failure by taking up matters that transcend what they understand and know. Nevertheless, my heart bleeds for you, oh reader!"[112]

3 • "KEEP AWAY FROM THE PRIMA DONNAS"

Hebrew Purpose and the Athletic Body

About three weeks after the Swedish swimmer Arne Borg won the gold medal at the Amsterdam Olympics (1928), the newspaper *Haaretz* published an editorial about his body.[1] According to the Hebrew journalist, an X-ray had revealed that Borg's triumphs were not the result of practice and perseverance but were actually attributable to an air-filled space in his belly, "a kind of fish bladder," that had formed in the aftermath of an operation he had undergone in childhood. "And lo and behold," declared the columnist, "the consequences of the surgery became, of all things, an advantage which, together with other physical virtues, played a decisive part in his remarkable athletic career: the abnormality served as the foundation and pillar of Arne Borg's optimal performance."[2]

Disregarding this questionable medical diagnosis, it is not surprising to learn that a record-breaking athlete has exceptional physical attributes. Certainly, at the international level athletic competition is not situated within the realm of the average. Nevertheless, the Hebrew author of the *Haaretz* article did not consider Borg's exceptional body an object of admiration. Instead, he viewed it as "scientific" proof of the national purposelessness of athletic achievement. "The results of this sort of research," the writer decreed, "serve those who believe that all such famous jugglers and tricksters are abnormal, and therefore argue that we must invest in educating the wider multitudes . . . rather than directing our efforts toward cultivating a select abnormal few."[3]

Concerns about the meaning of the athletic body were not limited to Hebrew culture. Against the backdrop of modernity and changing definitions of masculinity, physical culturists worldwide engaged in fervent debates on how and why to train the human body.[4] However, although athletes like the German Max Schmeling, the American Babe Ruth, and the Finnish Paavo Nurmi became national figures celebrated as heroes in the West, Asia, and the Middle East, in the Yishuv they were seldom regarded as anything more than a bunch of "famous jugglers and tricksters."[5]

Already in the early 1920s, the Zionist pioneer philosopher A. D. Gordon wrote to the heads of Maccabi, "I am aware that the basic premise of your association is 'a healthy soul in a healthy body' but I ask: where is the body, our national body?"[6] Asked Gordon, "Can gymnastics and sport truly make our national body whole? And if there is no [national] body, what is the purpose of this healthful regeneration?"[7] This concern was not limited to the pioneers. A decade after Gordon's letter, the Tel Aviv-based tabloid journalist Uri Keisari asked a similar question when commenting on a sketch of a muscular athlete on the front cover of a Maccabi pamphlet.[8] "The image does indeed attest to a body in full health," Keisari acknowledged, before adding "but what of the soul?"[9]

Thus, unlike gymnastics, which ostensibly makes its participants "into one [harmonious] unit, a solid, beautiful body," the competitive athlete was commonly perceived as a soulless and unrestrained object.[10] "We believe in the victory of ability," wrote sports journalist and Hapoel member Meir Benayahu in 1937, "not in the victory of the blind ecstasy that turns a man into a bull in a ring, inflamed by the scorching rod and the red cape."[11] Such worries were also addressed to the observing public. When the game is conducted with malicious savagery and the desire to win "no matter what," wrote *Davar* journalist Shimon Samet, "it is capable of awakening the most bestial instincts in the spectator and turning him into a vicious animal."[12]

Fearing the detrimental effects of sports enthusiasm, Hapoel members even formulated a "ten commandments" aimed at "improving the sporting level in Eretz Israel by promoting proper behavior worthy of a civilized public." Yet the Hebrew Athletes' fundamental solution for avoiding the transformation into a "vicious animal" was rejecting the distinctiveness of the athletic body and mind.[13] "We, therefore, have the right to demand that at the Hapoel gathering" maintained *Haaretz*, "we should see before us multitudes engaging in sports and gymnastics, *and not outstanding sportspeople* blessed with a gift for running and jumping. It is not the quality but the quantity that must serve as the measure of the actions of our [sporting] associations in Eretz Israel."[14] The Maccabi organization, ostensibly bourgeois, took a similar stance. The organization's senior figure, who held the position of inspector of physical education in schools, Yehoshua Alouf, wrote, "We here in the Land [of Israel] have become pampered in our demand for public performances and amusements. In our work in physical education for the young, we should be wary of the external glitter that usually accompanies the sports movements and give deeper attention to the content."[15] Similarly, a pamphlet from Maccabi Tel Aviv's athletics department stated, "Sports do not aspire to create 'stars,' and it is not the ultimate goal of sports to foster record-holding individuals. Our sportspeople must always stay humble and not think of themselves as special or outstanding . . . and keep away from the 'prima donnas.'"[16]

This expectation of not outshining or surpassing the people was intertwined with a growing anxiety stemming from the desire for sporting success.[17] "The aspiration to victory is cheap, chasing after 'goals' and whatnot," proclaimed an article in *Haaretz*. "After all, this is not the purpose of sports and competition. Certainly, everyone should aspire to be the winner, but not outside the limits of courtesy and patience toward one's opponent."[18] Or as the journalist for *HaBoker Sport* put it, one must commend the young wrestler who "always chooses to lose graciously rather than win disgracefully."[19]

In the void left after the purpose of sport was taken away, the athletic body was reimagined as being one with the people. Alouf, for example, advocated for a sporting approach in which "the individual stands out, not at the public's expense but as the public's agent."[20] Likewise an article about one of the leading footballers in Palestine, Avraham Beit Halevy, hailed him as "a European-level player" but also noted that he was "not just an excellent athlete on the playing field but a 'decent fellow' in day-to-day life," adding that "he knows how to draw people to him in a comradely and friendly manner."[21] The press coverage of Yaffa Cohen, one of the leading female Hebrew Athletes, also redirected attention from her competitive performance and accomplishments toward her everyday life. When a *HaBoker Sport* journalist visited her home, he proudly noted that her home life was the model of modesty and good hygiene. "This is the room of a true sportswoman," he wrote, "cleanliness, light, and flowers . . . sparse furniture. The walls hung with pretty pictures." Following this impression of her humble character and a brief overview of her athletic achievements, the interview ends with the question, "And what about [your life] outside of sport?" This question positions Cohen's body in the banality of the day to day. "My time is entirely taken up by domestic matters," she replied. "The only free time I have for sports is in the evenings and on Saturdays (*Shabatot*)."[22]

ATHLETIC PROFESSIONALISM AND THE MEANING OF THE HEBREW BODY

Concerns about the purposelessness ascribed to the Hebrew athletic body went hand in hand with the question of athletic professionalism.[23] Far from being a Zionist invention, the issue of sporting professionalism emerged in nineteenth-century Britain when payment for athletic competition became a social leverage, while also being a critical driving force behind modern sports' rapid dissemination and their transformation from a marginal cultural phenomenon into a global and popular industry.[24] Nonetheless, debates over professionalism often had a local element to them. In Britain, opposition to professionalism was part of the bourgeois attempt to prevent the lower classes from actively participating in sports, which reflected, among other things, the geographic tensions between north and south.[25] In Germany, the large sum of money involved in professional sports was often perceived as a sign of Americanization and was opposed by both sides of the political spectrum, while on Asia and the Middle East, it was often a symbol of westernization, modernization and colonization.[26]

In this sense, the prevalent criticism leveled in the Yishuv against athletic professionalism was just another reflection of specific national, social, and cultural tensions. Accordingly, local journalists tended not to use the Hebrew word "*Mikzo'anut*" but opted for a direct transliteration of the Latinate term "professionalism:" This word served as a kind of "mark of Cain" signaling the foreignness of the phenomenon and the cultural threat it represented. This condemnation of *Mikzo'anut*, however, transcended both class and political delineations, despite the fact there was almost no substantial practice of the phenomenon. Thus, more than a concrete social issue, athletic professionalism was frequently employed as an antonym for the Zionist cause. As one member of Maccabi's internal committee asserted, "We have brought forth a wave of football and *professionalism* while the cultural and national endeavor has been abandoned or greatly weakened."[27]

In other words, in Hebrew eyes, the financial elements of *professionalism* were always entangled with the mental and physical dangers associated with the autotelic modern sporting experience.[28] As early as 1921, *Do'ar HaYom* warned of the harmful tendency "to make 'sports' an interest for its own sake, a source of income and big profits, an institution of betting for large sums."[29] According to this journalist, athletic competitions are a moral threat because they do not ask "who is strong of body, healthy of spirit, quick of wit, but who might impart upon the public multitudes more competitive and pecuniary enthusiasm."[30] In this climate, when the Maccabi association defined its amateur status in 1926, only its coaches were allowed to receive payment, and compensating the athletes themselves—thereby commercializing Hebrew bodies—was strictly prohibited.[31]

The Hebrew unease about of athletic professionalism significantly shaped the evolution of Jewish sports in Palestine.[32] Its initial impact was likely felt by the local football teams that emerged in various corners of the Yishuv in the early 1920s. Despite not necessarily aligning with Maccabi (the sole Jewish physical-culture organization active in Palestine at that time), these popular "neighborhood" teams actively participated and garnered attention in numerous friendly games, small tournaments, and other competitions.[33] Such "innocent" and amateurish development was a requisite initial stage for many sporting clubs, undergone by numerous European football clubs two decades earlier. However, in Palestine, the Jewish local teams were a fleeting phenomenon, dissolving even before they had the chance to establish a clear identity and tradition.

"This great stirring among our sportspeople," a 1923 *Do'ar HaYom* article reads, "especially among the youth, is very gladdening, yet, on the other hand, it saddens the heart to see some members start pulling players from team to team whenever they form a new team." To this journalist's mind, the proliferation of clubs and the emphasis on the skills of the individual subverted the broader purpose that sports should serve in furthering the Jewish body's collective revival. "The exertion of energy and work of each for himself is harmful to the movement as a whole," the author of the article goes on to assert, "and let us not forget that our goal is not to hunt down particular souls [i.e., players] for the benefit of one team or the other, but to develop the Hebrew sports movement in general and the health of our youth in particular."[34]

A few years later, neighborhood teams began to disappear from the national sports landscape and consciousness. Some of the teams disbanded; others joined the mainstream physical-culture organizations Maccabi and the newly formed Hapoel. From a materialistic perspective, we can infer that the economic crisis experienced by the Jewish Yishuv in Palestine during the latter half of the 1920s, coupled with the shaky financial state of the small neighborhood enterprises, eventually led these independent associations to recognize the need to sell tickets and merge with larger national organizations.[35] The establishment of Hapoel and the subsequent transformation of Maccabi into an organization identified with the "middle class" were other catalyzing factors.

And yet, the official reason for the dissolution of the private teams was defined as fear of professionalization. In 1927, for example, members of the Balfour Jerusalem football team wrote, "In recognition of our team's need for great development, and in an effort to combat the *professionalism* that has been spreading through Maccabi of late, we hereby declare our departure from the Maccabi sports association and our entrance into the ranks of the Hapoel Physical Culture Association."[36] A very similar statement had been issued a month earlier by the Allenby football team from Tel Aviv, only three years after it was formed by students of the Hebrew-speaking school "Gimnasya Herzliya" who lived on the nearby Allenby Street. "In recognition of the need to combat professionalism in sports," wrote the heads of the team, "we hereby announce that we are severing all ties with Gibor [Hero]. We are entering the ranks of Hapoel and aligning our position with that of the organized labor movement of the General Organization of Workers."[37]

The merger between Hapoel and Allenby was the humble beginning of the popular football club Hapoel Tel Aviv, yet it was akin to a public announcement against sports professionalism as a whole. "We call upon our comrades in the field of sports in Eretz Israel," the team leaders wrote, "to fight against the disease of *professionalism* spreading today in several places in our land. And likewise, to prohibit the possibility of receiving a steady salary for playing, with no connection to any *productive work* toward the building up of our society, our nation and our land." In other words, the neighborhood football club decided to relinquish its independence for fear of the impact that professionalism would have on the revolutionary culture. As long as the Hebrew Athlete was in any way influenced by professionalism, claimed the members of the Allenby club, he was mired in a "poisonous atmosphere"; only after the venom was drained could he return to contributing to his people's "physical and spiritual health!"[38]

HEBREW BOXING AS A MASCULINE REAFFIRMATION UNDERMINED

The Hebrew objection to the purposelessness of sports was especially notable in the most masculine and professional sporting platform of the era: the boxing ring.[39] Outgrowing its British origins, boxing was transformed in the interwar years into a "mainstream" global cultural spectacle. and this development.[40] As Erik Jensen and other historians have noted, for the soldiers returning from the battlefield of the Great War, the rise of "rational" violence of the boxing ring made it a safe and controlled platform in which to cope with the destructive and shocking effects of their mental and bodily injuries.[41] Similarly, the sport became an attractive vocation for Jewish athletes in the Diaspora. Fighting against long-standing antisemitic stereotypes of weakness and effeminacy, the dozens of Jewish champions who emerged during the interwar gave rise to a "golden age" of Jewish boxing and a new modern image of the Jewish male as tough and violent.[42]

However, in contrast to this global celebration of "controlled violence," boxing in the Hebrew ring was often perceived as a potentially *unhealthy* activity. "The boxer does not do his job as the 'rewarding profession' of a healthy sportsman," read a 1932 article in a Hebrew sports journal. "Instead he does dangerous tricks, his inhuman and uncivilized antics inflaming the crowd of onlookers and transforming them into vicious beasts."[43] The main Zionist concern was that, in contrast to the graceful body produced by doing gymnastics, the spectacle of boxing constituted a degenerating influence. One *Haaretz* journalist argued, for example, that "it is necessary to make sure that the new sport does not become a kind of 'weakness,'" noting that "this sport possesses certain qualities that tug at the heart of youths, and we may worry that they will become obsessed from an early age and suffer from a disharmonious, unbalanced development."[44]

Proponents of physical culture therefore warned that "boxing requires, first of all, a healthy and developed body, and it is not enough to be skin and bones and have some agility, as some might have it."[45] Members of Hapoel praised their heavyweight boxer Loeb because "his favorite sport didn't become his bread and butter" [*Kardom lahfor bo*]. In addition to saving himself from the sin of "*professionalism*" and offsetting the perceived "uselessness" of his boxing by making a concrete contribution to the Zionist cause, Loeb's physical labor as a road worker, they argued, was a boon to his athletic activity, contributing to his abilities in the ring by making his fists stronger and his body sturdier.[46]

Simply put, it was the Zionist revival that imbued the Hebrew body and sports with meaning, and not vice versa. As part of this perspective and in line with the ethos of gymnastics, boxing in the ring was reimagined as a nonviolent and disciplined experience. "In athletic circles, there are those who see boxing in a negative light due to the bitter spirit of conflict it embodies and the manifestations of cruelty that sometimes accompany the competitions," claimed Benayahu in 1929. "However," he continued, "all admit that this sport, especially the preparatory and training exercises it requires, is unmatched in the harmonious advancement of the body and the development of certain positive psychological qualities." And so, whereas training was meant to teach participants to "purposefully use all the motions of the body in any situation," the aim of the competition should be merely to "demonstrate in the eyes of the crowd the accomplishments of groups and individuals as the result of systematic training."[47]

This nonprofessional, nonspectacular approach was also instrumental in shaping the spirit in which Hebrew culture approached the matches themselves. "Even as we take our first steps, we must refrain from the tasteless propaganda, the cheap advertising and the crude poster," maintained a *Davar* journalist in 1937. "The competition," he continued, "must take place in broad daylight, without blinding spotlights or tiresome turning on and off [of the lights]."[48]

Consequently, the boxing experience in the Yishuv often lacked both the appeal of the spectacle and the discipline of hygiene.[49] For instance, in 1935, the short film *Yoman Carmel* documented a random boxing match between the Maccabi and Hapoel teams.[50] It captures a modest, almost intimate scene: Ghostly nameless boxers clash in a makeshift ring at the heart of a cluttered room. One bare-chested combatant is set apart from his rival, who wears a sleeveless shirt as his insignia. Judges, ensconced behind white wooden tables, sit in a narrow crevice with their backs to the wall. Nearby a suited man leans back, hands deep in pockets, perched on a hefty cupboard crowned with a haphazard pile of mattresses. Tables draped in modest cloths are scattered around the ring's periphery, and the sparse crowd suggests that only those tethered to the event have gathered. Through a slender window, the encroaching night filters in, while a shadowy figure looms atop a closet, silently surveying the fray from above. A grand flag of Zion, adorned with a prominent Star of David, stretches across the wall, its commanding presence drawing the spectator's eye away from the frenetic dance in the ring.

Even in 1939, despite boxing being one of the most popular sports in the Yishuv, its events often remained underground affairs, held in warehouses and lacking proper equipment or budgets.[51] "Imagine a special canton over which the police have no control, where everything is tolerated and permitted," wrote a Tel Aviv resident in 1938, after watching a boxing match for the first time.[52] And yet, despite the general foreignness and the amateurish, spectacle-free atmosphere of the sport, Hebrew physical culture experts continued to strive for a sporting experience in which "order rules all."[53] Only then, according to a Hebrew sports journalist, would boxing acquire a purpose greater than any personal and momentary triumph: "an aim and will common to both sides: to foster an entire triumphant generation" [*Dor menazeah*].[54]

The story of the Hebrew boxer Ami'el Avineri (Emil Rebelski) serves as an apt illustration of the role of sports in the Yishuv. Avineri, son of the Hebrew educator Moshe Rebelski, was born in 1908 in the southern region of the Russian Empire. His first encounter with boxing took place in Berlin, and in 1926, after spending three years in the German capital, he emigrated to Palestine and set his sights on developing the sport in Tel Aviv.[55] Initially, Avineri operated within the framework of the Maccabi organization, and then from 1929 onward, he established his own private boxing club simply called "Box Club." The following year, the club's name was changed to "Benny Leonard" in honor of the great American Jewish boxer.[56]

The choice of the famous world champion "Benny Leonard" as the name might attest to wide-reaching international influences, yet the club did not attempt to challenge the prevailing attitudes toward professional sports in the Yishuv.[57] Like the athletic endeavors of Maccabi and Hapoel, the private boxing club's activities were amateurish and characterized by an unassuming, familial atmosphere where the participants were "just a bunch of Hebrew boys from Tel Aviv and the neighboring towns."[58] Moreover, the club supported the Hebrew desire for a disciplined and unemotional sporting atmosphere. In a flyer that it distributed, people in the crowd of spectators were depicted as a dog, a pig, and a monkey, all yelling out violent slogans, with the legend above their heads instructing "Do not shout!! The boxing ring is not an animal pen."[59]

In the early 1930s, after closing his club, Avineri returned to Berlin to pursue a career as a film actor, prompting the Maccabi journal to publish a short story on the departing boxer.

> On the Hebrew shore in Tel Aviv there appeared a young man, a youth almost, who attracted the attention of the passersby with his strange motions," the tale read. "The handsome-bodied youngster was swinging punches into the air.—'Lunatic!'—the kids who surrounded him on all sides called him.—'He has lost his mind'—the majority of women lounging in the sand called out mournfully. And the youth kept brandishing his fists in the air, as if hitting someone.[60]

The brief text underscores Hebrew culture's prevailing unfamiliarity with the rules and body language of boxing. However, it also reflects how Avineri's perceived lack of masculinity, in the eyes of Tel Aviv's women and children, is attributed not to aesthetics but to his ineffectual performance. Described as "handsome-bodied," Avineri's perceived "strangeness" stems not from his appearance but from the apparent triviality of his boxing skills.[61]

Consequently, the textual narrative of Avineri's "redemption" only materializes when his athletic body is imbued with a sense of national purpose. Having witnessed him knock out a "strong fellow of considerable heft and height" who had provoked him, the author declares, "All cheered for Emil. They stopped laughing at him and his contortions no longer seemed so strange." The account goes on to describe Avineri overcoming a British rival and even instructing "sixteen- and seventeen-year-old Hebrew youths, their skin tanned by the Israeli sun," how to defeat "the tall British soldiers hands down."[62]

Despite the narrative salvation, the Hebrew boxer's athletic pursuits ultimately failed to secure a significant place in Zionist collective memory. Although Avineri returned to Palestine and resumed his boxing career, his reintegration into Tel Aviv's life brought with it a shift toward a more practical role alongside the "frivolous" sport of boxing—that of a lifeguard.[63] Legends tell of his heroic rescues, claiming he saved thousands and even pioneered the stand-up paddleboard (*the hasakeh*). His ring exploits, therefore, often remain peripheral, overshadowed by his legacy as "Emil the Lifeguard" (*Emil hamatsil*) from the late 1930s until his death in the 1980s.[64]

THE AMBIGUOUS WELCOME FOR THE JEWISH ATHLETES OF CENTRAL EUROPE

Emil's transnational biography also reflects the contrasting attitudes toward athletic competitions held in the Diaspora and in Mandatory Palestine. In central Europe, for example, participating in football games became a symbolic act of fitting into the local culture as healthy and equal men.[65] Most notable was the Hakoah Vienna club. Founded in 1909 and expanding to become one of the most prominent Jewish sports clubs in the twentieth century, it included a successful football team, wrestlers, swimmers, fencers, and many other Olympic-caliber athletes. Hakoah's prominence also reached the Yishuv, where the locals portrayed the Jewish athletes as a "scrappy underdog"—"the small and skinny Hakoah" who had dealt with antisemitism with "courage, agility and technique."[66]

However, the Yishuv's reaction to Hakoah, and retrospectively, Jewish sports in Europe, came into question in 1924 when Austria's famous football team, the crown jewel of the Viennese club, decided to visit Palestine.[67] The short tour sparked debates about the meaning of sports in the Zionist Revolution and compelled the agents of Hebrew culture to "determine" whether it was an integral part of "Muscular Judaism" or, as *Do'ar HaYom* declared in 1923, "an imitation of the actions of others, and as such—it is no different than any other imitation in the world: it renders man into a monkey donning his owner's clothes."[68]

During their eight-day sojourn, the Jewish team traveled throughout Palestine and were festively welcomed wherever they went with speeches and ceremonies.[69] The hospitality shown to the team, which consisted largely of guided visits to holy places and historical attractions, reflected the common destiny shared by Hebrew culture and European Jewry.[70] Members of Maccabi, for instance, took out an ad to welcome the visitors and to express the hope that "Hakoah, who have managed to raise Hebrew sports to such a high degree, will open with their visit a 'new era' in Hebrew sports here."[71] Thus united in a common cause, "the sons of Eretz Israel are obliged to welcome Hakoah with the brotherly love it deserves."[72] Proponents of this approach linked the team's athletic activity in Europe thematically with the working of the land in Eretz Israel, claiming that Hakoah's endeavors were "pioneering work, like the work of the pioneers building up Eretz Israel, sacrificing their sweat and blood for the one single ideal they share with the members of Hakoah."[73]

However, although some voices sought to emphasize their common cause, others chose to focus on the foreignness of the non-Hebrew-speaking visitors.[74] As a *Haaretz* journalist put it, "It is certainly no sign of national unity when their representative greets the children of Tel Aviv in German."[75] Leading educator Eli'ezer Riger also wondered, in response to the Austrian team being honored with a ceremonial greeting by the Tel Aviv municipality, why Hakoah was being presented "as a symbol of our national vigor" when they "could not greet the children of Tel Aviv in Hebrew and did not find it necessary to write Hebrew words on the flag in Cairo. Are these the symbols of our national vigor in the eyes of the municipality?" asked Riger, "not the 'Hebrew Brigade,' the defenders of Galilee, or the pioneers?"[76] *Haaretz* claimed that the manager of the Austrian team admitted that the players were undeserving of the great praise they had received "because we still do not know your language."[77] Even those who wished to praise and embrace the European guests expressed doubts reminiscent of Keisari's concerns about sports producing a healthy body without a soul—noting that the Austrian Jews "still cling, it would seem, to the exterior and superficial order of things, without delving into their depths."[78]

In other words, despite their international success and their muscular physique, the members of Hakoah—and modern sports as a whole—found themselves excluded from the revolutionary experience. There were, among the Viennese footballers, quite a few Zionists who asked of their Hebrew brethren: "Light our way, give us your Israeli Hebrew-ness, and your wants—our wants will be fulfilled."[79] However, it seems that ultimately the Yishuv public ignored these sentiments, exhorting the Austrians to go home and send "young men who will take up shovels and plows."[80] As author Moshe Smilanski phrased it, "our nation's victory" must only be realized "the old and proven way: with the book and with the plow."[81] Simply put, the public consensus on the Hakoah visit ultimately arrived at the conclusion that sports were a phenomenon that belongs to the Diaspora.[82] A year later, Hakoah returned for a second visit to Palestine.[83] This time, their delegation elicited limited public interest, and the Hebrew media devoted only scant attention to these "youngsters who know how to kick a ball."[84]

A decade after the visitors from Hakoah came and went, tensions about Hebrew athletic competitions were reawakened with the return of German-speaking Jewish athletes to Palestine, this time not as guests but as immigrants and refugees. Following the rise of Nazism in 1933, approximately 250,000 people emigrated to the Yishuv, nearly doubling the Jewish population in Palestine and introducing a significant number of middle-class Jews from Central Europe, which dramatically changed the Yishuv's character. On the fringes of this mass migration, a considerable number of people, mostly from Austria and Germany, possessed athletic skill and knowledge and sought to continue their craft in the Levant. In June 1933, a *Do'ar HaYom* article proclaimed, "There is no doubt that the expert sportspeople from all the branches of sports, the coaches, the trainers, and the leaders . . . who disembark from almost every ship arriving on the land's shores, will raise the level of physical culture in Eretz Israel."[85]

As was the case in many other fields, the German-speaking athletes integrated relatively quickly, and within a few years, some held senior positions in Hebrew sports. Yet many had difficulty fitting into Hebrew culture. "It is with sorrow that we must mention the unhappy fact that, over the years, many immigrant athletes have left us," wrote Maccabi member Ernst Freudenthal. "Some have moved on to other sports federations," he continued, "while others—and these are the majority—scattered to the four corners of the Earth, among them those who had been loyal and devoted members in the ranks of Maccabi abroad."[86] A former player of Hakoah Vienna, Egon Pollak, for example, was appointed coach of the Maccabi Tel Aviv team in the 1930s and even served as the coach of the national team for a short period. Nevertheless, Pollak, who had taken part in the Hakoah Vienna delegation to Palestine a decade earlier, never managed to find his place in Palestine and emigrated to Australia in 1939.[87] Although he ultimately returned to Israel in the 1950s and served in a number of positions as coach and commentator, culminating in an appointment as the first coach of the Israeli national team, Pollack never seemed to have left his mark on Hebrew culture. In the 1970s, he returned to Germany and remained there until his death at the age of eighty-two. Pollak's story was not an unusual one: A 1939 article in *HaBoker Sport* noted, "Any incoming immigrant, even if he was immeasurably outstanding in sports in the Diaspora, is considered a foreigner here."[88]

The story of Nickolaus "Mickey" Hirschl is probably the starkest example of the failure of German-speaking athletes to integrate into Hebrew culture as athletes.[89] Hirschl, a heavyweight wrestler and member of Hakoah Vienna, emigrated to Palestine two years after winning two bronze medals at the 1932 Los Angeles Olympics.[90] Arriving in 1934 at the age of twenty-six, the wrestler—possibly the most prominent active athlete ever to emigrate to the Yishuv or the State of Israel—planned to continue competing in his favorite sport and to coach and foster a new generation of local wrestlers. In an interview he gave to *Davar*, he said, "The human material in Eretz Israel is excellent! I can already see in my mind's eye the strong Eretz Israeli brigade I have assembled, and how it surprises the European countries with its power and makes a name for the revivified land of the Hebrews."[91] Yet this was not to be. Despite his determination, the healthy and strong wrestler never achieved his ambition of representing the Yishuv in an official international competition and was all too soon erased from Hebrew culture and the Zionist collective memory.

Hirschl's failure to integrate is especially glaring, given the classical nature of the sport of wrestling. Unlike popular football or violent and consumerist boxing, Greco-Roman wrestling is stripped of many of the commercial aspects of modern sports. Instead, it is a kind of a "pure" masculine activity that had similar premodern traditions in the Americas, the Caucasus region, Oceania, and East Asia.[92] Accordingly, as early as the 1920s and 1930s, countries such as Japan, Turkey, and Egypt were already competing in the Olympics and coming away with medals. The Egyptian wrester Ibrahim Moustafa, for example, became a symbol of national masculinity following his gold-medal performance at the Amsterdam Olympics in 1928.[93] Even though this national pride was mixed with local doubts about whether modern sports were an effective tool in the nation's struggle against western colonialism,[94] that did not prevent the perennial presence of Moustafa's bare-chested image in the local press or his being a coach charged with shaping the next generation of wrestlers in Egypt. Hebrew culture, in contrast, did not afford Hirschl the privilege of playing a similar role in nearby Palestine. Despite hoping to fit in as an athlete and creating a new modern tradition of Zionist wrestling, the son of a Jewish butcher soon found himself working in the Tel Aviv slaughterhouse.[95]

Although it had an ignominious end, Hirschl's sporting career in Palestine initially showed some promise. When he began training and coaching on the Hapoel Tel Aviv wresting team, the newspaper *Davar* described him as "a model of dedication, devotion, and humility."[96] In 1936, Hirschl and his team competed successfully against a local Arab club, and he was even slated to take part in Hapoel's delegation to the "Popular Olympics" in Barcelona that same year. The event, in the Catalan capital, however, was canceled due to the outbreak of the Spanish civil war, and Hirschl never got the chance to put his prowess on display.[97]

Like that antifascist event, Hirschl's potential never materialized, and soon he vanished from the Hebrew sports landscape.[98] By 1938, it seemed Hirschl had given up on the sport he loved. "I am so tired; I have no desire to train," he told a journalist during a chance encounter on a football pitch.[99] In 1939, however, he attempted to resume training.[100] He joined Hakoah Tel Aviv and announced, "I feel capable of returning to a top performance level. But I must not work at the slaughterhouse as hard as I have been working until now. If I am allowed to cut back, I believe I can play an honorable role in the 1940 Olympics."[101] He requested special funding for a trip to neighboring Egypt to train with that country's excellent wrestlers, but this request went unanswered. In early 1940, he suffered a back injury at work and never returned to the Hebrew wrestling mat.[102] Shortly after, he joined the British Army and fought in World War II, after which he got married, moved to Australia, and opened a local beef-processing business.[103] About forty years later, he summed up his athletic career in a few words that seem to reflect the hardships endured by Central European Jewish athletes who had traded the deep-seated antisemitism of their homelands for national disregard in Palestine, proudly stating that he "was never interested in financial rewards from his athletic career" and had competed instead for "self-respect."[104]

Like Hirschl, many German-speaking athletes of the fifth wave of Jewish immigration (1932–1939) experienced difficulties because of the amateur nature of Hebrew sports; their lack of proper financial support led to hardships. In the summer of 1936, for instance, the Hapoel football club announced that it would be giving up the services of the team's coach and former Hakoah Vienna player Alexander "Nemesh" Neufeld because it could not "afford to spend the large sum of money that H. Nemesh's presence entails."[105] Roughly one month before Nemesh's departure, Ernst Freudenthal, who himself had emigrated to Palestine in 1933, made a suggestion on how to right the situation: "We must understand that this brand of immigrants (*Olim*) require a foundation to engage in athletic pursuits, which is why we must create the conditions for their basic sustenance by arranging work for them, in order to give them the possibility of devoting themselves [entirely] to athletic work."[106]

Freudenthal's suggestion, in fact, included a proposal to change the essence of Hebrew athletic competition. Like Alexandrovich and the "new sports journalists" (see chapter 2), Central European immigrants also saw sports as an integral part of national activity. As Walter Frankel, another notable Central European athlete in Palestine, wrote, "Hebrew sports also require pioneering . . . pioneers of sports, who pave new roads and prime the soil for a new and robust generation."[107]

The absence of a conflict between sporting competition and personal/national identity in the worldview of these recent immigrants also led to the formation and establishment of sports teams and clubs representing the athletes' countries of origin. Atid (Future), the Central European immigrants' club founded by Frankel and Freudenthal, was the largest and most prominent one, but it was joined by the Lithuanian community's Atzil (Noble), the Egyptian community's Hitkadmut (Advancement), and the Greek and Turkish communities' Degel Tzion (Flag of Zion).[108] However, as did the proliferation of neighborhood teams in the previous decade, this multicultural transformation of the map of Hebrew sports provoked a massive backlash from the physical-culture establishment. Maccabi member Aharon Rosenfeld wrote about this athletic schism: "It is a phenomenon that parades under the guise of an affinity for sports, but it is the fruit of moral degradation and organizational weakness that proves definitively that not all is well in our world of sports. . . . We must gather our forces by using them to the utmost and avoiding any kind of separatism." To counter the desire for local independent teams, which in Europe had served mainly as an expression of identity, Rosenfeld argued that the notion that sports could be a desirable end unto itself would be damaging to national solidarity:

> And if there are some sportsmen who would like to instill the idea of sport for the sake of sport . . . disconnected from any national responsibility—the time has come to sound the alarm about this danger that threatens to empty the movement of the little soul it has left. . . . There is no future for the various Atids ["futures"], there is no nobility in the Lithuanian immigrants' Atzil ["noble"], and there is no strength in Hakoah ["strength"]. The Hitkadmut ["Advancement"] team, comprising Jews of Egyptian origin and active mainly in the field of basketball, too, has no advancement, for it would be strange for every branch of sports to be an organization in and of itself. "Benny Leonard" has made no public appearance for years. . . . Inter-group rivalries will not breed athletic accomplishments, for they are destined, with time, to collapse from lack of spiritual ferment and sustainability.[109]

This criticism soon gave way to emphasizing the foreign nature of the new athletes. In a humorous article published in the Purim issue of *Davar,* the writer "wished" the Atid team to secure "at least one section manager who is not a [German immigrant]" and for "Hakoah Tel Aviv—a dozen fans made in Eretz Israel."[110] This criticism of the German immigrants' "foreignness" also led to outright conflicts. Maccabi North Tel Aviv, for instance, chose to sever its cooperation with Atid under the pretext that its own activities were mostly national in essence, whereas "the Atid children are educated and spend time in a German rather than Hebrew environment."[111]

Some of these "ethnic" teams continued their activity well into the second half of the twentieth century, but in the 1930s, Central European Jewish athletes were constantly faced with the charge that their profession lacked "national meaning." Thus, within this atmosphere of deliberate, idealistic amateurism, sportspersons who did manage to integrate into Zionist society had to see themselves as something other than *just athletes.*[112] Like Emil the lifeguard and ophthalmologist and cofounder of the Maccabi Health Fund Ernst Freudenthal, Walter Frankel too worked as a teacher of agriculture at the Hebrew Gymnasium in Jerusalem and was even one of the Hebrew developers of hydroponics—the art of cultivating plants without soil.[113]

About six months before the outbreak of World War II, *HaBoker Sport* summed up the cold shoulder given to the Jewish athletes who had emigrated to Palestine from Central Europe in the following words: "It is not at all hard to exclude the new man, the new immigrant who is mostly shattered in body and spirit due to the tortures he had undergone in the Diaspora. And on top of that, they also have their cares over their livelihoods and the relatives they had left behind back there, in the European inferno. And thus, the active sportsman gets 'out of shape.'" As the examples of Hirschl, Pollak, and Neufeld show, Hebrew culture only partly opened its arms to athletes wishing to pursue their craft. The sad result of such treatment was predictable: "National European champions, even European championship winners and Olympic medalists, [were] pushed aside by people who had never won even the tiniest competition in a land standing on the bottom rung of the sports world."[114]

SPORTS AESTHETIC, CONSUMERISM, AND PHOTOGRAPHY IN THE LATE 1930S

Despite the difficulties experienced by German-speaking athletes, their influence on the Hebrew sporting culture was not limited to their being athletes, coaches, and fans but also encompassed the different understanding they brought of the relationship between sports, consumerism, and individuality.[115]

Until the 1930s, sports commerce in the Yishuv was quite limited; it was often confined to local efforts such as giving away a pack of cigarettes with every ticket purchase.[116] However, many of the Central European athletes rarely had qualms about using their image to advertise a cigarette store in Tel Aviv and earning money as models and spokespeople.[117] As one immigrant athlete declared, "For sport to exist and to thrive, it requires money, money, and more money."[118]

The link between sports and commerce also included a different yet widespread aesthetic. The short-lived *HaSport* magazine, established by the German immigrant Kurt Benyamin (see chapter 2), for instance, did not shy away from emphasizing the individual and distinctive characteristics of the athletic body and its activity.[119] A bolder example can be found in the photography of the German-born photographer Liselotte Grschebina.[120] Similar to the representation of athletes in the work of Nazi director Leni Riefenstahl, Grschebina's visuals depict Hebrew Athletes, both men and women, dressed in white against the background of the sky of the Land of Israel.[121] The athletic body is positioned above the camera, gazing into the distance, back straight, and, like the athletes of ancient Greece, throwing a discus or a javelin. This common interwar aesthetic was not necessarily fascist, yet in Grschebina's eyes, the Hebrew Athlete was not a useless body but a mythical, bronze-skinned figure existing outside time and space.[122]

The consumerist and aesthetic aspects of this new approach were combined in the form of the *Mishmar VeSport* ("Defense and Sports") sticker book. Issued in 1939 by the German- immigrant-owned Dubek company, the booklet embraced an aesthetic that explicitly glorified the athletic body and individual Hebrew Athletes.[123] The previously anonymous athletes were photographed in motion, in the midst of athletic activity. Their running, swimming, boxing bodies were represented as vital entities, part of "the creation of a new Jewish archetype, a healthy, beautiful, self-confident person . . . [who] in knowing his own strength overcomes the reality of life and joins, as an individual and out of discipline, the entirety of the emergent nation."[124]

The financial considerations that might have motivated the publication are unclear, yet despite changes in aesthetics, the professionalization of the athletic body remained an unbreakable Hebrew taboo. Thus, even in the late 1930s, the athlete remained a secondary figure within the context of the Zionist Revolution and its challenges. As its name suggests, *Mishmar VeSport* was not exclusively devoted to athletes. Indeed, it opened and closed with images depicting pioneers "taming the frontier."[125] A similar, albeit even more regressive position, is allotted to sports in the first Hebrew movie *Zot Hi Ha'aretz* (This Is the Land) released in 1935.[126] Made by two Eastern European immigrants Baruch Agadati and Avigdor Hameiri, the film devotes only about three of its sixty minutes to depicting athletic activity as part of the urban revival in Eretz Israel. The montage focuses mainly on gymnastics rather than on athletic competition, and unlike the pioneers, the athletes do not speak but only move to the sounds of energetic music. Moreover, like *Mishmar VeSport,* the hour-long film begins and ends with descriptions of the exalted labor of pioneers working the land. In other words, in the years leading up to World War II, the Hebrew Athlete was rarely, if ever, able to stand alone.

In 1935, the organ of the Hapoel movement printed a small comic caricature under the optimistic title, "In the Not So Distant Future . . ." The sketch, which portrayed the pioneers and leaders of the Yishuv, such as Ben-Gurion and Moshe Sharett, as football players, stood in stark contrast to a series of German cartoons that depicted athletes as overestimating their cultural significance, claiming it surpassed that of figures like Goethe and Bismarck.[127] In other words, where the caricature presented the Hebrew Athlete as faceless details in the background of the drawing, the senior heads of the Labor Party were recognizable enough to be objects of exaggeration and emphasis. Below the drawing, a short legend exemplified the marginal place of sport in the desire for "revival": "No need for Hapoel's youth," it read, "we're young ourselves."[128]

In this revolutionary context, athletic competition produced a muscular body endowed with physical strength but with a limited ability to contribute to nation-building. In Hebrew eyes, sports may have been suitable in the Diaspora, but in Eretz Israel, it was separate from the revolutionary purpose of shaping the new Jewish body and mind. Therefore, in the words of Gordon, its place was limited to being "an addition to labor, a complement to labor, or a preparation for labor."[129]

This conception, which denied the athlete an exalted status, made it difficult to position the Hebrew athletic body as a desirable national model. As stated in in Maccabi's journal, "If we assume that the champion has to have exceptional qualities from birth . . . surely accomplishing a record based on this foundation cannot be a source of individual pride. This is all the more true for the nation to which the record-holder belongs." This kind of argument was not unique to Hebrew culture but was directly influenced by the sporting spectacles taking place in various places around the globe. However, in the Yishuv, it was given an additional revolutionary dimension that did not allow for the existence of athletic accomplishment in and of itself. In this vein, the same article declared, "Sports champions are for the nation nothing but luxuries, such as horse racing and cockfighting, and a 'world champion' cannot serve as a source of pride for the people any more than a winning horse or cockerel. Less, perhaps."[130] Thus, even in 1939, Hebrew spectators, as one journalist complained, "didn't care about being unable to see the games for which they had paid good money."[131]

The competitive athletic body's lack of revolutionary significance also affected the treatment of Jewish athletes who had emigrated to Palestine and wished to continue their athletic pursuits. "In any other place they would be treated with respect, and only here they are met with shouts of contempt," the manager of a Haifa-based football team wrote regretfully regarding the welcome received by his Hungarian players.[132] The difficulty of absorbing immigrant athletes stemmed partly from the amateur financial model adopted by Hebrew sports culture. However, as an immigrant athlete from Germany noted, "The 'unusual' attitude to the demands of sport" was also motivated by a deeper factor—"the lack of sports knowledge prevalent to this day in large sectors of the Yishuv."[133] Therefore, it is no coincidence that, throughout the interwar period, Hebrew culture was having trouble finding, fostering, and producing a Hebrew Athlete "qualified to participate in the Olympic Games."[134]

Nevertheless, by the end of the 1930s, the first signs of a broadening national discourse began to appear. For instance, a short time after his departure from Palestine, Mickey Hirschl was described as being "strong as a bear."[135] Although still animalistic, this image of the athlete positively singled out the body of the Jewish wrestler from that of common folk. After the establishment of the State of Israel, the consequences of this change took root, and Hebrew sportspeople born in Palestine in the interwar period, such as football players Yehoshua Glazer and Nahum Stelmach, were, for the first time, inducted into the Israeli collective memory. Today, too, however, the most devoted fans of Israeli sports, hardened by decades of international disappointment, still experience in their flesh the early twentieth-century Zionist revolutionary contempt for the outstanding body of the professional athlete.

4 • "THE WHOLE WORLD WILL KNOW OUR ANSWER"

Sports, Internationalism, and the Jewish Return to History

In January 1923, Yosef Yekutieli, wrote a satirical piece for the *Do'ar HaYom* newspaper titled "Basic Rules for the Game of Football." Humorously outlined a list of fictional football regulations, including "Arrive late to the field," "Make remarks to the referee," and "Anger your opponent," the prominent Maccabi member spoofed the violence and disorder that prevailed on the sports fields of the Yishuv.[1] Interestingly, however, Yekutieli's "new rules" did not "originate" in Britain but rather in Switzerland. In other words, despite living under the rule of football's inventors, he already understood by 1923 that the game had found new international ownership.

Indeed, the interwar ascent of modern sports cannot be fully understood without two organizations based in Switzerland: the International Association Football Federation (FIFA, founded in 1904) and the International Olympic Committee (IOC, founded in 1894). After World War I, interest in the role of international sports grew dramatically. Consequently, tournaments such as the FIFA World Cup and the Winter Olympic Games were established, along with a remarkable expansion of existing events like the Summer Olympic Games. The 1936 Berlin Olympiad, for instance, featured four thousand athletes from forty-nine countries, marking a 65 percent increase in participation compared to the 1912 Antwerp Summer Games held before the Great War. Moreover, Olympic traditions solidified during this period, introducing iconic elements such as the Olympic flag, oath, village, torch-lighting ceremony, and torch relay. The games also attracted substantial financial investments; most notably, the enduring partnership with the Coca-Cola Company that began in 1928 and continues to this day. Simply put, in less than twenty years , both FIFA and the IOC emerged as major entities, overseeing major events and wielding significant power, influence, and wealth.[2]

The rise of interwar internationalism was not unique to sports. As Glenda Sluga argues, modern internationalism was not the sole possession of radical socialists and naïve idealists; rather, it was a worldview that figured importantly in the efforts of liberal politics to defend "the needs of the free market," cultivate national rights, and restrain fascism and nationalism.[3] Thus, also the international sports scene was still in a state of multifaceted self-fashioning that was prone to continual change from within and without.[4] "Liberal" organizations such as FIFA and the IOC, which enjoy monopoly status today, then competed with a multitude of bodies, such as the Socialist Workers' Sport Internationale (SASI), that put forward a materially different vision of competitive sports.[5] Additionally, alongside the socialist or Soviet communist alternatives emerged numerous "independent" organizations and events with more focused agendas. These included the Jewish Maccabiah Games, the West Asian Games, and the World Women's Games, the premier venue for women's sports between the world wars.[6]

This fluid and inchoate nature of international sports had a direct impact on the Hebrew Athlete. It not only fueled the local rivalry between the Maccabi and Hapoel associations as a sports reflection of the liberal–socialist divide[7] but also gave the Hebrew Athlete a rare opportunity to gain entrée into the international arena. It is highly doubtful that, after World War II, an organization like Maccabi, representing a small minority of Palestine's inhabitants, could have become the de facto official representative of all Mandatory Palestine in relation to FIFA and the IOC. However, during that period of self-definition, when the rules were not yet fully established and international organizations were eager to expand their influence, Maccabi's members needed only a measure of obstinacy and persistence to secure their membership cards. To wit, in the eyes of a physical-culture aficionado, the development of international sports provided them with a rare propitious moment to earn a reputation in the international community, the Jewish world, and Hebrew culture.[8] "The value of sports today," wrote Walter Frankel, "is equal to that of politics itself... and a nation whose sons and daughters participate in international sporting life justifies its national existence and demonstrates its national political vitality."[9]

To join the international entities, however, the Hebrew Athlete had to learn the new "universal" language of modern competition. Yet this foray into the "great world" also unveiled the particularistic and predominantly emotional essence that Hebrew Athletes and perhaps Zionists at large imbued into internationalism during the interwar period.

RETURNING TO HISTORY WITHOUT LEAVING HOME

Yosef Yekutieli and several other Maccabi members initiated Zionist efforts to join the IOC—the gold standard of international sports—back in 1922. Driven by a naïve and optimistic fantasy that the encounter with the world's communities would give "the Hebrew people an opportunity to be like everybody else" [*ke-khol ha-goyim*],[10] joining the IOC did not make the "global stage" into a model of emulation for the Zionist movement. As an unnamed contributor to *HaBoker Sport* alleged, "Many among us who take an interest in sports fail to observe the big world and are utterly unconcerned about what has been achieved in sports there."[11] The detachment from goings-on outside the borders of the Zionist Revolution originated largely in the inability to perceive international sports as a source of inspiration at the level of values. "Hebrew sport is not an imitation of sports abroad," a writer for *Do'ar HaYom* asserted. "Its goal is not theirs and we should not learn from them."[12] Meir Benayahu went even further, claiming that one should not study the outcomes of competition "on the international scale" because Hebrew sports "should not amuse themselves with millimeters and seconds."[13]

This disinterest led to a basic Zionist misunderstanding of the international worldview. Thus, for the Hebrew Athletes, the primary goal of joining the IOC and FIFA was to establish official *Jewish* representation. As a contributor to *Haaretz* wrote ahead of the 1924 Olympiad, "Only we Jews have no official representation at the games and our flag will not be seen among the flags of all the nations on opening day. Yes, many Jews take part in the games, but they are fighting for the peoples among whom they dwell."[14] This perspective, which reflected the ethnocentric worldview of gymnastics, stood in stark contrast to the approach of the IOC and FIFA, which categorized athletes solely by their political citizenship. Accordingly, European Jewish athletes could be passionate Zionists but, at the international level, could represent only the state whose citizenship they held. Simply put, the athletes of Hakoah Vienna or Jewish boxers in the United States might be "proud Jews" who used sports in diverse ways to emphasize their Jewish identity, but they were always considered Austrians or Americans, respectively, on the international sports level. Hence, even though Maccabi wished to take part in international sports as a team from the Land of Israel, ostensibly representing all of world Jewry, international sports organizations agreed to recognize only the geopolitical entity that the League of Nations recognized: Mandatory Palestine. Moreover, they even demanded that the local body comprise all the inhabitants of that land.

Maccabi found this "civic" stance severely disappointing. As Yekutieli wrote after he first encountered the rigid international rules, "There seems no hope for Jews to appear at the Olympic Games as Jews." Despite the temporary setback, they persisted in their efforts for more than a decade. As Yekutieli wrote to his colleagues, "We must . . . not desist from the work; ultimately success and victory will be ours."[15] This determined Zionist perspective, which emphasized the value of action over words, eventually led Maccabi to "solve" the problem through deception. They enrolled a few "token" Arab members to provide a respectable picture for outside consumption while establishing Jewish-only controlled representation internally. It is unclear to what extent the international bodies were misled by the Zionist tactic; however, by granting official recognition, they also effectively enlisted Maccabi as local, boots-on-the-ground agents in Palestine.[16] As the secretary-general of FIFA wrote to his Zionist electees in the Middle East, "It is supposed that you inform me of every such permission given by you because the FIFA must know and authorize every encounter against non-affiliated organization."[17]

This dual perspective continued even after the official recognition. Thus, the Palestine Football Association and the Palestine Olympic Committee—their official names—were known within Hebrew culture as the Eretz Israel Olympic Committees and the Eretz Israel Football Association, respectively. Similarly, collaboration with the international community did little to hinder Yekutieli's ongoing efforts to enable Jews from other countries to officially represent "Palestine." Thus, for example, in 1935, he sent a personal letter to a higher-up in the IOC, Sigfrid Edström, asking "the International Olympic Committee [to] resolve that any Hebrew sportsman who wishes to represent in the Olympic Games the Land of Israel, which has been the national home of the Hebrew people since time immemorial and has been officially recognized [as such] by all nations in our times—be allowed to do so." Edström turned down the request, which would have required a major revision in the values of international sports. Nonetheless, Yekutieli, perhaps anticipating the initial refusal of his request, left an opening for future negotiations, writing: "I am very eager to continue discussing this clause with your excellency."[18]

This steadfast commitment to representing the Land of Israel was crucial to the Hebrew Athletes. Shortly after the Maccabi delegation returned from the 1934 World Women's Games in London, a short booklet titled *The Hebrew Flag in London* was published. Under the boldfaced title, the cover featured a photograph of young women athletes entering the stadium at the opening ceremony, carrying the national flag and a sign where the word "Palestine" was replaced with a photomontage captioned "Eretz Yisrael" in Hebrew. The camera, however, did not show the faces of most of the sportswomen, focusing instead on the artificial national emblem.[19] A member of the Maccabi delegation, Yaffa Cohen, summarized the trip similarly: "Look, our appearance served as lovely propaganda for Eretz Israel."[20]

Thus, Hebrew culture did not necessarily sanctify winning as the ultimate aim of international sports; rather, it celebrated the Jewish "return to history." "Be the score what it may," Alexander Alexandrovich wrote before a game of the football national team. "With raised head and erect steps shall we return to the field of competition, from awareness of our own value, the soothing sense that we have done our duty and exercised our entitlement amid straightforward and fair equality within the family of nations."[21] In much the same manner, when venturing abroad, the Hebrew Athletes fixed their gaze on the concrete symbol of their revolutionary passion: the national colors.[22] "The blue-and-white flag flutters over the hotel building alongside the flags of the other nations participating in the women's games," reported Lipa Levitan from the World Women's Games in London. "The heart rejoices at the sight of our blue-and-white flag with the Star of David waving in its glory alongside the American and the Italian, the Japanese and the French, the English, the Polish, and the German flags."[23] A member of the Maccabi delegation to New Delhi in 1934, Dov Rabinovitch, wrote in a similar vein, "I cannot describe to you our delight as we saw our flag, which the Indians hoisted over our tent."[24] Mentions of the importance of the flag also recurred in the Hebrew Athletes' personal writings. David Almagor, a member of the delegation to India, recounts in a letter home the physical sensation he experienced on seeing his national flag: "We winced under the burden of the difficulties of the road and our every limb cried out for rest. . . . The Zionist flag, fluttering from the staff, appeared before us . . . The sight of our national flag encouraged us and allowed us to forget our physical fatigue."[25]

Like the flag, the Hebrew body and identity were also seen as messengers of the Land of Israel. "They brought the blue light of our country into the narrow, smoke- and haze-filled hall," Uri Keisari wrote of the Hapoel delegation to Paris. "The azure of the sky of the Land [of Israel] radiated from their eyes."[26] Descriptions of the physical revival of Hebrew culture were also typical in the travelogue of a member of a Hapoel cycling delegation to Poland: "In an uplifted mood, members surround us at the table and are willing to hear us to no end. No matter how tired we are, it is a special pleasure to feel that we can satisfy some of these young children's aspirations for Eretz Israel."[27]

Accordingly, the heads of Maccabi-Hagibor Haifa received a verbal flogging when they chose to "strengthen" a delegation to the United States by adding several Jewish players from Hungary.[28] The Maccabi activist Ernst Simon decried the club's decision: "I protest . . . their wish to use Jewish professionals from other countries to put together the repatriation of Eretz Israel!"[29] The chair of the Haifa club, Haim Weisborg, who had emigrated to Palestine two years previously, tried to soften the criticism of his players' foreignness: "We are doing well and are doing good for our people and our land," he contended. "What we have in mind, among other things, is to show the whole world from here—our ancestors' land—that we are on par with the other peoples in every respect whatsoever."[30] Four months later, however, despite his wish to further the cause of "our ancestors' land," Weisborg had to admit that the trip had failed: "This attempt teaches us that henceforth it is no longer worth traveling to America either financially or spiritually. . . . In the future, we should try to appear only with our own forces."[31]

This affair was the last major attempt to use Diaspora Jews as sports emissaries of the Yishuv. Leading, for instance, members of the Maccabi delegation to India to Hebraized their names before setting out. Likewise, the Hebrew press noted proudly that, although they were expected to lose, all the young women athletes who had been sent to the World Women's Games in London had been born and raised in Eretz Israel.[32] The journalist Lipa Levitan, who had joined the Maccabi women's delegation in London, wrote, "It's literally a Babel of languages, and the main thing is that our language rings out here, too."[33]

In practice, however, it seems that the Zionist passion for a composite Hebrew identity abroad had the opposite outcome: It merely accentuated the foreignness of Jewish athletes from Palestine. "Their fine spirit of sportsmanship in accepting defeat with cheerfulness and dignity was one of the outstanding features of the meeting," concluded British Colonel J. H. Levey in his assessment of the performance of the Maccabi women's delegation to London. "In a world which is internationally selfish, it is good to see that athletes from Palestine can set an example of how to lose gracefully."[34] The IOC member Theodor Schmidt sent a similar message while visiting Palestine: "Sports in Palestine," he wrote, "are not following the old European paths but often take on original forms."[35]

The alterity of the athletes from Palestine was plain not only to the Europeans but also to some of the Hebrew Athletes themselves.[36] "They didn't know what to do and where to put their hands and feet," recalled Leah Lederman (Fletcher) about her comrades on the trip to London. "The members of the delegation," she said, "suffered from acute feelings of inferiority to the other delegations."[37] In a similar fashion, Meira Belkind, the supervisor of the London delegation, noted in her diary that two athletes got lost on the streets of Paris during their one-night stopover in the French capital: "A beat cop led them around, hoping they might identify their hotel. He finally took them to a police station. They sat down at the table and cried. All they could say was 'British Consul.'"[38] In other words, the young Jewish women were confident enough to take a nocturnal walk down foreign streets, but for better or worse, they were no longer part of the metropolises of the "Old Continent" because they were, both literally and symbolically, speaking another language.

THE HEBREW ATHLETE AND THE "NAZI OLYMPICS"

This particular Hebrew grammar found heightened public expression in the run-up to the Summer Olympic Games in Berlin in 1936. The Palestine Olympic Committee officially joined the IOC in May 1934. Two months later, they received an official invitation to participate in the 1936 Olympic Games. Hence, the first major issue the young Zionist body faced was also the most controversial: whether to take part in the "Nazi Olympics." This binary question, which had to be answered one way or the other, triggered coverage on a scale that few international sports events commanded in the 1930s Hebrew press.[39]

The polemic games compelled Maccabi members to confront the issue of joining an international entity that was organizing an event in an antisemitic state. The heads of Maccabi, who had worked for more than a decade to get this opportunity, responded with a multitude of tortuous wordings meant to preserve their international status while clearly boycotting the competitive sports festival in the Nazi capital. In a column in *Davar,* the most widely circulated Hebrew-language newspaper in Palestine, Maccabi wrote, "We hope to obtain the privilege [of participating in the Olympiad], too, and only then, of course, can we declare publicly to the entire sporting world that since the world Olympic Games are taking place in Hitlerian Germany this time, we sportspeople in Eretz Israel do not wish to participate in them even though we have the right to do so."[40] Public criticism of Maccabi, however, only escalated after the president of the local committee, Frederick Kisch, informed the IOC in November 1934 that the Zionist body would absent itself from the Games on the grounds of the IOC's insufficient resources and professional knowhow.[41] The decision of the Zionist diplomat, an alumnus of Cambridge University, not to mention German antisemitism as the reason for not participating was perceived in the Yishuv as a troubling sign of the "elements of the 'high diplomacy' that has begun to spread among Jewish functionaries in recent years."[42] That is, from the perspective of the Hebrew Athletes, international politics was arousing fear by its separation of language from action. "Instead of answering 'yes' or 'no' explicitly," it was written in *Uzenu,* "the board of Maccabi in Eretz Israel found a third way: yes and no together."[43]

This schism in the local sports arena was further widened by the international sports discourse. The official position of SASI and Hapoel was that the Olympic Games, regardless of their venue, represented a bourgeois occasion that deserved vehement condemnation and boycott.[44] In the eyes of the socialist sports establishment in Europe and Palestine, therefore, holding the Games under a racist regime only confirmed their claims about the pernicious essence of the "fascist" Olympic competitions. "In the most recent Olympiads," Emanuel Glickman of Hapoel wrote, "a few athletes from each country took part . . . and showed off their record achievements in an atmosphere of national and racist zealotry. . . . In the blood-drenched Nazi state . . . which has made physical culture a means of preparing for a new world war that will turn the human body into cannon fodder—not a trace of human culture, fraternity of peoples, and exaltation of man will be present."[45] This mordant, trenchant position, juxtaposed to Maccabi's apologia, served as a clear statement (and a subtle critique) of the identity of "the real sports representative" of the Jewish people: "Hapoel in Eretz [Israel], together with all Jewish sports organizations in Eretz [Israel] and the world that are true to human dignity, democracy, and peace, will respond to SASI's decision not to participate in showing respect for that heinous state and will unite in praise of the workers' forces in the world and their allies who promote peace and fraternity of humankind against fascism."[46]

Ultimately, however, despite the abundant spilled ink, fierce condemnations, and delicate answers, both Hapoel and Maccabi found themselves in a passive position without international influence. Consequently, despite their desire for action, Hebrew Athletes on both sides of the political divide had to settle for a few recycled propaganda articles and brief meetings at the local clubs.[47] This impotence only worsened as the public urged the country's body culturists to protest and take action in the international arena.[48] "It is therefore within the powers of the Palestine Olympic Committee," *Haaretz* ruled, "to organize sporting public opinion in all countries and demand that Germany not serve as the host of the international sports gathering."[49]

The opportunity for international action that the Hebrew physical culturists hoped to obtain came shortly before the opening ceremony in Berlin. Hapoel was planning to send a delegation to the "People's Olympiad" in Barcelona—an antifascist alternative to the "Nazi Olympics"—and Maccabi planned to send representatives to Germany in support of the local Maccabi chapter in Berlin.[50] However, the event in Barcelona was canceled when the Spanish civil war erupted, and the Maccabi trip was suspended due to concern at home that the dispatch of a Zionist delegation to Germany would be construed as support of Nazism.[51] Two weeks before the Nazi Olympics were to begin, that *Haaretz* reported the cancellation of the Jewish delegation to Germany: "It is hard to say what the right way should have been, but clearly it was every simple Jew's feeling that Maccabi should not go to Berlin."[52] The nature of the endgame was clear. Despite its pretense of playing a key role on the international sports scene, the Zionist body became a sideline observer with no real influence. As the Games were about to begin, "A. R." wrote on the sports page of *Haaretz*, "The fortunes of our athletes who had intended to go abroad this summer did not smile on them."[53] Simply put, the Hebrew Athlete stayed home.

HEBREW ATHLETES AND JEWISH ATHLETES

Of what, however, was this home constituted? The Hebrew physical culturists imagined themselves—and the Land of Israel—as the foundation stone of the Jewish sports hub. For example, before the Second Maccabiah (1935), Yekutieli described the event as a "national test" in which "hundreds and thousands of young people . . . who will immigrate to Eretz Israel . . . will inhale the air of the homeland."[54] Yet, the run-up to the Nazi Olympics demonstrated the distance between the Hebrew Athletes and their fellow Jews in Europe.

After it became clear that the Olympic Games would occur under the patronage of an antisemitic regime, Jewish sports enthusiasts in Palestine expressed their support for Jewish athletes in Europe. They suggested that "our sportsmen," suffering from discrimination and racism, should emigrate to Eretz Israel and even proposed taking action on their own for the sake of "their brothers" in exile.[55] N. Ben Aharon, for example, writing in *Do'ar HaYom,* stated that in view of the violence that Jewish athletes in Europe were experiencing, "a moral and public boycott should be declared and a special boycott committee representing all walks of the nation should spearhead it. [The committee] should be headquartered in Eretz Israel because it is from here that the call for a boycott should emanate."[56] Similarly, about two weeks after the Nuremberg Laws were passed in December 1935, "members of Maccabi" demanded that the Jewish Agency "issue Palestine immigration certificates [visas] . . . to those among our comrades who will suffer due to this decision in any country whatsoever."[57] Even after it became clear that the event in Berlin would take place undisturbed, the stalwarts of Hebrew sports continued to examine matters from a place of identity and a perspective that found it hard to believe "that Jews will be found who would prefer the Nazi Olympic wreath over the wreath of torments of the historical Jewish people [*yisrael saba*], which is fighting an existential war with mortal enemies."[58]

This deep-seated faith in international Jewish sports solidarity, however, began to fissure after it became known that the worldwide organizing body of Jewish sports, the World Maccabi Association, was not boycotting the Games collectively; instead, it was merely requesting that the IOC allow Diaspora Jews who so wished to boycott the Games on their own. The potentates of Hebrew sports considered the international Jewish organization's request "a watery and craven decision made thanks to the German Maccabis."[59] A journalist for *Haaretz,* for example, claimed, "Not only did it [World Maccabi] not know how to organize a boycott movement against the Olympiad and failed to support the first signs [of such a movement], but by its puzzling silence and its flaccid decisions ('absolving members from having to participate in the Olympiad') it even bothered to impose an atmosphere of 'patience' in its ranks that adds no dignity to this Association."[60]

Despite the World Maccabi Association's decision, the Hebrew physical culturists believed that their counterparts overseas would boycott the Nazi Games. A contributing editor of *Do'ar HaYom* wrote, "Although we must admit that the representatives 'betrayed their national calling,' the 'national conscience' will act in the right direction."[61] Even when rumors about Jewish athletes' intentions to take part in the Olympics began to crop up, the Hebrew Athletes tried to attribute their participation to an ulterior motive. "By means of passion, outstanding organizations, and an excellent external reception 'without distinguishing who is the guest is and where he came from,'" a commentator in *Haaretz* wrote, "Germany managed to reach out even to those who are foreign to the regime."[62] This outlook, which credited Jewish participation to the success of Nazi propaganda, persisted even after the international event was over. Simultaneously, however, the Hebrew Athlete began to realize that Jewish participation was a corollary not only of propaganda, coercion, and threats but also of the Jewish athletes' free will.[63]

As the news about Jewish athletes' willing participation in the Olympiad trickled in, attitudes toward them in the Yishuv took an increasingly radical turn. Jewish athletes who chose to boycott the Olympics were praised because "self-respect comes first."[64] Concurrently and contrarily, however, sharp criticism of the Jews who chose to represent themselves and their home countries began to appear on the pages of the Hebrew papers. "Who are these Diaspora Jews [*yehide huts*] who, despite the Hitlerite regime and the Nuremberg Laws," wondered a journalist for *Haaretz*, "seek Nazi Germany's hospitality . . . and was it knowingly that they chose to debase their dignity and self-awareness in order to travel to Germany at reduced prices as guests of Hitler's government?"[65] Similarly, *HaBoker Sport* proclaimed that the athletes of Hakoah Vienna who had decided to take part would be remembered "in eternal infamy [for] bringing disgrace on the entire Jewish people, which is fighting for its rights."[66] In another example, a journalist from *Do'ar HaYom* declared, "The Jews will remember in infamy these sportsmen's betrayal of their people's war of boycott against their tyrannizers-oppressors."[67] The secretary of the Palestine Olympic Committee Selig Rosecki wrote, "What the four Maccabi [members] did in Vienna revealed the deep wounds that are eroding the body of the Maccabi movement. And woe betide our future if these wounds are not [to] be removed by radical surgery."[68]

Even if one admits that the impending fate of European Jewry was unknown then, the biological metaphors invoked by Rosecki make for difficult reading. But, the Hebrew Athlete never wished to disengage from the "Jewish people." Throughout the 1920s, the German Jewish fencer Helen Mayer received enthusiastic treatment in the Palestine Hebrew press, which proudly called her "the queen of fencing."[69] After she decided to take part in the Berlin Games representing her German homeland, she became the subject of acidic condemnation in the Hebrew public sphere. The harsh words, however, did not absolve the collective Jewish responsibility: "Indeed, betrayers are as hard for Israel as psoriasis," *Do'ar HaYom* wrote about Mayer, mimicking a rabbinical dictum, "because even after they leave the camp, the responsibility for their actions falls upon us."[70]

Still, the Nazi Olympics forced the Hebrew Athletes to admit the limits of their strength. Several hours before the opening ceremony, Yosef Yekutieli wrote in his optimistic way, "We also know we are weak; therefore, our protests and demands go unheeded. . . . Our answer to the Olympic Games in Berlin will be . . . strong participation in the XII Olympiad. . . . We will bring together athletes who remain loyal to their country. . . . Then we will no longer be weak. Strong we shall be and the whole world will know our answer."[71]

A UNIVERSAL LANGUAGE FOR A PAROCHIAL EXPERIENCE

The Nazi Olympics affair revealed another parallel and largely abstract dimension of Hebrew Athletes' interaction with international sports: the perception of sport as an autotelic phenomenon. This perspective marked a shift in the athletes' view during the latter half of the 1930s, leading them to embrace and sanctify the "Olympic idea" or Olympism to safeguard and uphold the "purity" of the sporting virtues. This "universal" international "sporting worldview" or "philosophy" was not original; its roots could be traced to the British Isles in the nineteenth century when the emerging middle class implemented the idea of amateurism and fair play.[72] Furthermore, it was (and remains) eclectic and riddled with contradictions. Bluntly put, the innovators of modern sports, like Pierre de Coubertin, were not systematic philosophers. However, perhaps paradoxically, it is the numerous gaps in their scholarship that left room for multiple interpretations, thus accounting for the resonance of today's sports across various local cultures.[73] Indeed, the presence of sports in the Yishuv never deviated from the national outlook of the Hebrew Athlete; instead, it became an integral part of him or her. In other words, the Zionist revolutionary desire became one with the "true spirit of international sports."[74]

The integration of Olympism into Hebrew culture was not a haphazard occurrence. During his visit to Palestine in 1934, IOC member Theodor Schmidt took little interest in the local bureaucracy and its organizational abilities; he even overlooked the fact that the Jewish representatives represented only a small minority of the inhabitants of Palestine. Nonetheless, he devoted his lecture before a local audience to the purpose of the "Olympic idea." It seems his Hebrew listeners took his words to heart, going so far as to translate and publish them in the local press.[75] Shortly afterward, Schmidt's remarks reverberated even more strongly when, in its very first decision after joining the IOC, the Palestine Olympic Committee announced that it intended "to translate the propaganda pamphlet published by the International Olympic Committee into Hebrew and Arabic in order to distribute it in Eretz Israel for the purpose of explaining the Olympic idea and its value."[76]

The effort to disseminate information about the Olympic idea found special resonance against the background of the Nazi Olympics and the international debate about whether to hold the games in the capital of the Third Reich. Although the 1936 Summer Games were not the first sports event to take place under the patronage of controversial regimes, "Hitler's Olympics" marked the first time that the autotelic ethos of the compulsory separation of politics from sports was put to the test in serious public debate.[77] That is, most, if not all, of the participants in the debate supported the Olympic idea but disagreed about whether holding the Games in the Nazi state diminished or strengthened it. Did it sully athletic purity or perhaps substantiate it as something that transcended fleeting politics? With this background in mind, the Hebrew Athlete favored the former position. About seven months before the opening ceremony, Yekutieli wrote, "Honest sportsmen from all places of dispersion who learn fair play on the playing field every day will not lend a hand to the Berlin Games and will not take part in these Games. . . . All will be loyal to the Olympic idea and will remember the call of Baron de Coubertin, creator of the modern Olympic Games—'All games, all nations!'"[78]

This stance among those in the sporting community, however, differed from the prevailing view in Hebrew culture. According to the "official" line, which found expression mainly in the foreign-news pages of the Yishuv press, the Games in Berlin were part of a broad political struggle of the Jewish and Zionist people. As a corollary of this perspective, the leading powers in the global sports world and other supporters of holding the Games in Berlin were considered monolithically tethered to the heads of the Third Reich.[79] "American sportspeople who favored holding the Olympic Games," wrote a pundit for *Haaretz*, "are starting to speak literally in Goebbels's language."[80] In contrast to this commonly held Zionist position, in which "the Olympic Games are [seen as] more than a sports affair for us," the Hebrew Athletes emphasized the harm being done to "the Olympic idea" and pure sporting values.[81] Maccabi, for example, claimed that those opposed to holding the Olympics in Berlin event had "true sporting cognizance," whereas those in favor "did not act for the sake of sports.... The goal of their war ceased to be the Olympiad per se, and they intended more to endorse the Nazi regime writ large."[82]

Such expressions transcended public rhetoric and lip service. The wish to keep the "Olympic idea" pure appeared not only in the Hebrew Athletes' public remarks but also in their unpublished official documents. At a Palestine Maccabi conference, for instance, the decision to hold the next Olympic Games in Germany was vehemently protested; as written in the minutes, the Games were being held "in a country where all principles of freedom and human fraternity that underlie the Olympic idea are brutally trampled."[83] Similarly, the heads of Hapoel charged that participating in them would deal a blow to the "Olympic ideal" and clash with "human dignity, democracy, and peace."[84]

For the chair of the Palestine Olympic Committee Selig Rosecki, the injury to the "Olympic idea" appears to have been a real trauma. "I blame everyone, everyone who destroyed my soul-felt belief in the noble ideals of modern sports!" he cried out in an opinion piece on the inaugural day of the Olympics. "I accuse the representative sportsmen who will cross the threshold of the Berlin stadium: ... you have forsaken the noble ideals of the sporting man.... I accuse all of you of betrayal—in the name of... those vigilant for the idealistic principles of international sports." Rosecki's article, headlined "J'accuse!" and thus mimicking Émile Zola's famous precedent, did not spare the heads of the IOC from criticism: "You lords, sitting high and mighty on the International Olympic Committee... sweetly smiling and proclaiming fraternity, equality, and liberty... Nazi Germany, of all places; that land that inscribed on its banner, red as blood, slogans that stand in stark contrast to the principles of international sports: enmity toward people who belong to another race, hatred of a foreign nation, contempt for anyone whose views are different from its own."[85]

Despite the anguish that radiates from these words, they did not lead to Zionist secession from international sports.[86] Shortly before the Berlin Games began,

Rosecki and Yekutieli wrote to the heads of the IOC, again fiercely criticizing "holding the Games in grave and total contradistinction to the modern sporting spirit, which aspires to absolute equality of nations and races."[87] This time, however, they also turned their attention to the future: "All of our sportsmen are following what is being done at your honorable congress with great interest, because we all expect good hope from your work. We pray that your honorable and important mission for the development of physical culture for the benefit of mankind, irrespective of religion and race, will be crowned with great success."[88]

This renewed pledge of allegiance also made room for a new interpretation of the "Nazi Olympics." About a year after the games, Yekutieli wrote to a German colleague: "If it is not difficult for you and if it entails little expense, could you please obtain the sundry literature that was published for the Olympic Games in Berlin, the propaganda booklet in particular, I would thank you immensely because we are about to undertake a large international sports project and would dearly wish to have appropriate material before us."[89] Thus, even though "the pure and timeless underlying ideal of the Olympiad" had been undermined "by the demand of fleeting politics," the Hebrew Athlete's revolutionary vision remained fixed on a future in which Olympism was already an integral part.[90]

Two years later, the Yishuv shifted its focus to the football pitch as the national team faced off against a Greek squad in the World Cup preliminaries. "For the past week, strong jitters ahead of the binational contest have been rife in the sporting circles of Eretz Israel," *Haaretz* reported. "Everywhere, in the cafés, the institutions, the buses, the street, and at the associations, they have been speaking about this competition."[91] The widespread public interest led to extensive coverage, including the launch of *Haaretz*'s sports supplement and a special evening edition of *HaBoker*.

The coverage was indeed exceptional. Four years earlier, in 1934, when a Zionist team from Palestine first competed at this level, it faced its neighbor Egypt. Then, too, the event attracted considerable attention from the Hebrew cultural scene.[92] Several fans accompanied the Hebrew team to Egypt, and in the second match, held in Tel Aviv, eleven people were injured after "hundreds pressed against the unfinished fences and wooden structures."[93] Despite the popularity of football in the Yishuv and the lengthy combined history of the Jewish and Egyptian peoples, stretching back to Pharaoh and the account of the Exodus, most coverage of the event took place at the technical and informational levels. The Hebrew press emphasized information of importance to the fans who were about to travel to their southern neighbor, noting the date of the game, describing the composition of the teams in brief and utterly anodyne terms, and offering terse coverage of the game itself.[94]

This informative approach underwent a substantial transformation with the approach of the games against the Greek squad. "Through the fog of hatred and villainy, a beam of light breaks through," Benayahu wrote. "The two historical peoples meet again after thousands of years, on the battlefield of—peace."[95] The game on the field was now imagined as a temporal bonding of past and future, the ancient and the modern. Thus, about a year after his frustration with the Nazi Olympics, Rosecki reverted to his earlier glorification of sports: "May this international contest between the Hebrews and the Greeks in Tel Aviv," he wrote, "serve as a symbol of new times to come, of new trends in the history of humankind." The sporting encounter, however, also came with a universal commentary that carried clear moral weight. "Now we will meet in a delightful sports contest on the football field, in a battle waged under the international rules of the sport, in an atmosphere of high-mindedness and mutual respect," Rosecki wrote. "It is a war of peace in which, even if it stirs the greatest of passions, the rivals remember that they are brethren, members of the great family of world sports."[96]

The reports on the match, which framed sports as an ethical and autotelic phenomenon, reflected a subtle shift in the "Hebrew" language of sports. The coverage included more photographs, new visuals, and more descriptions of the athletes and the "sports moment" (see chapter 3). The veteran sports journalist Yisrael Paz went so far as to argue that the accounts included the first pun in Hebrew sports journalism.[97]

The content itself also changed. For the first time, it included personal information about the players. Although their Hebrew identity remained central, each athlete was also presented in the press with his own backstory. The special newsletter published by the football association ahead of the game included this descriptions: "It is noteworthy that the large majority of the team's players . . . were born in Eretz Israel or immigrated long ago. They began to play in Eretz Israel, and only five of them have a glittering past in football abroad and here received an opportunity to take their game to a higher level. . . . *The story of sporting life of each and every player should be observed,* and we should derive hope from his past playing for the future of sports as coming up this Sabbath."[98] Thus, the Hebrew Athlete was no longer a faceless messenger of the nation but was now a person with a history and characteristics who was capable of finding a place in the collective memory.

However, the process was not linear: The extensive and detailed descriptions of the players also attracted public criticism. The association's newsletter "told the players' history in detail and did not forget to note the languages they're fluent in," a commentator for *Davar* wrote, subsequently adding, "Would it not have been better to note whether the players are fluent in kicking, at least on one leg?" "But the [newsletter]," the socialist journalist continued, "is missing the main thing: a few words about the World Cup games."[99] On the political right flank too, similar demands emerged for a return to informative reporting. The Revisionist sports journalist Lipa Levitan, for example, accused that, instead of giving a lesson in sports history "they lavished hundreds of lines on the members of the team, lessons about the game of football, and just plain babbling. . . . In hundreds of boring lines [they] 'described' Israel's representatives on the football field, [saying] that the goalie, Klein, is 'slender and tall' and is a 'dark guy,' etc. etc."[100]

Although Hebrew culture may not have been fully prepared to sanctify the athlete as an autotelic being, the rising significance of international sports sparked acknowledgment of winning as a national goal and a calling card to "the international arena of sports."[101] From this standpoint, the bottom line of the twin outcomes—losing to Greece and not advancing to the World Cup—was resounding failure. "The thousands of spectators left the game, some silently, some complaining, some mocking, and some with a one-word remark: Bad!" Confessed a correspondent for *Sport Haaretz*. "And the last word, no few days will yet pass, much water will flow into the Jordan, until we will be able to say: Here before us is an Eretz Israel football team of which we may brag at home and on the road as well."[102]

The nexus between modern internationalism and the Jewish and Zionist world has an extensive history.[103] From philanthropic organizations such as the Alliance Israélite Universelle, the American Jewish Committee, and the American Jewish Joint Distribution Committee to the League of Nations and the Mandate system, Jews have turned to various forms of internationalism to secure, support, and defend Jewish minorities in Palestine and other parts of the globe.[104] Against this background, the Hebrew Athlete's encounter with the international sports community is a small part of a broad tapestry. Nonetheless, it adds an emotional dimension to the existing scholarly debates, which primarily focus on the legal and social aspects of that nexus.

International sports underwent a redesign between the world wars. The Hebrew Athletes wished to exploit the ascendancy of sports internationalism for national goals such as gaining influence among European Jews and improving the fortunes of Zionism in the international arena. However, despite the considerable accomplishment of joining the three main international sports organizations of the time—IOC, FIFA, and SASI—Hebrew Athletes never achieved the active revolutionary experience of "returning to history" that they so desired.[105] As Meir Benayahu asserted firmly, "The actions of the [Football] Association were always off-target. Nothing constructive was done."[106]

Consequently, Hebrew Athletes' eagerness to leverage the international arena for the official representation of Hebrew culture remained constrained. As Moshe Shertok (Sharett), a senior figure in the Jewish Agency, noted, the Maccabi delegation to India appeared "dubious in many people's eyes."[107] Author Yitzhak Demiel, expressed this common view even more acridly:

> And as nonsensical and frenetic as it is, they also took the national, political, [and] class flags and emblems and dragged them here. No! May it never happen here that some group of young guys, idlers or non-idlers from another people and

> land, clash at football or boxing with a group of young guys, idlers, from another people and another land. No! Here envoys are dispatched. Agents. Consuls! . . . Oh the folly, oh the tastelessness, oh the superficiality—a worldwide, intercountry, international superficiality![108]

Furthermore, the Zionist outlook that tightly linked Jewish identity to representation in the Olympic Games created underlying tensions and disillusionment between the Hebrew Athlete and the international sports community.[109] As IOC official (and eventually its president) Sigfrid Edström wrote to Yekutieli after once again rejecting the request to allow all Jews to represent Eretz Israel, "I hardly think the International Olympic Committee will change his fundamental rules to assist you. . . . We will certainly be happy to have Palestine take part in the Olympic Games in Helsingfors and hope you will send a small but good team."[110]

And still, in the second half of the 1930s the Hebrew Athlete began to speak an international sports language that viewed sports as essentially autotelic. As an unnamed contributor to *HaBoker Sport* wrote in 1939, "Obviously, lots of 'foreign entities' are picking at the mighty movement . . . but the sports idea is pure and noble."[111] By World War II, the language that would shape competitive sports in Israel and around the world managed to appear only in initial bursts. As we see in the next chapter, this global process overlapped in Palestine with local events, endowing the Hebrew sports experience with a more "useful" and violent purpose.

5 • "WE HAVE TO LEARN TO SACRIFICE EVERYTHING"

Militarism and the Zionist Desire for a Useful Experience

About a month after the Berlin Olympiad, the September issue of *HaMaccabi* led with a statement on the Jewish year just ending. "The year 1935/36 [5696]," a contributor to the journal wrote, "is a stopover on our lengthy path, the path of redemption and building—redeeming the nation and building the land. And it is our ardent and steadfast wish to uphold these two national fundamentals no matter what. No obstacle and no inhibition, overt or covert, will frighten or deter us: despite and notwithstanding everything, we will arise, build, avenge, and be redeemed!" The Hebrew Athletes' redemptional obstacles were attributed to the capital of Germany and the International Olympic Committee but also and mainly to the domestic arena and what the writer, alluding to the destruction of the Temple, called the "blood, fire, and pillars of smoke that accompanied the year 5696 in our land."[1]

It was about six months earlier, in April 1936, that the Arab Revolt had erupted. The Palestinian uprising against the mandatory regime lasted for three years, resulting in the loss of thousands of lives and leaving tens of thousands wounded. From the standpoint of the Hebrew Athletes, however, the blood and fire that were stalking their country not only represented danger but also accentuated the need to imbue autotelic sports with revolutionary meaning.

"One should not, however, turn a blind eye to the truth," a Maccabi member wrote a few weeks after the Arab Revolt began, "because for much time this gateway [sport] was open to Zionism not as a gateway to the world but only as the point of a needle. The powerful connection was blurred: a connection of Maccabi and Zionism [like that of] a father and [his] offspring. The organic nature of this connection often succumbed to superficial, flaccid linkages of symbols and representations only." This state of affairs also led the author to a clear conclusion: "The ideological power," he wrote, "that obligates Maccabi as a complete and comprehensive revival movement, whose essence is Zionism with all its principles and commandments, and whose attire is sports—this force did not manifest itself firmly."[2]

Against this revolutionary failure of sports, *HaMaccabi* claimed, that in the year 5696, the foundations were laid for a new area of *action* that has been unjustifiably neglected and forgotten thus far."[3] With these new foundations in place, Hebrew Athletes began to believe in their ability, "to fulfill . . . the purpose of their longing" and to "contribute their share in resolving the great and difficult obligations yet to be imposed on us."[4]

SEARCHING FOR MEANING ON LAND AND SEA

Much of this new fundamental concerned itself with the Hebrew Athletes' urban identity. As supporters of gymnastics and the *Lebensreform* discourse, their inevitable position in the urban sphere constituted a problem and an antithesis. Therefore, in the early 1920s, the Maccabians still hoped that "a special place for a gymnastics and a sports field"—"a free and healthy place away from town, far from the befouled smoky air"—would be designated in every new neighborhood built.[5] Similarly, they imagined their sports activity as part of the national frontier: "Indeed, it should be noted happily that 'country folks' [*Anshey ha-kefar*], those who lack the time to devote themselves to sports as 'urbanites' do, have done wonders on the playing field and have earned trophies."[6] Accordingly, in 1923, a victory by a football team from the Nes Tsiyyona village yielded the following observation: "The entire Yishuv in Eretz Israel can find glory in these nice young men, who were capable of being both good and diligent farmers and successful athletes. Hurray, Nes Tsiyyona!"[7]

The fulfillment of this aspiration was far from complete. Not only did almost all sports activity take place in city centers but even there the Hebrew Athletes also struggled to obtain adequate facilities and land for practice and competition.[8] In practice, most body-culture activity in the Yishuv took place in cramped cellars, crowded gymnasiums, and sandy fields full of "befouled smoky air."[9] With this as background, one of the Hebrew Athletes' recurrent complaints concerned the need to obtain funding for the construction of sports centers worthy of the name. "We have no *home* of our own that can serve as a suitable club where members can gather frequently and hold appropriate activities," Maccabians rued at a meeting in 1935.[10]

For the Hebrew Athletes this lack of space reflected the unimportance given to sports in the Zionist Revolution. Therefore, even though many in the Yishuv considered athletic centers and playing fields a purposeless use of space, the athletes commonly called them "homes." As early as 1926, the Jewish National Fund (JNF), the leading land buyer among Zionist organizations, turned down a request from the heads of Maccabi to subsidize the establishment of a playing field on grounds of economic disutility. "We must remark," JNF officials argued, "that we do not hope to earn much from competitive matches or a stadium. We are following the course of affairs in Europe very attentively and we know from them that all sports associations are wrestling with deficits and that stadiums everywhere generate deficits and not profits."[11] In other words, the JNF executives plainly disregarded the possibility that sports might have virtues that were not merely economic.

Six years later, however, the Hebrew Athletes did get the sports facility for which they had pleaded. The 20,000-seat stadium, built in North Tel Aviv in 1932 for the Maccabiah Games, was the first modern sporting grounds in Palestine. Nevertheless, the particular purpose and meaning of the stadium, the construction of which began only ten days before the games were about to begin, was frequently disputed.[12] Thus, when the field hosted a large international trade exposition, the Levant Fair, the sports journalist Alexandrovich wrote, "We saw nothing wrong with it. After all, sports in Eretz Israel always walk hand in hand with the general building of the country."[13] Even the Hebrew Athletes themselves generously promoted its use for nonsporting activities.[14] The feeling of contributing to the country, however, promptly gave way to insult when the Maccabians discovered the construction of a temporary amusement park on the grounds. "Those in charge of the exhibition need to know that it is definitely forbidden to arrange public games in a place where sports culture is disseminated," Alexandrovich argued. "The emotion that fills us isn't protest but sadness. Pure and simple, it pierces our hearts when I see what's being done on our grounds in Tel Aviv."[15]

This Zionist "normalization" of the sporting space clashed once again with the inherent autotelic meaning of the ground. Even the Hebrew Athletes' multipurpose perspective overlooked the fact that, despite being positioned on valuable urban land, the magic of the stadium lies in its need to remain empty most days of the week. As Gumbrecht argued, the moment the stadium bursts into activity, "everything, all of life, including we ourselves, seems congregated in the stadium, and for a limited span the fullness of life and Being stands in irremovable opposition to the emptiness of the stadium during the week."[16] This sacred aspect of the aesthetic experience of modern sports was inherently foreign to the Zionist Revolution. Thus, although renovated in 1935, the Maccabiah stadium never became a site of pilgrimage that would claim a respectable place in the national memory. By 1950, it was decreasingly used for official sports events and was demolished in 2012 to make way for a parking lot and children's facilities.

Recognizing the sports venue as increasingly purposeless, the leaders of Maccabi shifted their focus toward building a settlement for athletes. Established in 1936 with sizable funding from German Jewry, Kibbutz Kefar Hamaccabi (The Maccabi Village), about twenty kilometers from Haifa, was originally intended to accommodate athletes from Central Europe who had come to Palestine in the 1930s for the Maccabiah Games. However, for the Hebrew Athlete, this endeavor was always intertwined with forging a Zionist meaning for sports. "The pioneers of Maccabi settled the land not for the act of settlement alone," the movement journal stated, "but also to plant the Hebrew sports movement in the soil of the national revival."[17] For the leaders of Maccabi, it was the fulfillment of a dream. "Maccabi! Lend a hand to the construction of Kefar Hamaccabi," the movement's poster implored, while the graphic presented a Maccabian against the background of the frontier land, settled and ready for cultivation. The illustrated Hebrew Athlete, dressed in sports attire, grins as he lifts a building with his hands.[18]

This literal feeling of Atlas-style support for the national building enterprise was mingled with a temporary disillusionment with international sports after the Nazi Olympics, making Kefar Hamaccabi a purposeful corrective measure against the Berlin Olympic village. "There's something we can put up as a foil to the fake Olympic village of 1936," a contributor to the Maccabi journal wrote. "It's a village, too—the Maccabi village. Admittedly, this village isn't as lovely, worry-free, light-hearted, and grand as those lovely photos and postcards from Berlin." Yet, "days of peace may yet come upon us and Kefar Hamaccabi will become an Olympic village for a few weeks." Then the world's athletes would no longer be guests of a showcase village set up by a government whose principles are antithetical to sports, but rather "the guests of true friends, true sportsmen who will lead them to their quarters, friends who will pledge the strength and vigor that they acquired through sports not to training for the specters of destruction and devastation but rather for the cause of building and peace, thus helping to spare the Olympic ideal from desecration."[19]

Thus, it was clear to the Hebrew Athletes that, the kibbutz would serve more than the fleeting purpose of "housing the agents of international athletics who have nothing [to do] in the world but to set the highest record" but would instead have "a lofty goal, a goal for which sports is but training—the building of The Land of Israel." In this spirit, those settling in Kefar Hamaccabi might have to shed their athletic identity and forgo their goal of setting records. "The day will yet come," the Maccabi journal desired, "that the runner will march slowly behind his plow and the fencer will clutch only the butt of the hatchet." In the Hebrew Athletes' eyes, therefore, the path to meaning was clear-cut. "We will not be ashamed to state aloud in that even a sports-less Jew should have a purpose of his own," a Maccabi member wrote in regard to the essence of Kefar Hamaccabi. "As we steel and train our bodies and deliver the strength that flows from a healthy and rugged body to our minds, we must mobilize these physical and mental strengths in only one direction—the service of our nation and our land. This alone is the content of Jewish sports."[20]

This hope was short-lived, as it was quickly realized the Maccabi Federation was organizationally and financially unprepared for settlement activity. Furthermore, the disconnection of sports and settlement made the Maccabians' involvement unnecessary. "Unfortunately," a member of the Maccabi Central Committee acknowledged in the minutes for 1938, "it is no longer within our movement's institutional and financial ability to undertake the supervision of the village—a matter of vast responsibility—and Kefar Hamaccabi, too, has not done what it should in order to share this responsibility with us."[21] Thus, in the following years, it was the European-controlled World Maccabi Association that funded the construction of additional settlements, primarily for Central European immigrants, yet this effort no longer had a strong connection to the Hebrew Athletes' activities in the Yishuv.

Another, more local avenue of meaning that emerged during the Arab Revolt was greater participation in water sports. Aligning with the harmonic ideals of gymnastics, Hebrew Athletes already embraced these activities, finding in them a natural affinity for the water "Everyone knows the physical value of sailing," a participant in a Maccabi meeting stated. "Whomever engages in this sport places all the muscles of his body in motion and develops [them] equally."[22] Similar arguments appeared in the movement's journal: "Our watchword for this year is broadening the bounds of action and winning over the masses, youth in particular, to this healthy and natural sport [swimming], which suits the climate and the geographic conditions of our land."[23] In the film *This Is the Land* (1935), too, footage devoted to the growth of urban areas shows gymnastics on the beach, seafaring, and swimming in the Mediterranean.[24]

However, when Jaffa port was shut down due to the Arab Revolt and the small Tel Aviv port opened on the basis of Hebrew labor, a wave of enthusiasm swept the Yishuv at large and the Hebrew Athletes in particular.[25] As with the building of Kefar Hamaccabi, Hebrew Athletes saw water sports as another welcome opportunity to take action. "A marine group will be needed—don't hesitate! You've been sent to Kefar Hamaccabi—Go!" the Maccabi journal wrote.[26] In that spirit, *HaMaccabi* concluded, "Eventually swimming should become our national sport in Eretz Israel."[27] This position was also echoed by the socialist newspaper *Davar*: "Swimming is indisputably the most appropriate sport for the conditions of our land. We should act quickly to make it our national sport."[28]

This nationalization of the untamed water also came to be viewed as a historical Jewish frontier, essential for the nation's rebirth. "Despite all our efforts to this day, in all walks of our regenerated lives, our people don't yet realize what the sea is for any nation and particularly for Israel on our soil," *HaMaccabi* stated. The sea was perceived as having been an arena of Jewish history since the days of the Bible, Noah's Ark, and the parting of the Red Sea—a place where "a wind from God still sweeps [cf. Gen. 1:2] as in those bygone days." Against the background of "our hidden yearnings for the restoration of our maritime glory," Hebrew Athletes, "who love sports loving generally and water sports particularly, demand a special role . . . because it is only the sea that will make us a nation—a nation in the full sense of the word."[29]

Like the dearth of sports facilities, however, "the geographic conditions of our land" proved to be deficient. "Even as learning and knowing how to swim are almost compulsory in the whole world," the Maccabians lamented, "the first and large Hebrew city, where they're so fond of talking about conquering the sea and water sports, hasn't a single swimming pool."[30] Even the Maccabi branch in Tiberias, a town that abutted the Sea of Galilee, struggled for lack of facilities: "We have not developed the main and most important sport that we can develop most successfully—water sport—and for lack of financial resources we have not set up a swimming pool on [Lake] Kinneret [the Sea of Galilee] to this day."[31] Furthermore, water sports were found to be costly and challenging to develop. "To our misfortune, we have no private property for marine training," a Maccabian in Tel Aviv noted in the minutes. "Training costs lots of money, and Maccabi cannot commit to the burden of large expenses at the present time."[32]

The photo on the cover of the June 1931 edition of the magazine *Kolnoa'* featured the Tel Aviv seashore. On the beach are men and women doing gymnastics, light athletics, and even sailing. Conversely, in contrast to this image of healthy and strong bodies, the inside pages paint a different tableau. In a cartoon on page eleven, the caption reads, "Going sailing . . . The sailing frenzy has attacked all inhabitants of the land: Maccabi opened up a sailing section, Hapoel built a boat, Betar went abroad for the first time, the elderly viewers have followed in their footsteps, the old, the women, and the children are going sailing."[33] The illustration, however, shows a typical lower-middle-class family: a skinny, bespectacled, and gangling father; an obese mother wearing a shower cap; and three children, all sailing with poor control and no skill in a little boat that is slowly sinking from its stern.

For the Hebrew Athletes, designing the urban, frontier, or marine space was a concrete act, the antithesis of vacuous speech. "The demagogue's situation is always easy," a contributor to *HaMaccabi* argued. "It's much easier to give a political propaganda speech than to build a gymnastics hall, obtain a sports pitch, or even redeem a quarter-acre (*dunam*) of land for Kefar Hamaccabi."[34]

These possibilities, however, were secondary to the Hebrew Athlete's renewed interest in military training. After the Arab Revolt as Yishuv culture and society increasingly embraced the soldier as an ideal, Hebrew Athletes turned their energy to the battlefield.[35] About fifteen years earlier, it was still the conventional wisdom in Hebrew culture that athletes are poor soldiers because they are not habituated to suffering and therefore run away at moments of crisis.[36] Now, however, from the Hebrew Athletes' standpoint, military training was "the call of the hour (*Tsav Ha-sha'a*)."[37] "Sports and defense, gravitas and games, ostensibly clash with each other," a writer reflected shortly before the outbreak of World War II. "Nevertheless, they are typified by the most exalted and sublime characteristics of man and nation."[38]

"USEFUL SPORT"

Shortly after violence erupted in April 1936, Hebrew Athletes began to vigorously engage in military training, which they referred to as "useful sport" (*sport shimushi*). The "Hapoel battalions" in Tel Aviv were established in May 1936, and a month later members of Maccabi set up a "mobilization committee" so that the Yishuv's Hebrew Athlete could train and educate his body "in discipline and order for his own utility and that of the collective."[39] In the ensuing three years, Hebrew Athletes established groups and "battalions" devoted to "useful sport" all over the country.[40] In 1939 alone, for example, the Maccabi Central Committee dedicated about half its budget to developing "useful sport" and even established a paramilitary unit that it called the Maccabi Guard.[41]

The nexus of "useful sport" and military preparation was evident. The newspaper *Davar* advised its readers that "useful sport" training included "sprinting, distance running, hurdles, crawling and jumping, throwing balls and stones, climbing, boxing, jujitsu, map-reading, signaling, and so on."[42] Similarly, the syllabus of Maccabi's "useful sport" course provided detailed instructions on how to take shelter, sprawl on the ground while in motion, march long distances with a heavy pack, evacuate casualties, provide first aid, engage in self-defense, and fire an air rifle.[43] In the eyes of the Hebrew Athletes, the importance of "useful sport" was beyond doubt. "Useful sport is the imperative of the moment," stated the National Council of Hapoel Gymnastics Instructors. "It should be given a place of honor in our work, injected into all areas of activity, and not restricted to special military formations only."[44] The Maccabi journal expressed this more sharply, proclaiming on its cover page: "It is useful sport . . . that now stands at the forefront of our work."[45]

The Yishuv was not alone in linking sports with military preparation.[46] At the very outset of competitive sports in Britain in the eighteenth century, the conceptualization of sports as a way to develop the mental and physical traits that a good soldier needs struck root.[47] The connection was also attested in de Coubertin's late nineteenth-century writings.[48] Although the founder of the modern Olympic Games hoped that sports would make the conduct of future wars more moral, even then sports education in his homeland France—which had been trounced in 1871 in its military confrontation with Prussia—trained the young for impending military challenges.[49] However, the connection only grew stronger after the Great War when both totalitarian and liberal regimes began to invoke the metaphor of athlete and soldier. Thus, especially as international peace accords crumbled in the second half of the 1930s, the sports act acquired more and more status in the East and the West as an indicator of a nation's readiness to function physically and mentally on the battlefield.[50]

The bond of army and sports existed in Hebrew culture too. In its initial form, it manifested at the level of discourse; the sparse Hebrew vocabulary did not differentiate, for example, between a "battle" and a "fight" and lacked an adequate way to express the restrained emotions and gentility embodied in the word "match."[51] Consequently, the interwar Hebrew press frequently described the sporting act with metaphors such as "a difficult and tenacious war."[52] This metaphoric environment (see chapter 2) did not necessarily create a presence for the domain of sports, but the association, articulated in language and consciousness, between events at the stadium and those on the battlefield predated the Arab Revolt in the Hebrew culture. Second, violence on the Yishuv sports field was not only rhetorical but also a frequent occurrence (see chapter 1). Third, the Hebrew Athletes' affection for discipline stemming from their roots in the values of the gymnastics world was consistently associated with military training. As far back as the nineteenth century, Jahn's gymnastics was conceptualized as a platform for paramilitaristic training (largely among peoples under occupation).[53] Similarly, Nordau connected gymnastics with military training in his *Muskeljudentum* speech. In Europe too, self-defense studies were inseparable from the regular activities of Jewish and, in particular, Zionist communities.[54] Fourth, Hebrew body-culture devotees maintained strong relations with early platforms for military training such as youth movements. Zvi Nishri and Aviezer Yellin of Maccabi were key figures in establishing the Yishuv's Scouts movement; in the second half of the 1930s, and *HaBoker Sport* regularly devoted an entire page to "Yishuvic Scouting."

Nor did leading representatives of the Hebrew athletic community flinch from using violence. In 1921, for example, Nishri and several members of Maccabi broke into the Yiddishist Borochov book club in Jaffa and threatened to prevent their use of a non-Hebrew language with the help of crowbars and batons.[55] Likewise, in 1927 Hapoel established an association called Ha-Sadran (The Order Keeper). Initially meant to maintain order on the sports pitch, it later, under pressure from Ben-Gurion, briefly served as the Histadrut's defense force against the Revisionists until it was closed down in June 1935.[56] Finally, a good number of Hebrew aficionados of body culture flirted with military training and even joined the Haganah and Irgun militias. To wit, Hebrew sports culture had an organizational, value, and linguistic infrastructure that underpinned military training as part of the Hebrew body culture. As a member of the Maccabi Central Committee argued in July 1936 about the onset of "useful sport," "the recent events in [Palestine] served as only a final push for its fulfillment."[57]

Despite this ingrained integration of militarization and sports, early attempts to turn the Hebrew body-culture organizations into platforms for military training were not successful. Yehezkel Henkin, for example, was involved in the establishment of Maccabi in the early twentieth century but remained active in it for a short time only and left to establish Bar Giora, the forerunner of the paramilitary organization Hashomer.[58] Even though Ben-Gurion and Zeev Jabotinsky typically envisaged the body-culture organizations solely as military platforms, the connection between Maccabi and the Revisionist leader Jabotinsky, for example, had not deepened by the early 1920s because the latter requested that "instead of holding conferences (*kinus*) they will organize an induction (*giyus*)."[59]

Furthermore, some body-culture devotees in the interwar Yishuv hoped that sporting events would build a bridge between Zionism and the Arab population. "Maccabi has the great advantage," a member of the movement wrote in 1926, "of possibly being able to increase peace between us and our Arab neighbors and drawing the various races' minds closer by attracting Arab youth to the public games as observers and competitors."[60] This optimistic hope did not prevent the Hebrew Athletes from representing the Jewish people in the international arena at the Palestinian athletes' expense (chapter 4); however, even after 1936, the Hebrew Athletes' direct rivals remained their Arab counterparts in Palestine, Egypt, and Lebanon.[61] Shortly before the revolt began, *HaMaccabi* defined their visit to Lebanon as an encounter on the stage of international sports: "A spirit of friendship and sincerity prevailed throughout the contests, and the Maccabis' victories were always received with thunderous applause by everyone present."[62]

This cooperative spirit waned severely with the onset of the revolt and the blow it dealt to sports activity in the region. "The riots are into their seventh week, and we do not yet know when life will get back to normal," stated the Maccabi Central Committee in a circular to the branches of the association. "We have had to cancel some national contests and activities. . . . Our work is suffering badly."[63] Five months later, the president of Maccabi, Nahum Heth, confessed, "The events have interfered with the fulfillment of many plans that had already been worked up and begun to be fulfilled. Our sports activity suffered badly. However, we may have suffered even more in the organizational and financial senses. The members were needed for guarding and defense and the club facilities were appropriated for refugees and there was no possibility of putting these matters in order for months on end."[64]

Amid the turmoil, voices in the Yishuv also began questioning the pursuit of sports during a national crisis. "No few doubt that this is an appropriate time to develop broad activity in the field of physical education," said Rosecki, "At a time of warfare in Eretz Israel, bombs exploding like flying balls and placid citizens being assaulted in broad daylight—should the [Maccabi] Association work at such a crazy time?"[65] Much of the criticism concerned international participation: "Lots of arguments have broken out on this topic," *HaBoker Sport* reported. 'Is this the right time to send healthy young men such as these abroad while we need them dearly as defenders of the homeland?'"[66]

Even those who initially hoped to carry on as usual and "not cancel any activity" were ultimately compelled to rethink their stance.[67] In May 1936, Alexandrovich still clung to the idea that the national importance of sports grew all the more at this time of mayhem: "Let's remember," he wrote, "that sports should take up one of the most important places in building our country."[68] However, soon afterward the prominent sports journalist realized that the status quo ante would not be restored soon: "But after it became necessary to limit sports activity to efforts in a different direction, the Maccabi Central Committee did not drag its feet for long and organized useful sport in each and every location because that was what the moment required."[69]

This embrace of "useful sports" was an existential response to the upheaval and violence that shook the very essence of the Hebrew Athlete's experience.[70] About two weeks after the revolt erupted, the Maccabi journal called for intensive action. "Neither with words nor with talk," the editorialist proclaimed, but "with deed and action, with building and with labor shall we sanctify the memory of our martyrs who fell on the altar of the re-establishment of our homeland."[71] Like most Jews in the Yishuv, the Hebrew Athletes had hoped that the days of pogroms had ended once they had reached their new land. Thus, the thought of returning to lives of passive victimhood was intolerable.[72] The exact nature of the required change was not yet clear to them, but they began to see the need for "far-reaching conclusions" that would fulfill their duty "to make the recurrence of events such as those in recent days impossible—even in the slightest." Even if the road to their new national calling was still shrouded in uncertainty, the Hebrew Athletes recommitted themselves to the revolution: to Zionist desire harnessing Zionist fervor to shape the world and history through purposeful action. "May we therefore remember," one wrote, "now more than ever: If I am not for myself, who will be for me?" (*'im 'eyn 'ani li mi li*; M. Avot 1:14).[73]

Initially, the Hebrew Athletes turned their energies to collective action.[74] About one month into the Arab Revolt, the heads of Maccabi decided "to start, without delay . . . , implementing the physical-training program by means of useful sport . . . and we will apprise you of the details soon."[75] Against this background, the Hebrew Athletes committed to be "vigilant for the honor of the nation and life and property of the Yishuv," because this "is the necessity and duty of the hour and they are not free to desist from it day in, day out."[76] They proposed to "steel [their] will in order to inject the idea of useful sport to all walks of the nation . . . from our youth to the adults and up to the aged . . . omitting no one, *all* for the safeguarding of the nation and the homeland."[77]

Under this "command," the Hebrew Athletes could once again engage in activities beyond sports. "Maccabi has reached a turning point," the movement's journal wrote. "Either Maccabi will become either a popular sports movement that will bring abundant benefit for the fulfillment of Zionism or a salon of high-achieving individual champions and no more."[78] "Classical sports are undoubtedly very important for strengthening the body and putting psychological traits to use," a member of Maccabi stated, "but even so, there are situations in daily life where sports are out of the question." The need, therefore, shifted to teaching people the ability "to run in his 'civilian' clothing and street shoes on broken ground, march long distances with a load on his back, climb walls and fences, or swim across a river wearing attire fit for 'dry land.'"[79] Even Yekutieli, perhaps the greatest supporter of competitive sports, admitted, "The method has to be replaced, with a new one based on thorough order training and discipline drills. It is this method—the military one—that befits us."[80]

The new emphasis on "applied" and "useful" military training transcended the technical aspect of the actions taken and proposed a step full of personal and collective meaning. "We need to define what our 'nationalism' expresses," a Maccabian named Yigal stated. "Until now, our nationalism found expression in waving blue-and-white flags, blue-and-white clothing, and pretty slogans. Let's admit that having created Hebrew sports is our only portion, but is that enough? . . . We will conquer the land not only with flags and a band (I don't totally dismiss this) but also with total sacrifice in this last battle, which may end, heaven forfend, in final defeat. . . . We have to learn to sacrifice everything."[81]

This new responsibility demanded "a great effort—both moral and material"; yet for the Hebrew Athletes it was an opportunity.[82] "And if the events [the Arab Revolt] disrupted us immensely in most areas of sport," a writer in *HaBoker Sport* explained, "we must admit that, by acting as they did, the events caused us to take giant strides toward fulfilling the idea."[83] "The recent events," a Maccabi member noted, "inspired the heads of the movement to plot course and make sure it fits the demands of the time. It is a good augury for [the movement] that it isn't resting on its laurels."[84] About five months into the revolt, a prominent figure in Maccabi advised, "A new flow of blood has burst . . . into our ranks," viewing the crisis as a crucial moment to prevent the movement from sinking into a state of degenerative pessimism.[85] One Maccabian even warned his colleagues against the day after the end of the "events": "There is a serious risk that this passion will wane after the fleeting menace blows over . . . as our ranks and our public return to their sloppy [negligent] course, to 'sweet' inaction that may banish the past from memory and mask the dangers of the future."[86] In other words, the Arab Revolt may have shredded the fabric of life in Palestine, but for the Hebrew Athletes, it was "an immeasurably important moment" that marked the beginning of "a new golden age."[87]

In their eyes, spirited and calculated action for the collective demonstrated the movement's maturity and revolutionary purpose. "Our Central Committee deserves praise," exclaimed the editor of *HaMaccabi*, Eliezer Yellin, "for having undertaken this action after weighing the matter at length and creating a clear and specific plan in both the organizational and the technical senses."[88] Thus, the Hebrew Athletes expected their new fitness to give them the national recognition that they coveted. After all, as stated in a lead article in *HaMaccabi*, "It is unimaginable that this lofty aspiration to bequeath 'useful sport' to the nation can be fulfilled by our own forces unless our leaders, the leaders of the nation, the leaders of the Yishuv, help us to fulfill it."[89] Nestled in the demand for recognition of their new collective endeavor was their hope for a change in the Yishuv leaders' marginal treatment of the body-culture organizations: "Perhaps the propitious hour will come, at which they will recognize the severe error they have made thus far and correct the distortion."[90]

Despite the Hebrew Athletes' enthusiastic yearning, their military training was fraught with challenges.[91] In the early days of July 1936, the Maccabi Central Committee stated, "To carry out a broad program, several tasks must be accomplished first, and this can happen only after the situation improves and tempers in the country subside."[92] This hope, however, never fully materialized. A year after the violence broke out, the heads of Maccabi had to admit sorrowfully that "the operation did not develop as it should have; on the contrary—after starting nicely in many places, it weakened badly and effectively ground to a halt."[93] In the following years, it continued to suffer from insufficient resources and poor training.[94] The Maccabi instructors' course, for example, was only thirty-six hours long, and the Hapoel branch in Haifa devoted only two weekly sessions to training in "useful sport."[95] Moreover, according to the associations' reports, only several hundred people received training during the three years of the revolt.[96] Thus, just six months before the outbreak of World War II, they were forced to acknowledge "the unlikelihood of demanding that the battalions acquire the experience and training of an army for which governmental resources and training are available."[97]

Hampered by organizational difficulties, "useful sport" struggled to achieve the desired personal and collective transformation of the Hebrew Athlete's body and mind. Ironically, one of the main problems was physical unfitness.[98] "The lack of daily sports activity was evident" according to a journalist for *Davar*, who expressed disappointment in Hapoel's useful-sport instructors' course. "The members showed that they understood the technique and the theory of this sport but they have to follow it with practical training, too."[99] About a year later, in April 1939, the Hebrew Athletes redefined what they expected of trainees in "useful sport": "We must remember that we are dealing neither with 'battalions' nor with saber-rattling, nor even with young people who are living with their parents and are free to indulge in the fad of drilling and militarism, but with working people who toil every day to support themselves and their households and devote only their moments of rest to the battalion exercises that are called 'useful sport'"[100]

In a photograph from a "useful sport" instructors' course at the Maccabi Tel Aviv branch, thirty-five men stand in uniform and shorts, arranged in four staggered rows intended to convey military-like unity and discipline.[101] Yet, in this Maccabi version, the rows are uneven, and the eight instructors strike varied poses. In the right-hand corner, one instructor presses his leg against a comrade seated beside him, whose own legs are crossed in a hunched, bowed manner. In the front, an athlete at the edge of the frame wears white sandals, exposing his feet to the elements. On the upper rows, a few trainees cast playful sidelong glances, caught off-guard by the photographer. They hold the national flag askew as if they are struggling to lift its weight.

This revolutionary failure was intertwined with an enduring lack of institutional and public recognition. In April 1939, a member of Hapoel wrote sadly about the way his organization's battalions were treated: "This time, all the accusing Satans from within and without seem to have formed an alliance to demean the new organization's image."[102] Later that year, in September, the Maccabi Guard was shut down at Ben-Gurion's express request after only five months.[103]

Also the principal of the Reali School in Haifa, the Maccabi member Arthur Biram, turned his gaze to other horizons and shortly after the Arab Revolt began, urging the members of his movement to revise the mission of their sports association to "educating men simply to do their duty."[104] However, more than three years passed until Biram launched Hagam (an acronym for *Hinukh gufani meyuhad*, Special Physical Education) in September 1939—in partnership with several higher-ups in Maccabi—as a program subordinate to the needs of the Haganah and the Jewish National Council (*Va'ad Le'umi*).[105] Thus, with Hagam and the creation of a physical training department under the Jewish National Council that year, several leaders at Maccabi managed to get a foot in the establishment's door but only as individual white-collar staffers with negligible influence.

The limited success in disseminating useful sport also led to a change in its place among the Hebrew Athletes' activities. At the outset of the Arab Revolt, some body-culture devotees hoped to create via "useful sport" a new purposive identity separate from competitive sports. Several years later, however, they reversed their stance and acted to internalize military training and integrate it into competitive sports activities. Thus, in May 1938, in the shadow of the financial woes that beset useful sport, the Maccabi Central Committee resolved "not to make useful sport a specific sport but rather to integrate useful sport—its basic idea and its practical manifestations—into the general action plan."[106] A month later "useful sport" was redefined in an opaque and vague way. For example, Hapoel's 1938 military training manual (*Ha-hoger*) stated, "All sport that is wisely managed by someone knowledgeable is a useful sport."[107] In other words, useful sport was no longer necessarily related to military training. Or as announced at a Maccabi national conference, useful sport "will run like a crimson thread through all sports performances."[108]

Simultaneously, the insertion of military training as a concrete and integral component of sporting endeavors had a powerful effect on the meaning of sports and its contribution to national defense. Boxing, for example, which was typified in the 1920s mainly as a dangerous amusement sport, was now perceived by Hebrew Athletes as a purposeful "defensive sport." "Boxing is the most useful sport in life in terms of self-defense," a writer for *HaBoker Sport* enthused and then asserted, "At times of trouble everyone should know how to confront all dangers of life face-to-face."[109] The new perspective on the role of boxing even gave the act of punching practical aesthetic baggage. "There's nothing lovelier," the *HaBoker Sport* writer continued, "than two boxers putting up a handsome fight. Not a bit of strength goes to waste."[110] The perception of wrestling went through a similar evolution. "At this time, it's not just a heartwarming showy sport," a writer in *Davar* stated, "but a useful defensive sport, and for this reason the aspiration should be to spread it and sink its roots in our midst."[111] The effect of this military purposing transcended pure combat sports such as boxing and wrestling. A *Davar* journalist approvingly reported, "Light athletics [track and field] have shed their classical form and have been tailored to the needs of the time. The transformation is evident in all areas of light athletics, from cross-country racing to the shot put, which has crowded out the javelin and the discus."[112]

Thus, "useful sport" may not have given Hebrew Athletes the desired experience in their eyes, but it worked its way into their worldview. A day after the national team played against Greece in the World Cup preliminaries, an article headlined "Defense? What's That?" appeared on the sports page of *Davar*. Alongside generous coverage of the international match, the rapporteur wrote about a player who was evidently not a practiced defender: "He didn't know how to take the first step and start 'moving.' . . . Defense is a theory that requires study, practice, and mental fortitude."[113] Against this background, defense (like universal sports) was treated as having a sublime aspect that gave the Hebrew identity its correct contours. Defense, a Hebrew Athlete wrote, was an *av-melakha,* a craft that underpins all others, the basis for human existence.[114]

Defense and sports now settled into the Hebrew Athlete's worldview as complements to revolutionary building. In the booklet *Mishmar VeSport,* the following is stated: "Without both of them, the lives of the young generation would be unimaginable."[115] In this light, defense and sports were construed as alien to the "ailments of the exile," and the Hebrew Athlete was presented as "an expression of the free man who controls his body . . . who has to fight and defend himself against the destructive forces that again have risen against a human civilization in order to obliterate it." Accordingly, the Hebrew Athletes sought "to awaken and enhance in the Yishuv, in all its walks, an understanding of the great value of sports education." This awareness, however, did not stand alone but was combined with "the direct and strong connection between defenders and sportsmen, between the sports movement and defense of the homeland."[116]

By late 1939, the metaphor of the Hebrew Athlete as a warrior—both on the sports field and on the actual battlefield—was starting to become ingrained. The coach of the Palestine football team, an immigrant from Central Europe named Arthur Baar, wrote, "There is no room for softies and sissies in the footballers' ranks because only rugged and hardened fighters count here." The sports pitch became a place where "selected groups from two nations march off to face each other. In a forthright battle in which the spirit of fairness prevails, they fight to win the wreath of victory." This nexus of the value of sports and national endeavors, Baar argued, finds expression in wartime. "It is the footballers' role," he wrote, "not just to perform and play in contests in peacetime. If one day they will . . . have to invoke and use all the noble traits that they acquired and internalized in the course of competition, then they will join the ranks of the warriors with great passion and content, underscoring and demonstrating their physical strength, the esprit de guerre that pulses in them, and the will to act for the sake and benefit of all."[117]

The mayhem of the Arab Revolt etched itself deeply into the body of the Hebrew Athlete. Yet, its violence was soon drowned out by the thunder of atrocities in Europe. In that context, the mid-1930s were a pivotal time when the universal "Olympic idea" clashed with the pressing need for active defense, reshaping the experience of Hebrew Athletes. Thus, although fulfillment of their revolutionary aspirations seemed to once again slip through their fingers, the intertwining of militarization and universal ideals only heightened the tension between the global and the local, the universal and the particular, the pure and the useful.

Two weeks after Germany invaded Poland, *HaBoker Sport* published a short story titled "Sports and War." The plot, written from the point of view of an anonymous soldier, expressed the universal influence of sports some twenty years earlier during World War I. "We didn't look at the national markings of the aeroplanes," the hero relates, "and we couldn't tell whether they were Italian, French, or British. In any event, they belonged to the mighty camp of sports lovers." It's doubtful this story would have been written amid the fighting, because viewing sports as a unifying and joyous force gained global significance only after the Great War, not during it. In September 1939, however, the illusion of sporting autotelic detachment faded, and athletic international delegations hurriedly returned to their own borders. Even the most impassioned fans of sports had to admit dejectedly, "There were many disruptions in the sports interactions between nations."[118] It was the end of an era.

After the fact, one may say that World War II merely imposed a moratorium on international sports. Indeed, once the Axis was trounced, men and women from all over the world rushed back to the bosom of competitive sports with heightened intensity.[119] What they found, however, was a different world. On the edges of the destruction of Jewish culture, the Holocaust also brought the sports' "golden age" of European Jewry to a conclusive end. Only a week after the fighting broke out, Baar, an erstwhile leading personality in Hakoah Vienna, stated, "Under Germany's pressure, Hungary began to purge its sports of Jews. . . . One should strongly doubt that Hungarian football will be able to recover from the blows it sustained due to these losses."[120] In the Yishuv, however, the Hebrew Athlete continued to play almost undisturbed, "because even in war one continues in all areas of life," proclaimed Rosecki as European Jewry was being interned in the ghettos.[121]

Nonetheless, even after the war, Hebrew sporting language retained a distinct militarized tone. Throughout the 1950s, officers in the Israel Defense Forces played a central role in overseeing Israel's international sports efforts.[122] Even today, Israel's elite athletes train at the Wingate Institute—adjacent to an army base and named after the famed Zionist soldier from the Arab Revolt era. While it is not clear when the infamous Israeli rallying cry *milhama-milhama* (war war) first resonated in international competitions, by 1936 the Zionist sports fans had begun, at the very least, to warm up their vocal cords.

EPILOGUE

I do not know when it will happen, but one day, modern sports will eventually fade. Perhaps the current murmurs of discontent over the social costs of this global phenomenon will grow into louder concerns.[1] Or maybe it will be the "promised" biotechnological and robotic advancements that will reshape the allure of autotelic sport and the human experience.[2] But until then, it is important to remember that just as every fashion eventually ends, it also had its own beginning

The current dominance of modern spectacles often gives the impression that they've always been there. Admittedly, modern sports and their associated rituals, symbols, and experiences, shaped after World War I, still define much of today's sporting culture—from the Olympic Games to emerging sports like skateboarding, mixed martial arts, and gaming. Therefore, disentangling the contemporary neoliberal imagination from the past is no simple task.[3] As a wise professor whom I like told me when I tried to explain the difference between gymnastics and sports, "You know, even when I'm doing yoga I'm competitive." I had no good answer to that. How can one even imagine, for example, a boxer participating in the workers' sports of 1920s Vienna or Warsaw who did not, at least rhetorically, see winning as the main goal, even as he took blows to his head? Perhaps such a person never really existed, which might explain why gymnastics and workers' sports have waned while modern competitive sports continue to thrive.

And still, between the world wars, as sport rapidly evolved into a global phenomenon with deep national and cultural significance, debates erupted about the value and purpose of these unfamiliar competitive events. Opinions ranged widely—from the full embrace of modern sports to calls for diversification and even outright rejection of what was seen as a newly constructed tradition. The debates surrounding militarism, amateurism, and purpose constantly wove local perspectives into the fabric of broader transnational concerns, mirroring the existential rupture in which scientific and social progress allowed intense physical pursuits to become popular leisure activities for the masses. Consequently, conversations were not merely about weekend scores but also touched on profound and vital issues like the transformation of the body as both metaphor and experience and, ultimately, the essence of modernity itself.

One key factor in this modern rise of competitive sports was the decline of gymnastics, which before World War I had been the dominant form of organized physical culture. Like the debates supporting sports, the clash with gymnastics was not merely a matter of exercise routines but a reflection of two worldviews with different models of discipline, health, and society. As the supremacy of gymnastics began to weaken, the allure of competitive sports grew stronger. However, this does not mean that gymnastics disappeared entirely: Its traces remained visible throughout the 1920s and beyond, including in contemporary gym and physical education classes. Nonetheless, by the 1930s, it was becoming evident that modern sports had become hegemonic.

The transnational tension-filled rise of sports manifested within the Yishuv as well. Driven partly by mass emigration from Central Europe and the newly established collaboration with international sporting bodies, a Jewish sports culture emerged in Palestine in the latter half of the 1930s. Predominantly led by new immigrants from Poland and Germany, this burgeoning sports culture differed from the largely apologetic and reactionary post-gymnastics competitive activities of the 1920s. Accordingly, it gave rise to a new Hebrew sports journalism that adopted a forthright approach, viewing sports as an integral part of the nation's challenges. It embraced a more prideful perspective on the athletic physique as contributing to the collective body and offered a more universal interpretation of the "pure" sporting spectacle. In essence, this sports culture marked the beginning of a Hebrew cultural appreciation for competitive sports as a phenomenon imbued with meaning, perhaps even occasionally autotelic.

However, those delicate times of beginning were always a glocal mélange. When examined more closely, it becomes clear that this evolution unfolded differently in various countries and cultures. In the United States, for instance, the popularization of sports began before World War I and gave rise to distinctly American activities like baseball and football. In Japan, in contrast, modern martial arts such as Judo were adapted into international sports, reflecting their cultural and national significance on a global stage. Similarly, in the Yishuv, the agents of the transnational process were rarely indifferent to ideological considerations and often sought to merge sports with Zionist revolutionary desires and worldview. Consequently, the new sports journalists did not develop a new syntax and vocabulary to describe the sporting experience, nor did they reject Hebrew culture's monolithic yet particular embrace of sporting amateurism.

Against this ambiguous background, this book "revisited" the interwar period to describe the initial encounter of the Zionist Revolution with modern sports. By so doing, it sought to say something not only about the meaning of the pre-Holocaust Hebrew experience in the Yishuv but also, although more subtly, about competitive sports themselves. From a historiographic standpoint, this account aimed to distance itself from several common assumptions, of which perhaps the most salient are the colonial discourse—which views history as a reflection of identity and power between the oppressed and oppressor—and the artificial globalized separation of ideology from daily lives in the urban sphere. Therefore, instead of presenting a cynical or nostalgic narrative that has clear moral impact and a foregone conclusion, my intention was, to the extent possible, to spend some time with people of the past and "listen" to individuals whom I neither know nor understand nor hate. Hence, the story I told does not ask for identification but rather to "hearing" what the Hebrew Athletes had to say about the forgotten difference between gymnastics and sports, experiencing the Hebrew language, the meaninglessness of the competitive body itself, the hope of "returning to history" by means of the international community, and also, finally around 1936, the paradoxical internalization of the universal grammar of sports and investing the sporting act with useful militaristic purpose. "Listening" to those discussions did not reveal a binary picture in which ideology—or Zionism—was either all-encompassing or merely empty rhetoric. Instead, it presented the Zionist revolution as a dynamic historical phenomenon that, at least in Mandatory Palestine, held significant and tangible presence in people's lives.

Indeed, much of the ontological and epistemological challenge in historiographically engaging with the "original" experience of Zionism is that its initial revolutionary moment is becoming increasingly obscured over time. In this context, the twenty-one posters from the Maccabiah Games over the past ninety years serve as a valuable lens through which to reflect on this change.[4] The First Maccabiah took place in 1932. At the center of its poster is the flag of the Maccabi movement, prominently displaying an emblem reminiscent of the Star of David. Clutched by a faceless figure, the billowing flag stands out, while the figure itself lacks specific traits and characteristics: its black silhouette serves no purpose other than to unfurl the movement's banner.

Three years later, the poster for the Second Maccabiah (1935) continues the motif of a man waving a flag. At first glance, the muscular, clean-shaven athlete with a chiseled chin seems to embody an "aesthetic of toughness," echoing the Zionist pioneer immortalized, for instance, in the iconic interwar Jewish National Fund poster.[5] Yet, although the athlete gazes intently toward the horizon, the sunlight caresses only half his face, casting the other half into a realm of shadow. In this chiaroscuro interplay, the legless Hebrew athlete is not anchored in the rugged soil of the frontier but rather pasted artificially onto a background of sky and sea.

After 1948 and the attainment of statehood, the colorful Maccabiah posters no longer focus on the athletic body, and the stadium and the flags of foreign nations claim center stage. In these happy adverts, the Israeli flag is only one more flag in the international community, symbolizing a nation like all the nations.

This international emphasis endured for around twenty years but changed sharply after 1973, when the famous graphic artist Dan Reisinger began to design the posters. True to the style of this Israel Prize laureate, the posters in the next twenty-five years are typified by modernism, conciseness, and formal abstraction. Thus, instead of an athlete, the flag, or the stadium, an abstract graphic illustration of the Star of David and the human body is given. These vivid compositions, stripped of all dimensions of space and time, play with and deconstruct national symbols to the point where decoding them requires prior knowledge. In 1997, during the opening ceremony of the fifteenth Maccabiah Games, a bridge collapsed, killing four Jewish athletes and injuring over sixty others, embodying the tragic decline of the Zionist vision of building and revival, turning it into a distant memory.

Reisinger ceased designing the Maccabiah posters in 2005, marking the end of the deconstructivist style. Since then, however, the posters have lacked a clear unifying theme. Some try to incorporate seemingly traditional elements; in others, the design emphasizes stark, industrial motifs. Similarly, symbols of nation and state have disappeared, and the focus has shifted to highlighting the year and number of the event. In other words, all that remains of the bold figure waving the flag in the first Maccabiah poster is a fragmented effort to cling to a random point in time.

Certainly, the revolutionary age of the pioneers is gone. As the literary scholar, 1930s-born Menachem Brinker, wrote in the early 2000s, "During the statehood period, too, of course, there have been Israeli aviation pioneers and industrial pioneers, Israeli cinema pioneers, feminism pioneers, and so on, but among all of Israel's active elites, it is hard to detect a [Zionist] 'pioneer' in the traditional and full sense of the word, a Jewish person who undergoes a revolution of mind and way of life in order to bequeath a new future to the entire nation."[6] This dilution of the pioneer self, however, also reconceptualizes our ability to sincerely imagine the revolutionary. Thus, Yosef Yekutieli, born in the nineteenth century, titled his 1971 autobiography *From Exile to Redemption* (Mi-gola le-ge'ula)[7]; fourteen years later, when his daughter completed her beloved father's opus in 1985, the revolutionary collective narrative of the book vanished, and a new title appeared, *The Dreamer* (Ba'al ha-halomot).[8]

In part, this new imagination is a result of the globalized era about which Hobsbawm ironically noted, "Private human behavior has had less trouble in adjusting to the world of satellite television, email, holidays in the Seychelles, and trans-oceanic commuting."[9] In terms of history and sports, this 1990s reconstruction of Israeli identity and experience is particularly embodied in the insightful work of Modi Bar-On. Renowned both for his documentary programs on Zionist/Israeli history and for his twenty-five years of service as a presenter and writer for the Israeli studio of the European Champions League, Bar-On was regarded as a Renaissance man who bridged various worlds with his innovative cultural contributions. Nonetheless, there is a strong connection between his non-ideological documentaries, which present history as "all about people"—a collection of anecdotes, needs, and desires—and the sports show that, since it first aired in 1995, has upheld European football as a benchmark of popular culture. It is no coincidence that before shifting his broadcasts from his studio in the tranquil town of Herzliya to a renowned "sports cathedral" on the continent, Bar-On would look directly into the camera and, in a serious tone, say just one word: "Enjoy!"

So, was the Zionist Revolution merely a fleeting dream or nightmare, leaving no lasting legacy beyond the lands it claimed? At least in the realm of sports, its heritage is not always visible on the surface, as twenty-first-century Israeli athletes often dress, coif, and tattoo themselves in line with the latest global trends, making them indistinguishable from their counterparts elsewhere. Moreover, since the 1990s—with the privatization of Israeli sports, the country's admission to UEFA, and the spread of sports professionalism—Israeli athletes have achieved significant milestones: occasional appearances in the UEFA Champions League group stage and earning twenty Olympic medals and numerous world and European championship medals.

And yet, after more reflection, something else emerges—less visible yet no less tangible and visceral. Israeli sports culture continues to grapple with its image of futility, most vividly captured in the persistent fixation on the football team's absence from the European National Championship and the World Cup over the past forty years. This perceived failure is reflected in the view of Israeli athletes, especially football players, who are often celebrated as local heroes of the "dabbler neighborhood," rather than embodying values like "hard work," "effort," or "competitiveness."[10] Similarly, Olympic medalists like heavyweight judokas Ori Sasson and Arik Zeevi, despite their exceptional size and strength, are particularly cherished for their gentle and amiable demeanor. This dissonance between inner sensitivity and outer strength has long been linked to the "New Jew" and the "sabra"—those born in Israel. Ultimately, however, much like in the interwar years, even at the heights of the Olympic Games, Hebrew athletes remain grounded in the humdrum of daily life.

There is a certain appeal in the way Israelis connect with their sporting legacy beyond mere achievements, yet this appreciation often casts a shadow on their attitude toward domestic athletes who either cannot or choose not to embody the essence of the Hebrew/Israeli experience.[11] This dynamic is most conspicuously reflected in the Arab footballers who have become key members of the national squad in recent decades. From this perspective, Member of Knesset Ahmad Tibi's quip, "No Arabs, no goals" (*sha'arim*), humorously echoes the radical right's slogan, "No Arabs, no terror attacks" (*pigu'im*), striking a chord of truth. However, unlike Algerian players in France or African American athletes in the United States, Israelis do not view competitive sports as a space to embrace and enrich the national culture; rather, they expect these Arab players to blindly represent Hebrew culture. Given this ignorance of the complexities of the Middle East, it is no surprise that the Arab presence on the Israeli national team and league is often fraught with frictions and tensions.

Likewise, athletes who arrived in Israel after the disintegration of the Soviet Union have often faced a challenging reception. Despite their remarkable skills and significant impact on Israeli sports since the 1990s—and in contrast to Sasson and Zeevi—they often struggle to penetrate the heart of mainstream Hebrew culture. Thus, nearly sixty years after Vienna-born Nickolaus Hirschl set foot in Palestine, elite athletes like Olympic medalist Michael Kolganov and high jumper Konstantin Matusevich have found themselves re-immigrating in search of recognition and a livelihood, leaving behind a competitive void in their fields.[12] In that context, even Artem Dolgopyat, perhaps the greatest Israeli athlete of all time, who emigrated to Israel from Ukraine as a boy in 2009, still remains somewhat anonymous to the Israeli public. "Two years have passed since I won the gold medal at the Tokyo Olympics," he said in July 2023, "Back then, people didn't identify me much; they asked me whether I'm from the ninja [the Israeli remake of *American Ninja Warrior*]. They remember my face but don't know where I'm from. After I identify myself, they say, 'Hey, that's great!'"[13]

Nonetheless, the Israeli athlete continues to serve as a national emissary. Although winning has become a significant indicator of success in this role—especially in contrast to the 1930s—this focus is primarily limited to two competitions: the Summer Olympic Games and the FIFA World Cup. Accordingly, these events, where the Israeli flag can be raised before the world's nations, serve as the two formative arenas through which the Israeli athlete is judged in popular culture and collective memory. As Zeevi recently said, "You have to remember that, yes, the Olympics are what counts most in Israel. In terms of [my] sport, they are only one contest . . . but in the weight of advertising and image in Israel, the Olympiad trumps everything and it's a bit ridiculous."[14] Or, as Dolgopyat recalled, "The year I won the world championship, they took me to some mall and no one identified me. After I won in Tokyo, they took me to the same mall, and I couldn't move ahead five meters in ten minutes."[15]

Similarly, whenever the supposed separation of sports from politics is shattered—such as when Muslim athletes boycott or refuse to shake a Hebrew athlete's hand—the Israeli public reacts with indignation, feeling that such actions expose and underscore their differences. In 2022, former Israeli football superstar Eli Ohana served as a commentator at the World Cup in Qatar. After he discovered that a local chauffeur would refuse to transport him if he were from Israel, Ohana asked in amazement, "But why?" "I'm Palestinian," the driver replied. After he got out of the car, Ohana summed up the incident in astonishment: "I don't even know how to explain this. It's crazy. He picked us up with a smile. . . . Unbelievable."[16]

The naive expectation of love and belonging, even in an Arab country that is overtly hostile to Israel, paradoxically coexists with a noticeable absence of the entertainment element in the Israeli sports experience. Despite Bar-On's call to "enjoy," the atmosphere within Israeli sports remains laden with stress, anxiety, and a pervasive sense of non-enjoyment. Even today, Israeli footballers fortunate enough to play for foreign teams express their surprise at the relaxed and easygoing atmosphere in the dressing room. "The perception in Israel is very different. In Israel everything's hard, everything's stressful," the former player Dan Roman relates. "When I was in Holland, everything was easy. You come to practice, and you have it easy, everything's orderly, they smile at you, and when the fans speak with you, even if you lost, they speak to you respectfully."[17]

This "tense" sporting culture is also evident in today prolific media coverage.[18] Yet even, despite the ability of Israeli fans to watch major sporting events worldwide via live broadcasts, the Hebrew language still struggles to articulate the autotelic essence of the sporting moment. "The criticism about the quality of Israeli football and Israeli sports in general is understandable," the famous sports journalist Oren Yosipovitch writes, "but nothing will improve here if the surroundings forever remain more famous and important than the purpose." Even though Israeli sports journalists have been complaining for years about the many ailments of the phenomenon they are covering, they continue, sometimes knowingly, to turn out yellow journalism that underscores above all the basic lack of a sports culture in Israel.[19] "This is the loveliest hour of the words 'humiliation,' 'failure,' 'contempt,' [and] 'trash,'" the journalist Tal Volk wrote to his colleagues. "There's no success anymore; instead, there's mighty success at least. If you won, you did the unbelievable, and if not, so at least you did the sensational. There are no losses anymore. There are resounding failures. There are heroic victories. If you falter, even just once, you'll be sent far away to the end of the second scale where you're a rag, with no way and no method, and you and all your players have to be fired."[20]

This hectic sports discourse is also reflected in Israelis' lack of physical activity. A 2023 survey revealed that 65 percent of the population did not exercise on a regular basis. This highlights a significant difference between Israeli and Western cultures. Moreover, even the Israelis who do train often prefer "useful" activities like running, cycling, and gym workouts over participation in organized sports clubs and institutions. In other words, even today, sports competition itself is not necessarily seen as a means to promote the health of the Hebrew body.

Against this unsettling backdrop, it seems that even at the start of the twenty-first century, Israeli culture still struggles to fully embrace sports as an autotelic spectacle. Instead, the demands placed on Hebrew athletes and on their pursuit of specific goals continue, for better or worse, to echo the revolutionary desires of their ancestors. However, this tension—between revolution and globalization, past and present—is never binary or simple but is constantly and intimately intertwined, morphing into a unique form that blurs the two.

To be acquainted with only one side of the experience, as we contemporaries often are, makes it easy to dismiss the other half as mere myth. We often label this rejection as rationality, science, or critical thinking, though it is often no less ideological than the revolutionaries it seeks to disprove. On the contrary, the Zionist Revolution was never a zero-sum game but more like a stone cast into the ocean, reveling in its newfound relationship with the water, the air, and gravity. Although we might claim that the stone has finally settled on the seafloor and is resting in the abyss, its ripples still spread across the surface, continuing to touch and shape the world above.

Amidst this convoluted and perplexing state of affairs, one might also wander to the Israeli beach, where a contemporary Israeli "sport" can be observed that embodies and reflects the original Zionist vision for physical activity, effortlessly and straightforwardly. Often dubbed Israel's "national sport," the game of Matkot is far from a sport in the conventional sense.[21] Played with no rules and no clear goal, this noisy paddle ball game's appeal lies not in competition or acclaim but in the sheer joy of presence—beneath the open sky, beside the shimmering sea, as friends bat the ball back and forth, enacting together the delightful futility of never letting it fall. The appeal of this playful and relaxing activity is hard to put into words because it is about doing, not speaking. It is not a spectacle to be judged or a history to be chronicled but a fleeting moment where life and play dissolve into one. As the Israeli rapper Jimbo J reflects in his 2020 song, "From Matkot, I learned to count to ten, and the ball always taught me about gravity. When it fell into the water, I learned to swim, and when it hit sunbathers, I learned to say sorry."[22]

The game's origins are elusive, surfacing in the joyful sketches of Nachum Gutman in 1930s Tel Aviv and echoing, to some extent, the forgotten worldview of gymnastics.[23] Yet, continuing down the path of context and deconstruction would inevitably dissolve the autotelic experience of the game itself. Thus, we might conclude by viewing Matkot as a metaphor for a different kind of historical thinking—one that is not concerned with victories or losses nor is tethered to a political agenda driven by relentless critique or suspicion, but one that embraces creativity, curiosity, and wonder, free from the shadows of cynicism and nostalgia. As Jimbo J sings, Matkot "makes noise with the sea's rubber ball; like the rubber balls used to disperse protests; but they don't write the instructions in blood; they write them with waves on sandcastles."[24] Like sandcastles or the bounce of Matkot, history too can be an aesthetic exploration—a space where we reflect on our ancestors and ourselves, not seeking final answers but reveling in the imperfect beauty of it all. Perhaps if we can make peace with the endless variety and mystery of those who came before, we might also find peace within and the necessary courage to strive to build a better future.

ACKNOWLEDGMENTS

The historiographical and theoretical foundations of this book were shaped in the History Department at Tel Aviv University. I owe a great intellectual debt to Boaz Neumann who, on a sunny day in the Gilman Cafeteria, advised me to abandon my initial idea of writing a comparative thesis and to focus solely on the Yishuv. Little did I know that. in doing so, he was also returning me to Zionism. Boaz passed away not long after, leaving me with a profound sense of loss—both professionally and personally; I will miss his insights and our conversations.

I also want to thank Michael Shapira and Motti Golani for stepping in to support the completion of this project. Aviad Kleinberg provided generous assistance and guidance during his tenure as head of the Zvi Yavetz School of Historical Studies. And although she may not remember, Billie Melman gave me some much-needed words of encouragement at a critical time. Igal Halfin, and his work on the communist self, offered a model for *real* critical thinking about past and present. Zohar Shavit provided valuable lessons on motivation and the inner workings of academia. Michael Brenner, together with the Leo Baeck Institute and the Humboldt and Minerva Foundations, gave me the time and space to complete this project while expanding my intellectual horizons. And finally, as I edit this book, with the Albertan snowy weather outside my window, I wish to thank Jenny Belzberg and her family for warmly welcoming me to the University of Calgary and allowing me to pursue further career peaks.

I have also been fortunate to have engaged in many valuable conversations with colleagues. It would be impossible to mention and remember them all; however, Rob Boddice, Ohad Kohn, Assaf Mond, Ella Ayalon, Tamir Karkason, and Ofri Ilany each demonstrated in their own way what academic curiosity and passion for the humanities are all about. I am especially grateful to Hannah Pollin-Galay, Yoni Furas, Gilad Halperin, and Tsafi Sebba-Elran for reading and commenting on drafts of the manuscript. Naftali Greenwood helped make this book readable in a language that is not my native tongue. Hans Ulrich Gumbrecht, once just a name on my reading list, became a source of support and encouragement for both me and this book. It is an honor to now call him a colleague and a friend.

"Friend" is also a word that describes Roni Cohen. Although he would probably correct me, I recall that we first met in his small office at the Tel Aviv University Library while we were both graduate students. Since then, our friendship has spanned three continents and provided me with invaluable support through the ups and downs of an early academic career. Roni has taught me about powerful curses, the album method, and much more: Above all, he has shown me that brilliance need not be at odds with kindness. He is truly a mensch and the best of people (*Ha-tov she-ba-'anashim*).

And finally, to my family. My parents Rachel and Nachman never wavered in their support of my unconventional vocation, while my brother Ohad was always just a phone call away. My wife Sandra joined me in the early stages of this journey and gave me the motivation to carry on. Together, we brought our two daughters Yael and Amalia into this world who, among many blessings, remind me that the best reason to write about the past is for the sake of the future.

NOTES

INTRODUCTION

1. Recent descriptions may include Netflix's *Fauda*, Apple TV's *Tehran*, and Steven Spielberg's *Munich*.
2. The sketch, written by the famous Israeli author Etgar Keret, appeared in the formative Israeli satirical show *Ha-ḥamishia ha-kamerit* (The Chamber Quintet).
3. Conversely, the recent success of Israeli athletes in the Olympic Games is often met with a sense of astonishment and disbelief.
4. For some examples from the last decade that illustrate this common Israeli view, see *Calcalsit*, October 1, 2012, https://tinyurl.com/2ekvfmc3; *Maariv*, July 1, 2015, https://tinyurl.com/y4ewe4e4; *Hazavit*, September 2, 2017, https://tinyurl.com/4af59wd9; *Timeout*, June 12, 2018, https://tinyurl.com/2p8236f8; *Israel Hayom*, May 3, 2023, https://tinyurl.com/yt968wke.
5. The cite is from Joan Wallach Scott, "The Evidence of Experience," *Critical Inquiry* 17 (1991): 793. On cultural reading of the New Jew, see George Mosse, *The Image of Man: The Creation of Modern Masculinity* (Oxford: Oxford University Press, 1996); Sander Gilman, *The Jew's Body* (London: Routledge, 2013); and Daniel Boyarin, *Unheroic Conduct: The Rise of Heterosexuality and the Invention of the Jewish Men* (Berkeley: University of California Press, 1997).
6. For example: John Zilcosky and Marlo A. Burks, eds., *The Allure of Sports in Western Culture* (Toronto: University of Toronto Press, 2019). On Hebrew culture, see Itamar Even-Zohar's pivotal essay, "The Emergence of a Native Hebrew Culture in Palestine: 1882–1948," *Studies in Zionism* (1981): 167–184; as well as Arieh Bruce Saposnik, *Becoming Hebrew: The Creation of a Jewish National Culture in Ottoman Palestine* (Oxford: Oxford University Press, 2008).
7. Kenneth Moss, *An Unchosen People Jewish Political Reckoning in Interwar Poland* (Cambridge, MA: Harvard University Press, 2021), 221–253.
8. Kenneth B. Moss, *Jewish Renaissance in the Russian Revolution* (Cambridge, MA: Harvard University Press, 2009).
9. Eyal Chowers, *The Political Philosophy of Zionism* (Cambridge: Cambridge University Press, 2012); Boaz Neumann, *Land and Desire in Early Zionism* (Waltham, MA: Brandeis University Press, 2011).
10. Sophie Wahnich, *In Defense of the Terror: Liberty or Death in the French Revolution* (New York, 2016), 3.
11. David A. Bell and Yair Mintzker, "Introduction," in *Rethinking the Age of Revolutions: France and the Birth of the Modern World*, ed. David A. Bell and Yair Mintzker (Oxford: Oxford University Press, 2018), xvi–xxix. The idea of cul-de-sac is from Lynn Hunt, "The Experience of Revolution," *French Historical Studies* 32 (2009): 671–678.
12. Bell and Mintzker, "Introduction," xix.
13. Notable examples are Gur Alroey, *An Unpromising Land: Jewish Migration to Palestine in the Early Twentieth Century* (Stanford, CA: Stanford University Press 2014); Anat Helman, *Young Tel Aviv: A Tale of Two* Cities (Waltham, MA: Brandeis University Press, 2010); and Liora R. Halperin, *Babel in Zion: Jews, Nationalism, and Language Diversity in Palestine, 1920–1948* (New Haven, CT: Yale University Press, 2014).
14. On the problems of "daily life" as historiographical concept, see Rita Felski, *Doing Time: Feminist Theory and Postmodern Culture* (New York: NYU Press, 2000), 77–99.

15. Gur Alroey, *Immigrantim: Ha-Hagira ha- Yehudit le-Eretz Yisra'el be-Reshit ha-Me'ah ha-Esrim* (Jerusalem: Yad Ben-Zvi Press, 2004), 232 [my translation].
16. Jochen Hellbeck, *Revolution on My Mind: Writing a Diary Under Stalin* (Cambridge, MA: Harvard University Press, 2009), 13. In that context, see also Igal Halfin, *From Darkness to Light: Class, Consciousness, and Salvation in Revolutionary Russia* (Pittsburgh: University of Pittsburgh Press, 2000).
17. Tony Collins, *Sport in Capitalist Society: A Short History* (London: Routledge, 2013), 85; Barbara Keys, *Globalizing Sport: National Rivalry and International Community in the 1930s* (Cambridge, MA: Harvard University Press, 2006).
18. George Eisen, "Jewish History and the Ideology of Modern Sport: Approaches and Interpretations," *Journal of Sport History* 25 (1998): 482–531; Steven Riess, ed., *Sports and the American Jew* (Syracuse, NY: Syracuse University Press, 1998); Peter Levine, *Ellis Island to Ebbets Field: Sport and the American Jewish Experience* (Oxford: Oxford University Press, 1992); Michael Brenner, and Gidon Reuvani, eds., *Emancipation Through Muscles: Jews and Sports in Europe* (Lincoln: Nebraska University Press, 2006).
19. *Haaretz,* January 10, 1924, 4.
20. *Kolnoa,* October 27, 1932, 14.
21. In May 1938 the Maccabi Physical Culture Organization had 6,360 members; a year before, in February 1937, the organization had only 4,580 members. *Din Ve-Heshbon,* May 11, 1938, *Maccabi Sports Union Archive* [henceforth, "MCA"], 1–0094.
22. For example, one of the most prominent Hebrew Athletes, Yosef Yekutieli, was the son-in-law of the founder of Tel Aviv, Akiva Aryeh Weiss. Similarly, another chief Maccabi member and future Israeli parliamentarian, Nahum Het, was married to the granddaughter of the founder of Petah Tikva, Joel Moses Salomon. For biographies of the two, see Edna Yekutieli, *Ba'al ha ḥalomot* (Safrot 'akhshav, 1995) and Shmuel Meiri, *Nahum Het* (Haifa: Gestlit, 1996).
23. For Hebrew Athletes' discussions on their purpose, see *Uzeno,* February 6, 1935, 2; Zeev Dorsani, "Le-berur darken," *Uzeno,* February 20, 1935, 2; *HaMaccabi,* November–December 1923, 2; *Uzeno,* 5687 [1926–1927], 13–14; "El Kol," June 10, 1938, MCA, 1–0094; "Le-berur darken," September 1, 1939, *Wingate Institute Archive for Physical Education* [henceforth, "WIA"].
24. *Haaretz,* January 10, 1924, 4.
25. *HaMaccabi,* December 27, 1930, 81.
26. *HaMaccabi,* May 25, 1936, 1.
27. Ofer Idels, *Zionism: Emotions, Language and Experience* (Cambridge: Cambridge University Press, 2024), 16–32.
28. In that context see Jan Plamper, "Sounds of February, Smells of October: The Russian Revolution as Sensory Experience," *American Historical Review* 126 (2021): 140–165; Rob Boddice and Mark Smith, *Emotion, Sense, Experience* (Cambridge: Cambridge University Press, 2020)
29. Rita Felski, *The Limits of Critique* (Chicago University Press, 2015). See also Bruno Latour, "Why Has Critique Run out of Steam? From Matters of Fact to Matters of Concern," *Critical Inquiry* 30 (2004): 225–248.
30. Felski, *Limits of Critique,* 1–52; Paul Ricoeur, *Freud and Philosophy an Essay on Interpretation* (New Haven, CT: Yale University Press, 1970), 32–36.
31. Toril Moi, "Nothing Is Hidden," in *Critique and Postcritique,* ed. Elizabeth S. Anker and Rita Felski (Durham, NC: Duke University Press, 2017), 34; See also Moi's tour de force: *Revolution of the Ordinary: Literary Studies After Wittgenstein, Austin, and Cavell* (Chicago: University of Chicago Press, 2017).
32. Elizabeth S. Anker and Rita Felski, "Introduction," in *Critique and Postcritique,* 26.
33. For a similar reading of Zionism, see Neumann, *Land and Desire.*

34. Hayden White, "The Public Relevance of Historical Studies: A Reply to Dirk Moses," *History and Theory* 44 (2005): 338.
35. Ricoeur, *Freud and Philosophy*, 28.
36. Barbara J. Keys, "Introduction," in *The Ideals of Global Sport: From Peace to Human Rights*, ed. Barbara J. Keys (Philadelphia: University of Pennsylvania Press, 2019), 1–20; Ofer Idels, "'The Idea of Sports Is Pure and Noble': Internationalism, Zionism and the Formation of a Global Universal Language," *International History Review* (2024): 1–15.
37. Hans Ulrich Gumbrecht, *In Praise of Athletic Beauty* (Cambridge, MA: Harvard Press, 2006), 25–30.
38. Gumbrecht, *In Praise of Athletic Beauty*, 25–30. For a Ricoeurian reading of sport, see Roger W. H. Savage, "Effort, Play, and Sport," *Sport, Ethics and Philosophy* 10 (2016): 392–402.
39. The Soviet case is a good comparison: see Robert Edelman, *Serious Fun: A History of Spectator Sports in the USSR* (Oxford: Oxford University Press, 1993).
40. Roni Gechtman, "Socialist Mass Politics Through Sport: The Bund's Morgenshtern in Poland, 1926–1939," *Journal of Sport History* 26 (1999): 326–352. On the link with Eastern Europe, see Kenneth B. Moss, Benjamin Nathans, and Taro Tsurumi, eds., *From Europe's East to the Middle East Israel's Russian and Polish Lineages* (Philadelphia: University of Pennsylvania Press, 2021).
41. Susan Cahn, *Coming on Strong: Gender and Sexuality in Twentieth-Century Women's Sport* (Urbana: University of Illinois Press, 2015), esp. 55–82.
42. Ofer Idels, "How to Lose Gracefully in An Internationally Selfish World: Gender, The 'New Jew,' and the Underestimation of Athletic Performance in Interwar Palestine," *Journal of Modern Jewish Studies* 21 (2022): 215–233.
43. Anker and Felski, "Introduction," in *Critique and Postcritique*, 26.
44. Much of this perspective was inspired by Igal Halfin's discussion of the communist self, *Terror in My Soul: Communist Autobiographies on Trial* (Cambridge, MA: Harvard, 2003), x.

CHAPTER 1 TEACHING NORDAU TO PLAY FOOTBALL

1. *Ba-maslul*, 1933, 3.
2. Keys, *Globalizing Sport*, 3.
3. On Nordau and *Muskeljudentum* see Michael Stanislawski, *Zionism and the Fin de SiËcle: Cosmopolitanism and Nationalism from Nordau to Jabotinsky* (University of California Press, 2001).
4. Keys, *Globalizing Sport*, 182.
5. Christiane Eisenberg, *"English Sports" und deutsche B‚rger: Eine Gesellschaftsgeschichte 1800–1939* (Paderborn: Ferdinand Schöningh, 1999), 250–261.
6. *Oxford English Dictionary*, accessed May 1, 2023, https://www.oed.com/view/Entry/187476.
7. Norbert Elias, "Introduction," in *Quest for Excitement: Sports and Leisure in the Civilizing Process*, ed. Norbert Elias and Eric Dunning (Oxford: Blackwell, 1986), 19–63; Eric Hobsbawm, "Mass-Producing Traditions: Europe, 1870–1914," in *The Invention of Tradition*, ed. Eric Hobsbawm and Terence Roger (Cambridge, MA: Cambridge University Press, 1992), 263–308.
8. Allan Guttmann, *From Ritual to Record: The Nature of Modern Sports* (New York: Columbia University Press, 1978), 15–57; J. J. Coakley, *Sport in Society: Issues and Controversies* (Boston: McGraw-Hill, 1998), 4–18; Bernard Suits, "Tricky Triad: Games, Play, and Sport," *Journal of the Philosophy of Sport* 15 (2012): 1–9; Johan Huizinga, *Homo Ludens: A Study of the Play-Element in Culture* (London: Routledge, 1980), 25–45, 195–200; Roger Caillois, *Man, Play, and Games* (Urbana: University of Illinois Press, 2001), 3–144; Stefan Szymanski, "A Theory of the Evolution of Modern Sport," *Journal of Sport History* 35 (2008): 1–64.

9. Tony Collins, *A Social History of English Rugby Union* (New York: Routledge, 2009), 1–21; Mike Huggins, *The Victorians and Sport* (New York: Palgrave, 2004); David Kirk, *Schooling Bodies: School Practice and Public Discourse 1880–1950* (Leicester: Leicester University Press, 1998).
10. A. Mangan, *The Cultural Bond: Sport, Empire, Society* (New York: Routledge, 2011); Brian Stoddart, "Sport, Cultural Imperialism and Colonial Response in the British Empire." *Comparative Studies in Society and History* 40 (1988): 649–667.
11. Mark Dyreson, "The Emergence of Consumer Culture and the Transformation of Physical Culture: American Sport in the 1920s," *Journal of Sport History* 16 (1989): 261–289.
12. Collins, *Sport in Capitalist Society*, 48–60.
13. Michael Hau, *Performance Anxiety: Sport and Work in Germany from the Empire to Nazism* (Toronto: Toronto University Press, 2017), 15–48; Eugen Weber, "Pierre de Coubertin and the Introduction of Organized Sport in France," *Journal of Contemporary History* 15 (1970): 3–26.
14. James Walvin, *The People's Game: A Social History of British Football* (London: Random House, 2014), 107; Allen Guttmann, *The Olympics: A History of the Modern Games* (Champaign: University of Illinois Press, 2002), 21–37.
15. Mosse, *The Image of Man*, 40–47; Michael Kruger, "Body Culture and Nation Building: The History of Gymnastics in Germany in the Period of Its Foundation as a Nation-State," *International Journal of the History of Sport* 13 (1996): 409–411.
16. Christiane Eisenberg, "Charismatic Nationalist Leader: Turnvater Jahn," *International Journal of the History of Sport* 13 (1996): 14–27.
17. One may even say that the problematic and subjective scoring system used in today's gymnastics, like the strong overemphasis on current Olympic gymnasts relative to athletes in other sports, is a corollary of the first days of gymnastics.
18. Ina Zweiniger-Bargielowska, *Managing the Body: Beauty, Health, and Fitness in Britain 1880–1939* (Oxford: Oxford University Press, 2010), 2; Michael Hau, *The Cult of Health and Beauty in Germany: A Social History, 1890–1930* (Chicago: University of Chicago Press, 2003), 1; Svenja Goltermann, "Exercise and Perfection: Embodying the Nation in Nineteenth-Century Germany," *European Review of History* 11 (2004): 333–346.
19. Eugen Weber, "Gymnastics and Sports in Fin-de-Siècle France: Opium of the Classes?" *American Historical Review* 76 (1971): 70–98; Gertrud Pfister, ed., *Gymnastics, a Transatlantic Movement: From Europe to America* (New York: Routledge, 2011); Annette Hofmann, ed. *Turnen and Sport: Transatlantic Transfers* (New York: Waxmann, 2004); Claire Nolte, *The Sokol in the Czech Lands to 1914: Training for the Nation* (Hampshire: Palgrave, 2002); Alan Tomlinson and Christopher Young, "Towards a New History of European Sport," *European Review* 19 (2011): 487–507.
20. George Eisen, "Zionism, Nationalism and the Emergence of the Judische Turnerschaft," *Leo Baeck Institute Yearbook* 28 (1983): 247–262; Daniel Wildmann, *Der Veranderbare Korper: Judische Turner, Mannlichkeit und das Wiedergewinnen Von Geschichte in Deutschland Um 1900* (Tübingen: Mohr Siebeck, 2009); Sebastian Conrad, "Globalizing the Beautiful Body: Eugen Sandow, Bodybuilding, and the Ideal of Muscular Manliness at the Turn of the Twentieth Century," *Journal of World History*," 32 (2021): 95–125.
21. Todd Presner, *Muscular Judaism: The Jewish Body and the Politics of Regeneration* (London: Routledge, 2007), esp, 106–154.
22. Max Nordau, "Muskeljudentum," *J, dische Turnzeitung* 2, June 1900, 11 [Möge der jüdische Turnverein blühen und gedeihen und zu einem an allen Mittpunkten jüdischen Lebens eifrig nachgeahmten Vorbild].
23. *HaZvi*, August 22, 1910, 3.
24. *HaZvi*, December 30, 1908, 3.

25. Minutes of the Maccabi Association in Jerusalem, Aviezer Yellin Archives for Jewish Education in Israel and the Diaspora (hereinafter: AYA), 8–11, November 5, 1911.
26. *HaMaccabi,* May 16, 1913, 13–16; Uriel Zimri, *Agudot ha-hit'amlut ve-ha-sport be-Eretz Yisrael lifne milhemet ha-'olam ha-rishona* (Netanya: Wingate Institute, 1969), 71–91.
27. "Le-tse'ire artsenu," Elul 5672 [September 1911], AYA, 8–11; Zimri, *Agudot ha-hit'amlut,* 91.
28. Minutes of the Maccabi Association in Jerusalem, January 21, 1912, AYA, 8–11, "Le-tse'ire artsenu," Elul 5672 [September 1911], AYA, 8–11.
29. *HaZvi* April 26, 1912, 6. Italics are in the original.
30. For example, *HaZvi,* July 31, 1912, 3.
31. Minutes of the Maccabi Association in Jerusalem, January 21, 1912, AYA, 8–11.
32. *Do'ar HaYom,* January 5, 1923, 4.
33. Zvi Nishri, *Mi-divre yeme ha-hinukh ha-gufani* (Tel Aviv: National Committee, 1940), 18–19.
34. Hau, *Cult of Health and Beauty,* 177.
35. *Hashkafa,* May 8, 1908, 2.
36. *HaZvi,* February 10, 1909, 3; *HaTsefira,* November 30, 1910, 1; *HaZvi,* April 28, 1912, 5.
37. *Ha-herut Yerushalayim,* April 12, 1912, 2.
38. *HaPo'el ha-Tsa'ir,* April 18, 1913, 1; Z. Orloff, *Kadur Regel* (Jaffa: Maccabi Palestine Federation, 1914).
39. *HaMaccabi,* Kislev 5684 [December 1924], 12–13.
40. *HaHerut,* July 1, 1913, 2. All references to football in this chapter and throughout the book refer to the game Americans call "soccer."
41. Yosef Yekutieli, "25 shana la-mis'hak kadur ha-regel be-Tel Aviv: 1911–1936," *Hesegav shel Maccabi Tel Aviv be-25 ha-shanim ha-aharonot* (Jaffa: M. Shoham, 1936).
42. *HaHerut,* July 12, 1912, 3.
43. *Haaretz,* June 1, 1929, 3.
44. *HaMaccabi,* September 22, 1936, 4.
45. Tony Collins, *Sport in Capitalist Society,* 85.
46. *Do'ar HaYom,* March 3, 1920, 4.
47. "Maccabi Tel Aviv Technical Report for 1935/36," MCA, 1–11.
48. *Do'ar HaYom,* November 26, 1922, 5.
49. Maccabi Tel Aviv, Report on Cash Income and Expenditure, October 1, 1936–August 31, 1937, MCA, 1–10–1; *HaMaccabi,* August 1931, 324.
50. *'Uzenu,* 1935, 3.
51. "Minutes of Annual Assembly of Delegates of Maccabi Associations," Hanukka 5687 [December 1927], MCA, 1–54.
52. For additional examples of resistance by the sports organizations and their support of gymnastics, see *'Uzenu,* July 1935, 3; "Central Committee Report to National Conference in Hadera," May 11, 1938, MCA, 1–55.
53. *Haaretz,* January 10, 1924, 4.
54. "Minutes of Annual Assembly of Delegates of Maccabi Associations," Hanukka 5687 [December 1927], MCA, 1–54.
55. *Haaretz,* April 1, 1931, 3.
56. Zalman Avni, *15 dakot ba-yom lema'an ha-beriyut* (Tel Aviv: Goldner, 1938). For additional examples, see *Eikh yishmor ha-pakid gufo?* (Tel Aviv: Central Committee of the Federation of White-Collar Workers in Palestine and Central Committee of the Hapoel Body-Culture Association, 1938), Yehoshua Alouf, *Mun'he ha-hinukh ha-gufani: Hit'amlut* (Tel Aviv: Physical Training Department, 1940).

57. Michael Krüger and Annette R. Hofmann, "The Development of Physical-Education Institutions in Europe: A Short Introduction," *International Journal of the History of Sport* 32 (2015): 739.
58. Eric Chaline, *The Temple of Perfection: A History of the Gym* (London: Reaktion Books, 2015).
59. Benzion Mossinson to Zvi Nishri, Tevet 22, 5684, AYA, 5–1635–73; in 1927 Nishri established an organization of gymnastics teachers. See *Davar,* December 25, 1938, 6.
60. *HaMaccabi,* December 27, 1929, 63–64.
61. *HaMaccabi,* December 27, 1929, 63–64.
62. *Davar,* October 23, 1938, 6.
63. *Davar,* October 23, 1938, 6.
64. Stefan Zweig, *The World of Yesterday* (Lincoln: University of Nebraska Press, 1964), 58.
65. For an analysis of the German literature in this context, see Wolfgang Paterno, *Faust und Geist. Literatur und Boxen zwischen den Weltkriegen* (Vienna: Böhlau, 2018); *'Uzenu,* Tammuz 5695 [Summer 1935], 12–13; *Haaretz,* January 22, 1924, 4.
66. A. Hameiri, 1944, *Ha-tsok,* electronic version, Ben-Yehuda Project, retrieved on May 30, 2020, https://benyehuda.org/read/16530. See also *'Uzenu,* Tammuz 5695 [Summer 1935], 12–13; *Haaretz,* January 22, 1942, 4.
67. *Haaretz,* August 1, 1928, 3.
68. *Haaretz,* November 27, 1928, 3.
69. *HaMaccabi,* Kislev 5689 [December 1928], 4.
70. On writing and translating rules in the interwar era, see "Rules of Sports," 1932, MCA, 1–6; "Rules of the New Games," 1929, AYA, 1–17–10; "Maccabi Contests," 1918–1927, AYA 1–22–10; "Maccabi Rules," 1931–1949; AYA, 1–10–10. See also training books: Ernst Simon, *Atletika kala* (Haifa, 1937); O. Glückman, *Atletika kala: Targili hakhana* (Tel Aviv: Hapoel Body-Culture Association, 1941); *Ha-hukim ha-rishmi'im lefi hitah'dut ha-benleumit le-kadur-sal* (Tel Aviv: Federation of Amateur Sports Clubs, 1939); Shneor Tsuri, *Mis'hake sport: Kadur-yad* (Haifa: Hapoel Body-Culture Association, 1928).
71. Orloff, *Kadur regel;* A. Rubinstein, *HaMaccabi,* December 11, 1923, 10–11; Palestine Football Federation, *Sefer shimushi li-shenat 1930/31* (Jerusalem: Palestine Football Federation, 1930); Yosef Yekutieli, *Sefer huke ha-kaduregel: Lefi ha-hahlatot ha-rishmiyot shel ha-va'ad ha-ben leumi* (Jerusalem: Y. Azrieli, 1927–1928).
72. Yekutieli, *Sefer huke ha-kaduregel,* 1.
73. *Haaretz,* January 10, 1924, 4.
74. *HaBoker Sport,* February 25, 1939, 2; Yosef Yehutieli, *HaBoker Sport,* March 18, 1939, 2.
75. *Haaretz,* November 17, 1932, 3.
76. *Kolnoa',* January 22, 1932, 12; *HaMaccabi,* Nissan 5685 [April 1925], 2–4; *HaMaccabi,* Kislev 5686 [December 1925], 4–5. As for attitudes toward women and sports elsewhere, see Susan Cahn, *Coming on Strong,* 82; Patricia A. Vertinsky, *The Eternally Wounded Woman: Women, Doctors, and Exercise in the Late Nineteenth Century* (Urbana: University of Illinois Press, 1994).
77. *Davar,* January 4, 1937, 9.
78. *Do'ar HaYom,* July 4, 1924, 4.
79. *Davar,* March 15, 1937, 9.
80. See, for example, *Do'ar HaYom,* June 4, 1926, 7; *Do'ar HaYom,* October 3, 1926, 3; *Kolnoa',* July 10, 1931, 7; *Do'ar HaYom,* January 19, 1934, 8.
81. *Davar,* February 28, 1929, 3.
82. *HaMaccabi,* C., March 31, 151.
83. *Do'ar HaYom,* January 9, 1923, 4; *Do'ar HaYom,* May 30, 1923, 3; *HaMaccabi,* Iyar 5685 [May 1933], 2–4; *'Uzenu,* March 8. 1935, 3; M. Hadshuni, "Sikum 'aluv," *'Uzenu,* February 6, 1935, 2; *'Uzenu,* January 3, 1935, 2–3; *Davar,* March 9, 1936, 3.

84. Barbara Keys, "Soviet Sport and Transnational Mass Culture in the 1930s," *Journal of Contemporary History* 38 (2003): 413–434; Gechtman, "Socialist Mass Politics," 326–352.
85. *Davar*, January 6, 1935, 5.
86. *Davar*, March 9, 1936, 14.
87. *HaBoker Sport*, February 4, 1939, 1.
88. Z. Orloff, *Shi'ure hit'amlut: Le-vate sefer, la-agudot ve-la-bayit* (Jaffa: A. Eitan and S. Shoshani, 1920), 12; *Haaretz*, September 19, 1928, 3. On the gradual integration of competition into the curriculum of the Herzliya Hebrew Gymnasium, see "Herzliya Hebrew Gymnasium: 5697 [1936/37] Curriculum," AYA, 8–103–110; "Herzliya Hebrew Gymnasium: 5686 [1925/26] Curriculum," AYA, 8–103–110; see also *Haaretz*, May 11, 1930, 3.
89. *Ma'arakhot*, September 1, 1939, 58. See also *Haaretz*, December 22, 1938, 6; *HaMaccabi*, April 5, 1936, 2–3.
90. *Davar*, August 27, 1939, 6.
91. *'Uzenu*, January 1934, 14.
92. *'Uzenu*, January 31, 1935, 5.
93. Haim Kaufman, "Yesoda shel 'Hitagdut ha-Sport Hapoel," *Cathedra* 80 (1996): 122–149. Exceptional in this context is his short article: "Ha-zika ha-re'ayonit ben sport ha-po'alim leven hitagdut 'Hapoel' bi-tekufat ha-Mandat," *BiTenu'a* 3 (1995): 56–71.
94. David Steinberg, "The Worker's Sport International 1920–1928," *Journal of Contemporary History* 13 (1978): 233–251; Michael Kruger, "The German Workers' Sport Movement Between Socialism, Workers Culture, Middle-Class Gymnastics and Sport for All," *International Journal of the History of Sport* 31 (2013): 1098–1117.
95. *'Uzenu*, Nissan 5687 [April 1927], 11; *Do'ar HaYom*, June 21, 1926, 1.
96. Minutes of the Committee for Preparation of a Cultural Workplan, December 23, 1929, AYA, 1.10–159–22.
97. For the original, see Nordau, "Muskeljudentum," 11. The new translation into Hebrew appears in *HaMaccabi*, November 10, 1923, 3.
98. .wikipedia.org/wiki/יהדות_שרירים (accessed September 1, 2024).
99. "Sport," *Even-Shoshan*, 1997, Vol. C, 1262.
100. "To All Delegates to the Maccabi Conference in Hadera," June 10, 1938, MCA, 1–0094.

CHAPTER 2 COMPETING IN HEBREW

1. Haim Hazaz, *Siporim Nevcharim* (Tel-Aviv: Dvir, 1977), 155 [author translation].
2. *Haaretz*, November 3, 1939, 4.
3. *Davar*, March 9, 1936, 3.
4. *IIuuretz*, February 12, 1932, 5. See also the discussion in Chapter 1 and Nahman Bialik's contemptuous dismissal of football at the first meeting of his public lecture forum *Oneg Shabbat*: Anat Helman, "Sport on the Sabbath: Controversy in 1920s and 1930s Jewish Palestine," *International Journal of the History of Sport* 25 (2008): 55.
5. This interpretation contrasts with Israeli sports sociologist Amir Ben-Porat, who viewed Hazaz's claim not as a dismissal of sport but as an assertion that it is more than just a game—it is a crucial element in national formation with "far-reaching significance.": "Isra'el safa kasha akh kulam dibru 'ota," *Iyunim* (2010): 144–168, quote on p. 144.
6. Erik Jensen, *Body by Weimar: Athletes, Gender, and German Modernity* (New York: Oxford University Press, 2010), 56; Richard Gruneau, *Sport and Modernity* (Cambridge: Polity Press, 2017), 4.
7. Bert[olt] Brecht, "Die Krise des Sports," in *Der Sport am Scheidewege*, ed. Willy Meisl (Heidelberg: Iris, 1928), 146. See also Jon Hughes, *Max Schmeling and the Making of a National Hero in Twentieth-Century Germany* (Cham, Switzerland: Palgrave Macmillan, 2018), 30–31.

8. For example, see Irena Martínková and Jim Parry, *Phenomenological Approaches to Sport* (London: Routledge, 2015); Andrew Edgar, *Sport and Art: An Essay in the Hermeneutics of Sport* (London: Routledge, 2014); and Steven Connor, *A Philosophy of Sport* (London: Reaktion Books, 2011).
9. Victor Turner, *On the Edge of the Bush: Anthropology as Experience* (Tucson: University of Arizona Press, 1985), 237. See also Sharon Rowe, "Modern Sports: Liminal Ritual or Liminoid Leisure," *Journal of Ritual Studies* 12 (1998): 47–60.
10. Elias, "Introduction," in *Quest for Excitement*, 19–63.
11. Gumbrecht, *In Praise of Athletic Beauty*, 214. See also Hans Ulrich Gumbrecht, "Epiphany of Form: On the Beauty of Team Sports," *New Literary History* 30 (1999): 351–372.
12. A. D. Gordon, *Ha-Adam ve'Hatavea*, edited by Yuval Jobani and Ron Margolin (Jerusalem: Magnes Press, 2020), 141–155.
13. Eelco Runia, *Moved by the Past: Discontinuity and Historical Mutation* (New York: Columbia University Press, 2014), 53.
14. Gumbrecht, *In Praise of Athletic Beauty*, 39–57.
15. *Davar*, March 9, 1936, 3.
16. *HaBoker Sport*, March 7, 1937, 2.
17. *HaBoker Sport*, May 13, 1939, 2.
18. Idels, *Zionism*, 16–32.
19. Benjamin Harshav, *Language in Time of Revolution* (Berkeley: University of California Press), 82.
20. A. D. Gordon, "Rashomot Hchronot," *Project Ben-Yehuda*, https://benyehuda.org/read/18893, accessed on September 8, 2022 [my translation].
21. Le-ze'irey 'arzenu, 1912, AYA, 8–11.
22. Neumann, *Land and Desire*, 150–180.
23. Gordon, "Rashomot."
24. C. H. Bialik, "Language Closing and Disclosing," in Joseph Dan, *The Heart and the Fountain: An Anthology of Jewish Mystical Experiences*, translated by trans. Yael Lotan (Oxford: Oxford University Press, 2003), 257–261. See also Chowers, *Political Philosophy of Zionism*, 158.
25. Maya Dar, "Ve-matay yesh zeman," *Haya Haya* (2003): 73–92. On the contrary, the Hebrew term for gymnastics (*hit'amlut*) is pre-modern.
26. *Davar*, December 12, 1937, 4.
27. *Haaretz*, February 12, 1932, 5. Italics are in the original.
28. *Davar*, March 31, 1937, 9.
29. *Davar*, July 17, 1930, 3.
30. *Davar*, December 12, 1937, 4.
31. *Davar*, June 24, 1937, 4; *Davar*, March 31, 1937, 9.
32. Meira Belkind, "Belkind Dairy," Rishon LeZion Archive [henceforth, "RLA"], 3-02-1-1.
33. *Haaretz*, February 12, 1932, 5.
34. *HaMaccabi*, February 27, 1936, 8–9.
35. Assaf Inbari, "Towards a Hebrew Literature," *Azure* (2000): 100. On biblical narrative, see Frank Polak, *Ha-sipur ba-mikra* (Jerualem: Mosad Bialik, 1999).
36. John Carvalho, "Communications and Journalism," in *The Oxford Handbook of Sports History*, ed. Robert Edelman and Wayne Wilson (Oxford: Oxford University Press, 2017), 159–161.
37. Duncan Wu, *William Hazlitt: The First Modern Man* (Oxford: Oxford University Press, 2010), 305–306.

38. David Snowdon, "Hazlitt's Prizefight Revisited: Pierce Egan and Jon Bee's Boxiana-Style Perspective," *Romantic Textualities: Literature and Print Culture* 20 (2011).
39. John Rickards Betts, "Sporting Journalism in Nineteenth-Century America," *American Quarterly* 55 (1953): 39–56; Michael Oriard, *Reading Football: How the Popular Press Created an American Spectacle* (Chapel Hill: University of North Carolina Press).
40. Jean K. Chalaby, "Journalism as an Anglo-American Invention: A Comparison of the Development of French and Anglo-American, Journalism, 1830s–1920s," *European Journal of Communication* 11 (1996): 303–326.
41. *HaMaccabi*, December 27, 1936, 1–2.
42. *Davar*, October 30, 1938, 5.
43. *Davar*, October 16, 1938, 7.
44. *Davar*, October 30, 1938, 5; *Davar*, January 16, 1938, 8.
45. *New York Times*, June 9, 1933, 21. See also the Hebrew media coverage of the famous fights between Schmeling and Joe Lewis: *Davar*, June 29, 1936, 9; *Haaretz*, June 4, 1938, 11; *Davar*, June 24, 1938, 1.
46. *Do'ar HaYom*, June 11, 1933, 1.
47. *The Palestine Post*, June 12, 1933, 3.
48. *Der Moment*, June 11, 1933, 5.
49. *Der Moment*, June 11, 1933, 5.
50. *Haynt*, June 11, 1933, 2.
51. In the American Yiddish press, there was also a photo of the knockout moment: *Forverts*, June 9, 1933, 2.
52. Yael Chaver, *What Must be Forgotten: The Survival of Yiddish in Zionist Palestine* (Syracuse, NY: Syracuse University Press, 2004); Zohar Shavit, "Can It Be That Our Dormant Language Has Been Wholly Revived? Vision, Propaganda, and Linguistic Reality in the Yishuv Under the British Mandate," *Israel Studies* 22 (2017): 101–138.
53. *Haaretz*, February 12, 1932, 5.
54. *Haaretz*, February 12, 1932, 5.
55. *New York Times*, September 24, 1926, 1.
56. *Do'ar HaYom*, October 27, 1926, 3.
57. *New York Times*, September 24, 1926, 1.
58. *New York Times*, September 24, 1926, 1.
59. Gumbrecht, *In 1926: Living at the Edge of Time* (Cambridge, MA: Harvard University Press, 1997), 49–50.
60. *Davar*, September 24, 1937, 7; *Davar*, October 1, 1937, 7; *HaBoker*, November 13, 1938, 4.
61. *Sport Haaretz*, February 6, 1938, 3.
62. Ibid.
63. Yosef Yekutieli, March 8, 1923, MCA, 23-001-5.
64. *Haaretz*, December 29, 1935, 6.
65. *Haaretz*, December 29, 1935, 6.
66. *HaBoker Sport*, December 5, 1936, 2; *Davar*, January 16, 1938, 8.
67. Bialik, "Language Closing and Disclosing," 257.
68. *Davar*, September 18, 1938, 6.
69. *Haaretz*, February 26, 1937, 4.
70. *Haaretz*, December 29, 1935, 6.
71. *Sport Haaretz*, February 21, 1938, 1.
72. *Sport Haaretz*, January 23, 1938, 2.

73. *HaBoker Sport,* April 29, 1939, 2.
74. *Sport Haaretz,* January 23, 1938, 2.
75. Meir Shkedi, "Hazhaara," June 19, 1931, MCA, 0054–1.
76. Joan Tumblety, *Remaking the Male Body: Masculinity and the Uses of Physical Culture in Interwar and Vichy France* (Oxford: Oxford University Press, 2012), 107; Hughes, *Max Schmeling,* 20–25; Jensen, *Body by Weimar,* 9–12; Murat C. Yildiz, "Mapping the 'Sports Nahda': Toward A History of Sports in the Modern Middle East," in *Sport, Politics and Society in the Middle East,* ed. Danyel Reiche and Tamir Sorek (Oxford: Oxford University Press, 2019), 22–32.
77. *Kolnoa,* April 10, 1931, 5.
78. Shkedi, "Hazhaara," MCA, 0054–1
79. *Kolnoa,* October 9, 1931, 13.
80. Deborah Bernstein, *Nashim Ba-Sholaim: Migdar Ve-Le'umiut Be- Tel Aviv Ha-Mandatorit* (Jerusalem: Yad-ben Zvi, 2008), 159.
81. *Sport Haaretz,* February 21, 1938, 4. See also *HaBoker Sport,* September 2, 1939, 2.
82. Israel Paz, "Ha-sport ba-'aitonut Haktova," in *Tarbut ha-guf ve-ha-sport,* ed. Haim Kaufman and Hagi Harif (Jerusalem: Yad-Ben Zvi Press, 2002), 245. In addition, *Davar* began publishing its own sports supplement that reflected the "informative approach."
83. *HaBoker Sport,* December 5, 1936, 2. Italics added.
84. *HaSport,* March 19, 1936, 2–3.
85. *HaBoker Sport,* June 28, 1936, 2.
86. *HaBoker Sport,* June 28, 1936, 2.
87. *Sport Haaretz,* January 23, 1938, 1.
88. *HaBoker Sport,* April 29, 1939, 2. Italics added.
89. *Sport Haaretz,* January 23, 1938, 2.
90. *Sport Haaretz,* January 23, 1938, 2.
91. *HaSport,* March 25, 1935, 1.
92. *HaBoker Sport,* December 5, 1936, 2.
93. *Sport Haaretz,* January 23, 1938, 1.
94. *HaSport,* April 20, 1938, 2.
95. *Sport Haaretz,* February 21, 1938, 3.
96. *HaBoker Sport,* May 7, 1936, 1; *Sport Haaretz,* June 2, 1938, 2.
97. *Sport Haaretz,* February 21, 1938, 3.
98. *Sport Haaretz,* February 21, 1938, 4.
99. For example, see *HaSport,* March 25, 1932, 2; *Sport,* March 19, 1936, 6.
100. *HaSport,* September 24, 1931, 1.
101. Gilad Halpern, "For King and Country: The Palestine Post and Zionist Propaganda in Pre-State Israel, 1932–1950" (PhD diss., Haifa University, 2024).
102. *The Palestine Post,* December 21, 1936, 11.
103. *HaBoker Sport,* December 26, 1936, 2.
104. *HaBoker Sport,* December 26, 1936, 2.
105. *The Palestine Post,* 21 December 1936, 11.
106. *The Palestine Post,* 21 December 1936, 11.
107. *HaBoker Sport,* December 26, 1936, 2.
108. *Davar,* September 18, 1938, 6.
109. *Davar,* September 18, 1938, 6.
110. *Even-Shoshan Dictionary 1997,* s.v. "Sport."
111. *HaSport,* September 12, 1940, 3.
112. *Davar,* January 23, 1938, 4.

CHAPTER 3 "KEEP AWAY FROM THE PRIMA DONNAS"

1. During his athletic career, Borg won five Olympic medals and eight European Championships medals and held a number of world records. The most prestigious of these was being the first man to sum 1,500 meters in under twenty minutes.
2. *Haaretz*, August 29, 1928, 3.
3. *Haaretz*, August 29, 1928, 3.
4. Jensen, *Body by Weimar*, 102; Conrad, "Globalizing the Beautiful Body," 95–125; George Mosse, *The Image of Man*, 41–47; Hau, *Performance Anxiety*, 49–83; Anson Rabinbach, *The Human Motor: Energy, Fatigue, and the Origins of Modernity* (Berkeley: University of California Press, 1992), esp. 174.
5. *Haaretz*, August 29, 1928, 3.
6. Gordon, "Letter," 2. The Hebrew word for soul—*nefesh*—is encompassing both "mind" and "spirit."
7. Gordon, "Letter," 2.
8. *BaMaslul*, December 1932, 10.
9. *Do'ar HaYom*, January 22, 1933, 2.
10. *HaZvi*, March 15, 1912, 3. For more examples see *HaZvi*, December 26, 1912, 3; *Hashkafa*, March 28, 1908, 2; and *HaHerut Yerushala'im*, April 24, 1914, 3.
11. *Davar*, March 31, 1937,9.
12. *Davar*, July 17, 1930, 3
13. *Uzenu*, February 1935, 3.
14. *Haaretz*, September 19, 1928, 3. Italics added.
15. *Ha'sport be-batai Hasfer*, May 19, 1938, 1.
16. *BaMaslul*, December 1932, 10.
17. *HaBoker Sport*, February 4, 1939, 1.
18. *Haaretz*, September 10, 1931, 2.
19. *HaBoker Sport*, March 4, 1939, 2. In Hebrew, this sentence carries an additional, aesthetic component: The words translate literally as "losing pretty" vs. "winning ugly."
20. *Ha'sport be-batai Hasfer*, May 19, 1938, 1.
21. *HaBoker Sport*, April 1, 1939, 2.
22. *HaBoker Sport*, January 28, 1939, 3.
23. *Do'ar HaYom*, December 12, 1925.
24. Adrian Harvey, *The Beginnings of a Commercial Sporting Culture in Britain 1793–1850* (Burlington, VT: Ashgate, 2004); Neil Wigglesworth, *The Evolution of English Sport* (London: Frank Cass, 1996); Neil Tranter, *Sport, Economy and Society in Britain 1750 1914* (Cambridge, MA: Cambridge University Press, 1998); and Wray Vamplew, *Pay up and Play the Game: Professional Sport in Britain 1875–1914* (New York: Cambridge University Press, 2004).
25. Collins, *Sport in Capitalist Society*, 27–37.
26. Hughes, *Max Schmeling*, 20. On Italy, see Victoria De Grazia, *The Culture of Consent: Mass Organization of Leisure in Fascist Italy* (Cambridge: Cambridge University Press, 1981), 178.
27. "Protocol," December 23, 1929, WIA, 1.10-159-22. Italics are in the original.
28. *HaBoker Sport*, April 29, 1939, 4; *HaBoker Sport*, March 18, 1939, 3.
29. *Do'ar HaYom*, July 5, 1921, 2.
30. *Do'ar HaYom*, July 5, 1921, 2.
31. *Do'ar HaYom*, December 10, 1926, 3.
32. See for example, Ila Committee, "Committee of the 'Maccabi' association for gymnastics," June 16, 1919, MCA, 1–0094; "The Ila football team," MCA, 1–0090; *Do'ar HaYom*, June 24, 1926, 4; *Do'ar HaYom*, September 24, 1923, 2. This development was not limited to football. See,

for example, HaKvutza HaLevana (The White Team) Jerusalem athletics club established in 1923.

33. Committee of the Maccabi Association Tel Aviv, "Opening Games of the 1922–23 Football Season," *HaMaccabi*, December 1922, 12–13. See also Haim Kaufman and Yair Galili, "The Early Development of Hebrew Football in Eretz Israel, 1910–1928," *Soccer & Society* (2008): 81–95.

34. *Do'ar HaYom*, June 29, 1923, 8. For more criticism of professionalism, see *Davar*, February 28, 1929, 3.

35. *HaMaccabi*, November 1926, 12; *Do'ar HaYom*, November 25, 1922, 3.

36. *Davar*, May 10, 1927, 3.

37. "Declaration," *Davar*, April 3, 1927, 3. *Gibor* was another forgotten local football club once associated with Maccabi

38. "Declaration," *Davar*, April 3, 1927, 3.

39. On the early days of boxing in the United States see Elliott J. Gorn, *The Manly Art: Bare-Knuckle Prize Fighting in America* (Ithaca: Cornell University Press, 2010); Jeffrey T. Sammons, *Beyond the Ring: The Role of Boxing in American Society* (Urbana: University of Illinois Press, 1988), 48–72; and Matthew Taylor, "Round the London Ring: Boxing, Class and Community in Interwar London," *London Journal* 34, no. 2 (2009): 4

40. Erik Jensen, "Crowd Control: Boxing Spectatorship and Social Order in Weimar Germany," in *Histories of Leisure*, ed. Rudy Koshar (Oxford: Berg, 2002), 79–101. This link between the battlefield and the boxing ring was also evident in the key place of military service (or lack of) in the public images of prominent interwar boxers such as Jack Dempsey, Gene Tunney, and Georges Carpentier.

41. See Sammons, *Beyond the Ring*, 49–50; Maxence Pascal Philippe Leconte, "Reexamining Violence and Trauma in the French Boxing Literature of the Interwar Period: Henri Decoin Quinze Rounds (1930) and Alfred Menguy Gueules Aplaties (1933)," *International Journal of the History of Sport* 36, nos. 1–2 (2019): 207–224.

42. Mike Silver, *Stars in the Ring: Jewish Champions in the Golden Age of Boxing* (Lanham, MD: Rowman & Littlefield, 2016), 90–266; Allen Bodner, *When Boxing Was a Jewish Sport* (New York: SUNY Press, 2011); David Dee "'The Hefty Hebrew': Boxing and British-Jewish Identity, 1890–1960," *Sport in History* 32, no. 3 (2012): 361–381.

43. *HaSport Hasavoa*, March 25, 1932, 6.

44. *Haaretz*, March 19, 1929, 3.

45. *Haaretz*, March 19, 1929, 3.

46. *Uzenu*, January 17, 1935, 3.

47. *Haaretz*, February 19, 1929, 3.

48. *Davar*, December 12, 1937, 4.

49. *Uzenu*, January 3, 1935, 5; *Uzenu*, January 10, 1935, 3; *HaBoker Sport*, October 19, 1936, 4.

50. "Yoman Carmel," Winter 35, Israel State Archive, 046–1. https://youtu.be/REsipFYiGS4.

51. For evidence of the relative popularity of the sport, see *HaBoker Sport*, March 3, 1939, 3.

52. See. for example, the description of man witnessing a boxing match for the first time in *Davar*, May 15, 1938, 4.

53. "The Future of Boxing in Our Land," 4.

54. "The Future of Boxing in Our Land," 4.

55. David Tidhar, "Amiel (Emil) Avineri (Rebelski)," in *Intseklopedia le-halutse ha-Yishuv u-vonav*, Vol. 5 (Herzliya: Sifriyat Rishonim, 1959), 2259.

56. *Davar*, December 1, 1934, 2.

57. The Jewish American boxer received almost zero coverage in the Hebrew press: *Davar*, June 23, 1930, 3.

58. *Haaretz,* July 10, 1930, 3; "Benny Leonard Club Rules," May 4, 1930, WIA, 1.10-159-22; Benny Leonard, June 26, 1933, MCA, 1–0090; *Uzenu,* January 10, 1935, 3.
59. Unmarked flyer 1929, WIA, AR25.
60. *HaMaccabi,* January 1931, 27.
61. On interwar athletics body aesthetics, see Zweiniger-Bargielowska, *Managing the Body,* 4.
62. *HaMaccabi,* January 1931, 28.
63. *Do'ar HaYom,* December 28, 1934, 3; *Do'ar HaYom,* December 14, 1934, 4; *Haaretz,* July 10, 1930, 3; *Haaretz,* December 7, 1934, 10; *Haaretz,* May 14, 1930, 3; As a lifeguard, see *Davar,* February 24, 1950, 29.
64. Anat Helman, "Zionism, Politics, Hedonism: Sports in Interwar Tel Aviv," in *Jews, Sports, and the Rites of Citizenship,* ed. J. Kugelmass (Champaign: University of Illinois Press, 2007), 95–113.
65. Nathan Marcus, "Zionist Football and Jewish Identity in Weimar Germany," *Judaica* (2005): 147–166.
66. *Haaretz,* January 7, 1924, 2.
67. For more on German Jewry, see Sharon Gillerman, *Germans into Jews: Remaking the Jewish Social Body in the Weimar Republic* (Stanford, CA: Stanford University Press, 2009).
68. *Do'ar HaYom,* February 4, 1923, 4.
69. "Plan," *Tel Aviv Municipal Archive* (TAMA hereafter), 2-56-540; *Haaretz,* January 7, 1924, 2; *Do'ar HaYom,* January 3, 1924, 3; *Haaretz,* February 13, 1924, 3.
70. *Do'ar HaYom,* January 9, 1924, 1; *Haaretz,* January 11, 1924, 4.
71. *Haaretz,* January 7, 1924, 3.
72. *Haaretz,* January 7, 1924, 2.
73. *Haaretz,* January 7, 1924, 2; *Haaretz,* January 22, 1924, 4.
74. *Haaretz,* January 10, 1924, 3; *Do'ar HaYom,* January 16, 1924, 4; on Hebrew, see *Haaretz,* February 13, 1924, 4; *Haaretz,* February 14,1924, 3.
75. *Haaretz,* January 10, 1924, 2.
76. *Haaretz,* January 1924, 2.
77. *Haaretz,* January 17, 1924, 4.
78. *Haaretz,* January 10, 1924, 2.
79. *Do'ar HaYom,* January 9, 1924, 1.
80. *Haaretz,* January 17, 1924, 4. The statement was made by the Haifa-based agronomist and educator Pinchas Hacohen. See also *Do'ar HaYom,* January 9, 1924, 1; and the satirical poem in *Haaretz,* January 18, 1924, 4.
81. *Haaretz,* January 10, 1924, 4.
82. A notable example is the speech of the mayor of Tel-Aviv Meir Dizengoff in *Haaretz,* January 7, 1924, 2; See also "Greeting Speech Given by Tel Aviv Mayor Meir Dizengoff," January 7, 1924, TAMA, 2-56-540.
83. *Haaretz,* January 2, 1925, 2; *Haaretz,* January 14, 1925, 2.
84. *Do'ar HaYom,* January 8, 1925, 2.
85. *Do'ar HaYom,* June 16, 1933, 7.
86. *HaMaccabi,* July 3, 1936, 6.
87. "Letter to Egon Pollak," September 2, 1939, MCA, 1–0043.
88. *HaBoker Sport,* April 1, 1939, 2.
89. Before he emigrated to Palestine, Hirschl had only a few mentions in the Hebrew press. See, for instance, *Davar,* May 24, 1932, 3, where it was claimed that Hirschl was the victim of antisemitism.
90. William D. Bowman, "Hakoah Vienna and the International Nature of Interwar Austrian Sports," *Central European History* 44 (2011): 646–667.

91. *Davar*, December 25, 1934, 2.
92. Joseph S. Alter, *The Wrestler's Body: Identity and Ideology in North India* (Berkeley: University of California Press, 1992); Dennis J. Frost, *Seeing Stars: Sports Celebrity, Identity, and Body Culture in Modern Japan* (Cambridge, MA: Harvard University Press, 2010), 19–68.
93. Wilson Chacko Jacob, *Working out Egypt: Effendi Masculinity and Subject Formation in Colonial Modernity, 1870–1940* (Durham, NC: Duke University Press, 2011), 142.
94. Jacob, *Working out Egypt*, 145.
95. *Davar*, December 25, 1934, 2.
96. *Davar*, December 25, 1934, 2; *Davar*, February 27, 1936, 10.
97. *Davar*, March 2, 1936, 9; *Davar*, March 12, 1936, 10.
98. As late as 1939, residents of the Yishuv could not tell the difference between boxing and wrestling: *Davar*, April 9, 1939, 5.
99. *Haaretz*, February 21, 1938, 2. It appears that Hirschl's physical abilities came in handy on the Yishuv's football fields. In 1938, for example, he leapt from the stands to save a referee from the clutches of an angry crowd. See *HaYarden*, January 21, 1938, 10.
100. *Mitteilungsblatt*, April 2, 1939, 5.
101. *HaBoker Sport*, March 25, 1939, 3.
102. *Davar*, April 8, 1940, 5.
103. *Wrestling USA Magazine*, October 1, 1985.
https://web.archive.org/web/20101012200407/http://homepage.mac.com/gdemarco1/WA/Hirschl.html
104. *Wrestling USA Magazine*, October 1, 1985.
105. *HaBoker Sport*, August 29, 1936, 4.
106. *HaMaccabi*, July 3, 1936, 6.
107. *HaBoker Sport*, October 19, 1936, 4.
108. *Davar*, September 8, 1938, 5. Local teams were also founded by the Yemenite and Spanish community, such as the Bnei Yehuda football club.
109. *Haaretz*, January 2, 1937, 12.
110. *Davar*, March 20, 1938, 4. Note that in the Hebrew source, this reads "at least one section manager who is not a doctor," in reference to a common joke in the Yishuv at the time, according to which *all* German Jewish immigrants were doctors.
111. *HaBoker Sport*, November 7, 1936, 1.
112. In this context, see Liat Kozma's article regarding the emigration of German sexologists to the Yishuv in the 1930s: "Sexology in the Yishuv: The Rise and Decline of Sexual Consultation in Tel Aviv, 1930–39," *International Journal of Middle East Studies* 42 (2010): 231–249.
113. Walter Frankel, *Ha-gan lelo 'adama* (Tel Aviv: Hadar, 1958). For more about Frankel's agriculture work in Palestine see *HaSport Hasavoa*, March 25, 1932, 3.
114. *HaBoker Sport*, April 1, 1939, 2.
115. Jensen, *Body by Weimar*, 3–14.
116. *Do'ar HaYom*, June 15, 1927, 4.
117. *HaSport*, April 20, 1938, 2.
118. *HaBoker Sport*, September 9, 1939, 4.
119. Like others in his country of origin, Benyamin was embracing photography as a medium that was less conducive to depicting racist Jewish stereotypes. Matthias Marschik, "Depicting Hakoah: Images of a Zionist Sports Club in Interwar Vienna," *Historical Social Research* 43, no. 2 (2018): 129–147.
120. The Israel Museum, Jerusalem, https://www.imj.org.il/he/collections/342021, accessed May 21, 2022.

121. It seems that Grschebina's athletic imagery resembles the aesthetics of known German filmmaker Leni Riefenstahl. See Michael Mackenzie, "From Athens to Berlin: The 1936 Olympics and Leni Riefenstahl's Olympia," *Critical Inquiry* 29, no. 2 (2003): 302–336; and Daniel Wildmann, "Desired Bodies: Leni Riefenstahl's Olympia, Aryan Masculinity and the Classical Body," in *Brill's Companion to the Classics, Fascist Italy and Nazi Germany*, ed. Helen Roche and Kyriakos Demetriou (Leiden: Brill, 2018), 60–81.
122. Joan Tumblety, "Rethinking the Fascist Aesthetic: Mass Gymnastics, Political Spectacle and the Stadium in 1930s France," *European History Quarterly* 43, no. 4 (2013): 707–730; Ina Zweiniger-Bargielowska, "Building a British Superman: Physical Culture in Interwar Britain," *Journal of Contemporary History* 41, no. 4 (October 2006): 595–610.
123. *Davar*, December 31, 1939, 4.
124. *Davar*, December 31, 1939, 65.
125. *Davar*, December 31, 1939, 49–64.
126. The Spielberg Archive—This Is the Land (*Zot Hi Haaretz*), https://youtu.be/eex9Kij, accessed May 21, 2022. See also Hizky Shoham, "Of Other Cinematic Spaces: Urban Zionism in Early Hebrew Cinema," *Israel Studies Review* 26, (2011): 109–131.
127. *Uzenu*, July 1935, 12.
128. *Uzenu*, July 1935, 12.
129. Gordon, "Letter," 2.
130. *HaMaccabi*, September 22, 1936, 11.
131. *HaBoker Sport*, June 10, 1939, 4.
132. *Do'ar HaYom*, May 12, 1927, 3.
133. Dubek Cigarette Company, *Mishmar VeSport: Osef ha-temunot shel "Dubek" me-haye ha-no'ar ha-'ivri ba-arets* (Tel Aviv, Dubek Ltd., 1939), 65.
134. "*HaBoker Sport*, January 28, 1939, 3.
135. *HaBoker Sport*, March 25, 1939, 3

CHAPTER 4 "THE WHOLE WORLD WILL KNOW OUR ANSWER"

1. *Do'ar HaYom*, January 11, 1923, 3.
2. Keys, *Globalizing Sport*, 40–63.
3. Glenda Sluga, *Internationalism in the Age of Nationalism* (Philadelphia: University of Pennsylvania Press, 2013), 1–10; Glenda Sluga and Patricia Clavin, eds., *Internationalisms: A Twentieth-Century History* (Cambridge: Cambridge University Press, 2016); Erez Manela, *The Wilsonian Moment: Self-Determination and the International Origins of Anticolonial Nationalism* (New York: Oxford University Press, 2007); F.S.L. Lyons, *Internationalism in Europe, 1815–1914* (Leyden: A. W. Sythoff, 1963); Martin Geyer and Johannes Paulmann, eds., *The Mechanics of Internationalism: Culture, Society, and Politics from the 1840s to World War I* (New York: Oxford University Press, 2001).
4. Keys, *Globalizing Sport*, 1–16; Matthew P. Llewellyn, "Olympic Games Are an International Farce," *International Journal of the History of Sport* 28, no. 5 (2011): 751–772.
5. Steinberg, "The Worker's," 233–251; Arnd Krüger and James Riordan, eds., *The Story of Worker Sport* (Champaign, IL: Human Kinetics, 1996), 1–10.
6. Ron Kaplan, *The Jewish Olympics: The History of the Maccabiah Games* (New York: Simon & Schuster, 2015).
7. Haim Kaufman, "Maccabi versus Hapoel: The Political Divide That Developed in Sports in Eretz Israel, 1926–1935," *Israel Affairs* (2007): 554–565.
8. *Do'ar HaYom*, April 2, 1935, 10.

9. *Kolnoa*, October 27, 1932, 14.
10. *BaMaslul*, August 1932, 4.
11. *HaBoker Sport*, July 29, 1939, 2.
12. *Do'ar HaYom*, June 21, 1926, 1.
13. *Haaretz*, October 17, 1928, 3.
14. *Haaretz*, July 16, 1924, 4.
15. Yekutieli to Gur Arye, July 8, 1924, WIA, 1.19-61.
16. To I. Chalutz, 3 September 1935, Fédération Internationale de Football Association Archives (hereafter: FIFA, Palestine/Israel 1932–1950; To Mr. I. J. Chalutz, 16 August 1938, FIFA, Palestine/Israel 1932–1950.
17. To Mr. I. Chalutz, 4 May 1938, FIFA, Palestine/Israel 1932–1950. Conversely, Maccabi used its membership in FIFA to impede the football activity of Hapoel and Arab groups in Palestine. On Hapoel, see I. J. Chalutz to Dr. Schricker, 6 September 1932, FIFA, Palestine/Israel 1932–1950; "Palestine Football Association," 17 January 1933, FIFA, Palestine/Israel 1932–1950; To Mr. I. J. Chalutz, 6 April 1935, FIFA, Palestine/Israel 1932–1950; General Secretary to Mr. J. Chalutz, 30 March 1936, FIFA, Palestine/Israel 1932–1950; I. J. Chalutz to Dr. Schriecker, 14 March 1937, FIFA, Palestine/Israel 1932–1950.On the Arab teams in Palestine, see I. J. Chalutz and Eng. S. Torok to General Secretary, 1932; FIFA, Palestine/Israel 1932–1950.
18. Yekutieli to Edström, March 7, 1935, MCA, 5-1-23.
19. July 21, 1934, WIA, 4.06-191-2.
20. July 21, 1934, WIA, 4.06-191-2.
21. *HaBoker Sport*, January 19, 1938, 4.
22. *Haaretz*, November 17, 1933, 4; *Haaretz*, July 6, 1933, 2; *Sport Haaretz*, August 10, 1934, 9; *Sport Haaretz*, August 3, 1934, 9; March 29, 1933, MCA, 1-4-39. On the importance of flying the national colors, see Uri Nadav and Yehoshua Alouf to Jewish Agency for Palestine Executive, January 25, 1934, Central Zionist Archives (hereinafter: CZA), S25/6711.
23. *HaYarden*, August 22, 1934, 3.
24. *Kolnoa*, April 25, 1934, 19.
25. 1934, WIA, 1-4-36.
26. *Kolnoa*, January 22, 1932, 6.
27. A. Valinčiaim, Travelogue, July 3, 1934, The Lavon Institute for Labour Research, IV-244-11
28. Haim Kaufman, "Mas'ot shel kevutsot sport lehul, masa Maccabi Haifa le-artsot ha-berit bi-sh'nat 1927," *Ha-hinukh ha-gufani ve-ha-sport* 4 (2001): 19–21.
29. *Davar*, April 27, 1927, 3. For other responses, see *Davar*, April 19, 1927, 3; *Uzenu*, April 1937, 35; and *Davar*, April 5, 1927, 3.
30. *Do'ar HaYom*, May 12, 1927, 3.
31. *Do'ar HaYom*, September 6, 1927, 3.
32. *Kolnoa*, January 25, 1934, 18–20; *HaYarden*, September 7, 1934, 2.
33. *HaYarden*, August 22, 1934, 3.
34. J. H. Levey to Maccabi Eretz Israel, October 10, 1934, MCA, 4.06-191-2. On the delegations to India and London in their gender context, see Ofer Idels, "How to Lose Gracefully," 215–233.
35. "A conversation between our writer Mr. S. Rosecki and Dr. Schmidt," 1934, WIA, 1-19-61.
36. Consider, for example, the four members of the Maccabi football delegation to Australia who used the occasion to emigrate to the southern continent. See September 2, 1939, MCA, 1-5-43; *Davar*, August 27, 1939, 6.
37. *HaBoker*, July 18, 1957, 3.
38. Meira Belkind, Travelogue, 1934, RLA, 3.02-1-1.

39. For discussion of the Yishuv's attitude toward Nazi Germany, see Yfaat Weiss, "The Transfer Agreement and the Boycott Movement: A Jewish Dilemma on the Eve of the Holocaust," *Yad Vashem Studies* 26 (1998): 129–171.
40. *Davar*, April 24, 1934, 3.
41. For a critique, see "On Kisch's official response: Kisch to President of the Organizing Committee of the XI Olympiad," November 4, 1934, WIA, 1.19.61.
42. January 24, 1935, *Uzenu*, 2.
43. January 24, 1935, *Uzenu*, 2.
44. Ofer Idels, "Mis'hakim medumyanim: Sport, ha-Yishuv, ve-ha-Olympiada ha-ahat 'esre, 1931–1963," *Cathedra* 167 (2018): 92–97; Idels, "The Idea of Sports," 1–15.
45. *Davar*, February 3, 1936, 9.
46. "The Olympic Games in Nazi Germany," 1935, WIA, uncataloged.
47. *Davar* evening extra, January 1936, 3; *Davar*, February 7, 1936, 10; *Davar*, February 6, 1936, evening extra, 1.
48. *Haaretz*, May 15, 1933, 7; *Haaretz*, October 20, 1933, 6; *Do'ar HaYom*, October 13, 1935, 4.
49. *Haaretz*, August 2, 1935, 12.
50. On Barcelona and the trip to Berlin, see *Haaretz*, July 3, 1936, 7.
51. *Davar*, June 29, 1936, evening extra, 3; *HaBoker Sport*, July 5, 1936, 1.
52. *Haaretz*, July 14, 1936, 14.
53. *Haaretz*, July 31, 1936, 11.
54. *Do'ar HaYom*, April 2, 1935, 10.
55. *Haaretz*, June 16, 1933, 7; *Do'ar HaYom*, October 8, 1935, 4.
56. *Do'ar HaYom*, October 13, 1935, 4.
57. *Do'ar HaYom*, December 19, 1935, 6.
58. January 7, 1936, 4. See also *Haaretz*, January 31, 1936, 2; *HaMaccabi*, January 31, 1936, 15; *Haaretz*, July 16, 1936, 2.
59. *Do'ar HaYom*, October 8, 1935, 4; see also *Haaretz*, October 4, 1935, 13; *Haaretz*, October 18, 1935, evening extra, 12.
60. *Haaretz*, December 6, 1935, evening extra, 12.
61. *Do'ar HaYom*, October 13, 1935, 4.
62. *Haaretz*, August 21, 1936, 16. For additional examples, see *HaBoker Sport*, August 1, 1936, 2; *Haaretz*, August 10, 1936, 2; *Haaretz*, August 7, 1936; 15; *Haaretz*, July 30, 1936, 11; *Haaretz*, August 6, 1936, 2; *Haaretz*, August 9, 1936, 2.
63. *Haaretz*, February 27, 1936, 5.
64. *HaBoker Sport*, August 8, 1936, 1. For similar coverage, see *Haaretz*, August 10, 1936, 12; *HaBoker Sport*, July 5, 1936, 2; *Haaretz*, July 24, 1936, 2; *Haaretz*, July 24, 1936, 2; *HaBoker Sport*, July 26, 1936, 1; *HaBoker Sport*, July 25, 1936, 1; *HaBoker Sport*, August 8, 1936, 1; and *Haaretz*, August 10, 1936. On the affair from a Czechoslovak–Jewish angle, see Tatjana Lichtenstein, "'An Athlete like a Soldier Must Not Retreat': Zionists, Sport, and Belonging in Interwar Czechoslovakia," *Shofar: An Interdisciplinary Journal of Jewish Studies* 15 (2015): 1–26.
65. *Haaretz*, July 24, 1936, 2.
66. *HaBoker Sport*, August 1, 1936, 1.
67. *Do'ar HaYom*, February 25, 1936, 5.
68. *HaBoker Sport*, August 8, 1936, 2.
69. For previous favorable references to Mayer in the Yishuv press, see *Davar*, August 23, 1932, 3; *Haaretz*, June 16, 1933, 7; and *Kolnoa*, August 1932, 6. For criticism of Mayer after her decision to participate, see *Davar*, February 24, 1936, evening extra, 3; and *Haaretz*, December 10, 1935, 2.
70. *Do'ar HaYom*, February 25, 1936, 5.

71. *HaBoker Sport*, August 1, 1936, 2.
72. J. A. Mangan, *Athleticism in the Victorian and Edwardian Public School* (New York: Routledge, 2000); Collins, *Rugby Union*, 6; Walvin, *The People's Game*, 31–49; Collins, *Sport in Capitalist Society*, 25.
73. David Young. *The Modern Olympics: A Struggle for Revival* (Baltimore: Johns Hopkins University Press, 1996); John J. MacAloon, *This Great Symbol: Pierre de Coubertin and the Origins of the Modern Olympic* (London: Routledge, 2013).
74. Kisch to President of the Organizing Committee of the XI Olympiad, November 4, 1934, WIA, 1.19.61.
75. *Hed haMaccabi*, Passover 1934, 12.
76. *Do'ar HaYom*, June 28, 1934, 1.
77. David Clay Large, *Nazi Games: The Olympics of 1936* (New York: W. W. Norton, 2007), 69–110. For example, only two years earlier the World Cup had been held in Fascist Italy.
78. *HaMaccabi*, January 31, 1936, 6.
79. *Haaretz*, January 11, 1935, 1; *Davar*, November 6, 1935, 1; *Haaretz*, December 8, 1935, 1.
80. *Haaretz*, December 10, 1935, 2.
81. *Davar*, July 27, 1936, 9.
82. *HaMaccabi*, February 14, 1936, 21. Italics added.
83. *Do'ar HaYom*, December 19, 1935, 6.
84. Hapoel Association for Physical Culture, Central Committee: "The Olympic Games in Nazi Germany," 1935, WIA, uncatalogued
85. *HaBoker Sport*, August 1, 1936, 2.
86. For example, tackling the question of why the Yishuv should participate in international sports after Berlin, Shimon Samet argued for its national and cultural importance: *Eretz Yisrael–Yavan*, January 19, 1938, 2.
87. *HaBoker Sport*, August 1, 1936. For the original letter, see Yekutieli and Rosecki to Edström, July 24, 1936, WIA, 1.19-61.
88. Yekutieli and Rosecki to Edström, July 24, 1936, WIA, 1.19-61.
89. Yekutieli to Friedenthal, June 8, 1937, MCA, 5.1.24.
90. *HaMaccabi*, September 22, 1936, 2.
91. *Sport Haaretz*, January 23, 1938, 1. For a critique, see *Davar*, January 23, 1938, 4.
92. *Do'ar HaYom*, April 4, 1934, 1; *Do'ar HaYom*, April 8, 1934, 1; *Davar*, March 13, 1934; *Haaretz*, March 18, 1934, 1.
93. *Haaretz*, April 8, 1934, 4.
94. See, for example, *Haaretz*, March 23, 1934, 7; *Haaretz*, April 13, 1934, 7; *Davar*, April 9, 1934, 7; and *Hed HaMaccabi*, April 1934, 4–5.
95. *Eretz Yisrael–Yavan*, January 19, 1938, 2.
96. *Eretz Yisrael–Yavan*, January 19, 1938, 3.
97. Yisarel Paz, "Ha-sport ba-'itonut ha-ketuva," in *Tarbut Hagof Ve-hasport*, ed. Haim Kaufman and Haggi Harif (Jerusalem: Yad-Ben Zvi, 2002): 347. The pun is *hishivu hatkafa sha'ara* (literally, "returned offense to the gate")—a play on the biblical phrase, *hishivu milhama sha'ara* ("hit back"), with "offense" replacing "war" and the "to the gate" supplanted by "to the goal"—*sha'ara* in Hebrew football jargon.
98. *Eretz Yisrael–Yavan*, January 19, 1938, 4.
99. *Davar*, February 6, 1938, 4.
100. *HaYarden*, February 4, 1938, 6.
101. *Eretz Israel–Yavan*, January 19, 1938, 2.
102. *Sport Haaretz*, January 23, 1938, 3. The epithet "failed the test" was rather common in the coverage of the game; it appeared in *Davar* and *Haaretz*, among other organs.

103. Abigail Green, "Nationalism and the 'Jewish International': Religious Internationalism in Europe and the Middle East C. 1840–c. 1880," *Comparative Studies in Society and History* 50 (2008): 535–558; Gil Rubin, "A State of Their Own: Jewish Internationalism and Human Rights," *Marginalia*, June 6, 2018; Samuel Moyn, "René Cassin (1887–1976): Human Rights and Jewish Internationalism," in *Makers of Jewish Modernity: Thinkers, Artists, Leaders, and the World They Made*, ed. Jacques Picard, Jacques Revel, Michael Steinberg, and Idith Zertal (Princeton: Princeton University Press, 2015), 278; Sluga, *Internationalism*, 2.

104. James Loeffler, *Rooted Cosmopolitans: Jews and Human Rights in the Twentieth Century* (New Haven, CT: Yale University Press, 2018). See also Jaclyn Granick, *International Jewish Humanitarianism in the Age of the Great War* (Cambridge: Cambridge University Press, 2021); Yehuda Bauer, *My Brother's Keeper: A History of the American Jewish Joint Distribution Committee, 1929–1939* (Philadelphia: Jewish Publication Society of America, 1974); Carole Fink, *Defending the Rights of Others: The Great Powers, the Jews, and International Minority Protection, 1878–1938* (New York: Cambridge University Press, 2004); Rebecca Korbin, "American Jewish Philanthropy, Polish Jewry and the Crisis of 1929," in *1929: Mapping the Jewish World*, ed. Hasia Diner and Gennady Estraikh (New York: New York University Press, 2013), 73–93; and Simon Rabinovitch, *Jewish Rites, National Rights: Nationalism and Autonomy in Late Imperial and Revolutionary Russia* (Stanford, CA: Stanford University Press, 2014).

105. Consider, for example, the decision to transfer Yekutieli to a meaningless sinecure: "Minutes of Palestine Olympic Committee meeting, April 20, 1039, WIA, 1.19-61.

106. *Haaretz*, August 4, 1936, 3.

107. Shertok to Maccabi, April 23, 1934, CZA, S25/6711. For early criticism from within Maccabi, see *Do'ar HaYom*, July 29, 1925, 5.

108. *Hapoel Hatzair*, December 14, 1934, 16–17.

109. The Yishuv was the only national team that turned down an invitation to participate in the Berlin Olympiad for reasons associated with German antisemitism.

110. Edström to Yekutieli, January 10, 1939, WIA, 1.19-61.

111. *HaBoker Sport*, February 4, 1939, 1.

CHAPTER 5 "WE HAVE TO LEARN TO SACRIFICE EVERYTHING"

1. *HaMaccabi*, September 2, 1936, 1–2.
2. *HaMaccabi*, May 25, 1936, 2–3.
3. *HaMaccabi*, September 22, 1936, 1–2. Italics added.
4. Dubek, *Mishmar VeSport*, 4.
5. *Do'ar HaYom*, January 22, 1923, 4.
6. *Do'ar HaYom*, May 3, 1923, 4.
7. *Do'ar HaYom*, March 2, 1923, 4.
8. *Do'ar HaYom*, October 23, 1923, 2.
9. *Do'ar Ha-Yom*, January 22, 1923, 4.
10. "D'var haverim," June 9, 1937, MCA, 1–0094.
11. "Jewish National Fund to Maccabi Association in Eretz Israel," July 26, 1926, MCA, 1–0011.
12. Nina S. Spiegel, *Embodying Hebrew Culture: Aesthetics, Athletics, and Dance in the Jewish Community of Mandate Palestine* (Detroit: Wayne State Press, 2013), 66–67.
13. *HaMaccabi*, April 30, 1936, 16–17.
14. *Haaretz*, November 16, 1927, 4.
15. *HaMaccabi*, April 30, 1936, 17.

16. Hans Ulrich Gumbrecht, *Crowds: The Stadium as a Ritual of Intensity* (Stanford, CA: Stanford University Press, 2021), 9.
17. *HaMaccabi*, December 27, 1936, 8–9.
18. Kraus Meyer, "Maccabi! Ten yad le-vinyan Kefar Hamaccabi 'al admat ha-Keren Kayemet le-Israel," 1936, National Library collection, retrieved from https://www.nli.org.il/he/sheets/NNL_EPHEMERA997003250960405171/NLI
19. *HaMaccabi*, December 27, 1936, 8–9.
20. *HaMaccabi*, December 27, 1936, 8–9.
21. "Report of the Central Committee to the National Conference," May 11, 1938, MCA, 1–0055.
22. Emanuel Lappin, "Shayit," 1938, MCA, 1–0058.
23. *HaMaccabi*, May 25, 1936, 11.
24. Spielberg Archive—*This Is the Land* [Zot hi ha-arets], https://youtu.be/eex9Kijm accessed May 21, 2022.
25. Emanuel Lappin, "Shayit," 1938, MCA, 1–0058.
26. *HaMaccabi*, September 22, 1936, 7.
27. *HaMaccabi*, May 25, 1936, 13.
28. *Davar*, October 23, 1938, 6.
29. *HaMaccabi*, July 3, 1936, 3–5.
30. *HaMaccabi*, July 3, 1936, 3–5.
31. "D'var haverim," June 9, 1937, MCA, 1–0094.
32. Emanuel Lappin, "Shayit," 1938, MCA, 1–0058.
33. *Kolnoa*, June 12, 1931, 11.
34. *HaMaccabi*, July 3, 1936, 2–3.
35. Anita Shapira, *Land and Power: The Zionist Resort to Force, 1881–1948* (Oxford: Oxford University Press, 1992).
36. *Haaretz*, January 10, 1924, 4.
37. *Davar*, October 23, 1938, 6.
38. *Mishmar VeSport*, 4.
39. "Ha-va'ada ha-megayeset," Tammuz 5696 [July 1936], MCA, 1–0050.
40. *Davar*, April 2, 1939, 6; *Omer*, February 25, 1939, 2.
41. Central Committee of the Maccabi Federation in Eretz Israel, MCA, "Doh ha-hakhnasa ve-ha-hotsa'a," *Din ve-heshbon sefer ha-Maccabi*, November 2, 1939, 52.
42. *Davar*, November 30, 1936, 9.
43. Maccabi Federation in Eretz Israel, "Kurs mekhin le-sport shimushi," Kislev 5697 [December 1936], MCA, 1–0083.
44. *Davar*, June 26, 1938, 5.
45. *HaMaccabi*, August 20, 1936, 1.
46. Derek J. Penslar, *Jews and the Military: A History* (Princeton, NJ: Princeton University Press, 2013).
47. J. A. Mangan, ed. *Militarism, Sport, Europe: War Without Weapons* (London: Cass Publishers, 2003).
48. Norbert Muller, ed., *Olympism: Pierre De Coubertin: Selected Writings* (Lausanne: International Olympic Committee, 2000), 63.
49. Guttmann, *The Olympics*, 7–21.
50. David L. Hoffman, "Bodies of Knowledge: Physical Culture and the New Soviet Man," in *Language and Revolution: Modern Political Identities*, ed. Igal Halfin (London: Cass Publishers, 2002), 228–242; Hau, *Performance Anxiety*, 127–171; De Grazia, *Culture of Consent*, 176; Tumblety, *Remaking the Male Body*, 135–149; Zweiniger-Bargielowska, *Managing the Body*, 280–330;

Kevin Gray Carr, "Making Way: War, Philosophy and Sport in Japanese 'Jûdô,'" *Journal of Sport History* 20, no. 2 (1993): 167–188; J. A. Mangan, ed., *Superman Supreme: Fascist Body as Political Icon: Global Fascism* (London: Cass Publishers, 2000).

51. On war and play, see Huizinga, *Homo Ludens*, 89–104.

52. *The HaMaccabi*, Passover 5694 [April 1934], 8.

53. Collins, *Sport in Capitalist Society*, 22.

54. Jan Rybak, *Everyday Zionism in East-Central Europe: Nation-Building in War and Revolution, 1914–1920* (Oxford: Oxford University Press, 2021), 151–198; Mihály Kálmán, "Hero Shtetls: Reading Civil War Self-Defense in the Yishuv," in *From Europe's East to the Middle East Israel's Russian and Polish Lineages*, ed. Kenneth B. Moss, Benjamin Nathans, and Taro Tsurumi (Philadelphia: University of Pennsylvania Press, 2021), 305–342.

55. *Do'ar HaYom*, March 2, 1912.

56. Ya'akov Goldstein, "Ha-me'oravut ha-politit shel 'Hapoel': Parshat igud Ha-Sadran,'" in *Tarbut ha-guf ve-ha-sport be-Yisrael ba-me'a ha-'esrim*, ed. Haim Kaufman and Haggai Harif (Jerusalem: Yad Izhak Ben-Zvi, 2002), 129–158.

57. *HaMaccabi*, July 24, 1936, 9.

58. David Tidhar, "Yehezkel Henkin," *Intseklopedia le-halutse ha-Yishuv u-vonav*, 1959, 3627.

59. "Minutes of the Maccabi Association in Jerusalem," November 5, 1911, AYA, 8–11,

60. *Do'ar HaYom*, May 3, 1926.

61. *HaMaccabi*, April 5, 1936, 26–27.

62. *HaMaccabi*, April 30, 1936, 16.

63. Circular no. 10, June 4, 1936, WIA, 1.10–39.

64. *HaMaccabi*, September 22, 1936, 25.

65. *HaBoker Sport*, August 22, 1936, 4.

66. *HaBoker Sport*, September 26, 1936, 4.

67. Circular no. 1, WIA.

68. *HaMaccabi*, May 25, 1936, 13. For the same argument in Hapoel, see *Davar*, July 27, 1936, 9.

69. *HaBoker Sport*, September 12, 1936, 4. See also earlier Alexandrovich's testimony, *HaBoker*, July 26, 1938, 4.

70. The Maccabi journal, for example, led with a list of persons killed in the violence. *HaMaccabi*, May 25, 1936, 1.

71. *HaMaccabi*, April 30, 1936, 1–2.

72. Shapira, *Land and Power*, 219–276.

73. *HaMaccabi*, April 30, 1936, 1–2; see also *Davar*, June 19, 1938, 8.

74. "Ha-va'ada ha-megayeset," Tammuz 5696 [July 1936], MCA, 1-0050; *Davar*, November 30, 1936, 9.

75. Circular no. 10, WIA.

76. *HaMaccabi*, July 3, 1936, 1; *HaMaccabi*, April 30, 1936, 1.

77. *HaMaccabi*, July 3, 1936, 1.

78. *HaMaccabi*, August 20, 1936, 10.

79. *HaMaccabi*, May 25, 1936, 11.

80. *HaBoker Sport*, September 19, 1936, 2.

81. *HaMaccabi*, September 22, 1936, 7.

82. *HaMaccabi*, July 24, 1936, 9.

83. *HaBoker Sport*, September 12, 1936, 8.

84. *HaMaccabi*, August 20, 1936, 1.

85. *HaMaccabi*, September 22, 1936, 1.

86. *HaMaccabi*, December 27, 1936, 7.

87. *HaMaccabi*, September 22, 1936, 2–3.

88. *HaMaccabi*, September 22, 1936, 1.
89. *HaMaccabi*, August 20, 1936, 1.
90. *HaMaccabi*, August 20, 1936, 1. Maccabi writers repeatedly used the concept of *me'uvat* (distortion/degeneration) as a recurrent metaphor in this context.
91. *Davar*, April 2, 1939, 6.
92. *HaMaccabi*, July 24, 1936, 4.
93. "Report on Meeting of the Council for Useful Sports," April 2, 1937, MCA, 1–0011; "Report of the Central Committee to the National Conference," May 11, 1938, MCA, 1–0055.
94. "Decisions of the Maccabi Council," July 23, 1937, MCA, 1–0095.
95. "At the Hapoel Association: Haifa Branch," *Davar*, April 13, 1937, 4.
96. "Sport shimushi," MCA, 1–0011.
97. *HaBoker Sport*, September 12, 1936, 1.
98. "Useful Sports," MCA, 1–001.
99. *Davar*, September 4, 1938, 6.
100. *Davar*, April 16, 1939, 6.
101. *HaBoker Sport*, September 12, 1936, 1.
102. *HaBoker Sport*, September 12, 1936, 1.
103. David Ish Shalom, "Maccabi Eretz Israel Union 1906–1948" (PhD diss., Hebrew University of Jerusalem, 2004), 130.
104. *HaMaccabi*, April 5, 1936, 2–3.
105. *Haaretz*, December 22, 1938, 6.
106. "Report of the Central Committee to the National Conference," May 11, 1938, MCA, 1–0055.
107. *Davar*, June 6, 1938, 4.
108. *Omer*, December 17, 1938, 2; *Davar*, June 12, 1938, 4.
109. *HaBoker Sport*, September 12, 1936, 7.
110. *HaBoker Sport*, September 12, 1936, 7.
111. *Davar*, May 22, 1938, 4.
112. *Omer*, December 17, 1938, 2.
113. *Davar*, January 3, 1938, 4.
114. *Davar*, January 23, 1938, 4.
115. Above we noted the Central European Jewish interpretation of the nexus of sports and war. The pamphlet *Mishmar VeSport*, many of whose authors originated in Germany and Austria, is to some extent an importation of this interpretation into Hebrew culture.
116. *Mishmar VeSport*, 4.
117. A. Baar, *Kadur ha-regel, Mishmar VeSport*, 38.
118. *HaBoker Sport*, September 16, 1939, 3.
119. Robert Edelman and Christopher Young, *The Whole World Was Watching: Sport in the Cold War* (Stanford, CA: Stanford University Press, 2019).
120. *HaBoker Sport*, September 9, 1939, 4.
121. *HaBoker Sport*, December 17, 1939, 1.
122. Udi Carmi, "Me'uravutam shel ketsine Tsahal ba-sport ha-Yisraeli," *Yisrael* 25 (2018): 171–196.

EPILOGUE

1. Andrew Zimbalist, *Circus Maximus: The Economic Gamble Behind Hosting the Olympics and the World Cup* (Washington, DC: Brookings Institution Press, 2016); Chris Dempsey and Andrew Zimbalist, *No Boston Olympics: How and Why Smart Cities Are Passing on the Torch*

(Boston: New England University Press, 2017); Barrie Houlihan and Jinming Zheng, "The Olympics and Elite Sport Policy: Where Will It All End?" *International Journal of the History of Sport* 30 (2013): 338–355.

2. Tara Magdalinski, *Sport, Technology and the Body: The Nature of Performance* (London: Routledge, 2009).

3. Arjun Appadurai, *Modernity at Large: Cultural Dimensions of Globalization* (Minneapolis: University of Minnesota Press, 1996).

4. To view the Maccabia posters, see https://he.wikipedia.org/wiki/%D7%94%D7%9E%D7%9B%D7%91%D7%99%D7%94, accessed December 31, 2023.

5. Jan Nederveen Pieterse, "Aesthetics of Power: Time and Body Politics," *Third Text* 22 (Spring 1993): 33–42; Spiegel, *Embodying Hebrew Culture*, 8–11, 158–159.

6. Menachem Brinker, "Halutsiyut," in *Siman Yehudi hadash: Zehut Yehudit be-'idan hiloni* (Jerusalem: Keter, 2008), 40 [author's translation].

7. Yosef Yekutieli, *Mi-gola le-ge'ula* (Tel Aviv: self-published, 1971).

8. Edna Yekutieli-Cohen, *Ba'al ha-halomot* (Tel Aviv: Akhshav Books, 1995). The title is a reference to the biblical Yosef (Joseph) in Genesis 37:19.

9. Eric Hobsbawm, *The Age of Extremes: The Short Twentieth Century, 1914–1991* (London: Abacus Books, 1995), 15.

10. Consider, for example, the nostalgic fan community "Kaduregel Shefel."

11. *Ynet*, May 15, 2015, https://www.ynet.co.il/articles/0,7340,L-4657470,00.html.

12. *Yedioth Ahronoth*, November 22, 2017, https://www.yediot.co.il/articles/0,7340,L-5046808,00.html; *Ynet*, September 1, 2015, https://www.ynet.co.il/articles/0,7340,L-4696429,00.html.

13. *Ynet*, July 23, 2023, https://www.ynet.co.il/sport/article/h1hjsskq2.

14. *Israel Hayom*, January 9, 2020, https://www.israelhayom.co.il/article/723117.

15. *Ynet*, July 23, 2023, https://www.ynet.co.il/sport/article/h1hjsskq2.

16. See https://twitter.com/i/status/1596198639151374337, accessed December 31, 2023.

17. *Walla*, August 26, 2017, https://sports.walla.co.il/item/3091725.

18. Yahiel Limor, Ilan Tamir, and Orly Shifman, "Ha'Hatzlacha she'harga et ha'iton," *Kesher* 45 (2013): 95–103.

19. *Walla*, January 5, 2014, http://news.walla.co.il/?w=//2709299.

20. *Globes*, September 11, 2019, https://www.globes.co.il/news/article.aspx?did=1000878624.

21. Lama Matkot," *Kan Digital*, YouTube, https://youtu.be/_Ja-FgBIWXY?si=Cd5bvMS-4JpfBiaol, accessed September 30, 2024.

22. Jimbo J, "Matkot," *Ovedi Namal* (2021), track 4.

23. *Davar Le-Yeladim*, July 15, 1932, 1.

24. Jimbo J, "Matkot," track 4.

BIBLIOGRAPHY

ARCHIVES AND LIBRARIES

Aviezer Yellin Archives for Jewish Education in Israel and the Diaspora (AYA)
Central Zionist Archives (CZA)
Fédération Internationale de Football Association Archives (FIFA)
Israel State Archive (ISA)
Maccabi Sports Union Archive (MCA)
National Library Collection of Israel
Pinchas Lavon Institute for Labour Movement Research (PLI)
Rishon LeTsiyon Municipal Archive (RMLA)
Spielberg Archive (SA)
Tel Aviv Municipal Archive (TAMA)
Wingate Institute Archive for Physical Education (WIA)

DICTIONARIES AND ENCYCLOPEDIAS

David Tidhar, *Intseklopedia le-halutse ha-Yishuv u-vonav* (1947–1971)
Even-Shoshan, 1997
Oxford English Dictionary

NEWSPAPERS AND JOURNALS

BaMaslul
Calcalsit
Davar
Davar Le-Yeladim
Der Moment
Do'ar HaYom
Eretz Yisrael–Yavan
Forverts
Globes
Haaretz
Haaretz Sport
HaBoker Sport
Ha-herut Yerushalayim
HaMaccabi
HaPo'el ha-Tsa'ir
Ha'sport be-batai Hasfer
HaSport Hasvoea
Hashkafa
HaSport
HaTsefira
HaYarden
Haynt
HaZvi
Hed haMaccabi
Israel Hayom
J, dische Turnzeitung
Kolnoa
Maariv
Ma'arakhot
Mitteilungsblatt
The New York Times
The Palestine Bulletin
The Palestine Post
Uzeno
Wrestling USA Magazine
Yedioth Ahronoth

Websites

Ben-Yehuda Project
Hazavit
Mako
Marginalia
Timeout
Twitter
Walla
Ynet
YouTube

BOOKS

Alroey. Gur. *Immigrantim: Ha-Hagira ha-Yehudit le-Eretz Yisra'el be-Reshit ha-Me'ah ha-Esrim.* Jerusalem: Yad Ben-Zvi Press, 2004.

———. *An Unpromising Land: Jewish Migration to Palestine in the Early Twentieth Century.* Stanford, CA: Stanford University Press 2014.

Alouf, Yehoshua. *Ha'sport be-batai Hasfer*, May 19, 1938, 1.

———. *Mun'he ha-hinukh ha-gufani: Hit'amlut.* Tel Aviv: Physical Training Department, 1940.

Alter, Joseph S. *The Wrestler's Body: Identity and Ideology in North India.* Berkeley: University of California Press, 1992.

Anker, Elizabeth S., and Rita Felski, eds. *Critique and Postcritique.* Durham, NC: Duke University Press, 2017.

Appadurai, Arjun. *Modernity at Large: Cultural Dimensions of Globalization.* Minneapolis: University of Minnesota Press, 1996.

Avni, Zalman. *15 dakot ba-yom lema'an ha-beriyut.* Tel Aviv: Goldner, 1938.

Bauer, Yehuda. *My Brother's Keeper: A History of the American Jewish Joint Distribution Committee, 1929–1939.* Philadelphia: Jewish Publication Society of America, 1974.

Bell, David, and Yair Mintzker, eds. *Rethinking the Age of Revolutions: France and the Birth of the Modern World.* Oxford: Oxford University Press, 2018.

Ben-Porat, Amir. *Mi-mis'hak li-sehura: Ha-kaduregel ha-Yisraeli 1948–1999.* Beersheva: Ben-Gurion University of the Negev, 2002.

———. "Isra'el safa kasha akh kulam dibru 'ota." *Iyunim* (2010): 144–168.

Bernstein, Deborah. *Nashim Ba-Sholaim: Migdar.Ve-Le'umiut Be-Tel Aviv Ha-Mandatorit.* Jerusalem: Yad-ben Zvi, 2008.

Betts, John Rickards. "Sporting Journalism in Nineteenth-Century America." *American Quarterly* 55, no. 1 (Spring, 1953): 39–56.

Boddice, Rob, and Mark Smith. *Emotion, Sense, Experience.* Cambridge: Cambridge University Press, 2020.

Bodner, Allen. *When Boxing Was a Jewish Sport.* New York: SUNY Press, 2011.

Bowman, William D. "Hakoah Vienna and the International Nature of Interwar Austrian Sports." *Central European History* 44 (2011): 646–667.

Boyarin, Daniel. *Unheroic Conduct: The Rise of Heterosexuality and the Invention of the Jewish Men.* Berkley: University of California Press, 1997.

Brenner, Michael, and Reuvani Gidon, eds. *Emancipation Through Muscles: Jews and Sports in Europe.* Lincoln: University of Nebraska Press, 2006.

Brinker, Menachem, ed. *Siman Yehudi hadash: Zehut Yehudit be-'idan hiloni.* Jerusalem: Keter, 2008.

Cahn, Susan. *Coming on Strong: Gender and Sexuality in Twentieth-Century Women's Sport.* Urbana: University of Illinois Press, 2015.

Caillois, Roger. *Man, Play, and Games.* Urbana: University of Illinois Press, 2001.

Carr, Kevin Gray. "Making Way: War, Philosophy and Sport in Japanese 'Jûdô.'" *Journal of Sport History* 20, no. 2 (Summer 1993): 167–188.

Carmi, Udi. "Me'uravutam shel ketsine Tsahal ba-sport ha-Yisraeli." *Israel* 25 (2018): 171–196.

Chalaby, Jean K. "Journalism as an Anglo-American Invention: A Comparison of the Development of French and Anglo-American Journalism, 1830s–1920s." *European Journal of Communication* 11, no. 3 (1996): 303–326.

Chaline, Eric. *The Temple of Perfection: A History of the Gym.* London: Reaktion Books, 2015.

Chaver, Yael. *What Must Be Forgotten: The Survival of Yiddish in Zionist Palestine.* Syracuse, NY: Syracuse University Press, 2004.

Chowers, Eyal. *The Political Philosophy of Zionism: Trading Jewish Words for a Hebraic Land.* Cambridge: Cambridge University Press, 2012.

Coakley, J. J. *Sport in Society: Issues and Controversies.* Boston: McGraw-Hill, 1998.

Collins, Tony. *A Social History of English Rugby Union*. New York, Routledge, 2009.

———. *Sport in Capitalist Society: A Short History*. New York: Routledge, 2013.

Connor, Steven. *A Philosophy of Sport*. London: Reaktion Books, 2011.

Conrad, Sebastian. "Globalizing the Beautiful Body: Eugen Sandow, Bodybuilding, and the Ideal of Muscular Manliness at the Turn of the Twentieth Century." *Journal of World History* 32 (2021): 95–125.

Dan, Joseph. *The Heart and the Fountain: An Anthology of Jewish Mystical Experiences*. Oxford: Oxford University Press, 2003.

Dar, Maya. "Ve-matay yesh zeman." *Haya Haya* (2003): 73–92.

Dee, David. "'The Hefty Hebrew': Boxing and British-Jewish Identity, 1890–1960." *Sport in History* 32, no. 3 (2012): 361–381.

De Grazia, Victoria. *The Culture of Consent: Mass Organization of Leisure in Fascist Italy*. Cambridge: Cambridge University Press, 1981.

Dempsey, Chris, and Andrew Zimbalist. *No Boston Olympics: How and Why Smart Cities Are Passing on the Torch*. Boston: New England University Press of, 2017.

Diner, Hasia, and Gennady Estraikh, eds. *1929: Mapping the Jewish World*. New York: NYU Press, 2013.

Dubek Cigarette Company. *Mishmar VeSport: Osef ha-temunot shel "Dubek" me-haye ha-no'ar ha-'ivri ba-arets*. Tel Aviv, Dubek, Ltd., 1939.

Dyreson Mark. "The Emergence of Consumer Culture and the Transformation of Physical Culture: American Sport in the 1920s." *Journal of Sport History* 16 (1989): 261–289.

Edelman, Robert. *Serious Fun: A History of Spectator Sports in the USSR*. Oxford: Oxford University Press, 1993.

Edelman, Robert, and Wayne Wilson, eds. *The Oxford Handbook of Sports History*. Oxford: Oxford University Press, 2017.

Edelman, Robert, and Christopher Young. *The Whole World Was Watching: Sport in the Cold War*. Stanford, CA: Stanford University Press, 2019.

Edgar, Andrew. *Sport and Art: An Essay in the Hermeneutics of Sport*. London: Routledge, 2014.

Eikh yishmor ha-pakid gufo? Tel Aviv: Central Committee of the Federation of White-Collar Workers in Palestine and Central Committee of the Hapoel Body-Culture Association, 1938.

Eisen, George. "Zionism, Nationalism and the Emergence of the Judische Turnerschaft." *Leo Baeck Institute Yearbook* 28, no. 1 (1983): 247–262.

———. "Jewish History and the Ideology of Modern Sport: Approaches and Interpretations." *Journal of Sport History* 25, no. 2 (1998): 482–531.

Eisenberg, Christiane. "Charismatic Nationalist Leader: Turunvater Jahn." *International Journal of the History of Sport* 14, no. 3 (1996): 14–27.

———. *"English Sports" und deutsche Bürger: Eine Gesellschaftsgeschichte 1800–1939*. Paderborn: Ferdinand Schöningh, 1999.

Elias, Norbert, and Eric Dunning. *Quest for Excitement: Sport and Leisure in the Civilizing Process*. Oxford: Blackwell, 1986.

Even-Zohar, Itamar. "The Emergence of a Native Hebrew Culture in Palestine: 1882–1948." *Studies in Zionism* (1981): 167–184.

Felski, Rita. *Doing Time: Feminist Theory and Postmodern Culture*. New York: NYU Press, 2000.

———. *The Limits of Critique*. Chicago: University of Chicago Press, 2015.

Fink, Carole. *Defending the Rights of Others: The Great Powers, the Jews, and International Minority Protection, 1878–1938*. New York: Cambridge University Press, 2004.

Frankel, Walter. *Ha-gan lelo 'adama*. Tel Aviv: Hadar, 1958.

Frost, Dennis J. *Seeing Stars: Sports Celebrity, Identity, and Body Culture in Modern Japan.* Cambridge, MA: Harvard University Press, 2010.

Gechtman, Roni. "Socialist Mass Politics Through Sport: The Bund's Morgnshtern in Poland, 1926–1939." *Journal of Sport History* 26, no. 2 (1999): 326–352.

Geyer, Martin, and Johannes Paulmann, eds. *The Mechanics of Internationalism: Culture, Society and Politics from the 1840s to World War I.* New York: Oxford University Press, 2001.

Gillerman, Sharon. *Germans into Jews: Remaking the Jewish Social Body in the Weimar Republic.* Stanford, CA: Stanford University Press, 2009.

Gilman, Sander. *The Jew's Body.* London: Routledge, 2013.

Glückman, O. *Atletika kala: Targili hakhana.* Tel Aviv: Hapoel Body-Culture Association, 1941.

Goltermann, Svenja. "Exercise and Perfection: Embodying the Nation in Nineteenth-Century Germany." *European Review of History* 11 (2004): 333–346.

Gordon, A. D. *Ha-Adam ve'Hatavea,* edited by Yuval Jobani and Ron Margolin. Jerusalem: Magnes Press, 2020.

Gorn, Elliott J. *The Manly Art: Bare-Knuckle Prize Fighting in America.* Ithaca, NY: Cornell University Press, 2010.

Granick, Jaclyn. *International Jewish Humanitarianism in the Age of the Great War.* Cambridge: Cambridge University Press, 2021.

Green, Abigail. "Nationalism and the 'Jewish International': Religious Internationalism in Europe and the Middle East c. 1840–c. 1880." *Comparative Studies in Society and History* 50 (2008): 535–558.

Gruneau, Richard. *Sport and Modernity.* Cambridge: Polity Press, 2017.

Gumbrecht, Hans Ulrich. *In 1926: Living on the Edge of Time.* Cambridge, MA: Harvard University Press, 1998.

———. "Epiphany of Form: On the Beauty of Team Sports." *New Literary History* 30 (1999): 351–372.

———. *In Praise of Athletic Beauty.* Cambridge, MA: Harvard Press, 2006.

———. *Crowds: The Stadium as a Ritual of Intensity.* Stanford, CA: Stanford University Press, 2021.

Guttmann, Allen. *From Ritual to Record: The Nature of Modern Sports.* New York: Columbia University Press, 1978.

———. *The Olympics: A History of the Modern Games.* Urbana: Illinois University Press, 2002.

Ha-hukim ha-rishmi'im lefi hitah'dut ha-benleumit le-kadur-sal. Tel Aviv: Federation of Amateur Sports Clubs, 1939.

Halfin, Igal. *From Darkness to Light: Class, Consciousness, and Salvation in Revolutionary Russia.* Pittsburgh: University of Pittsburgh Press, 2000.

———. ed. *Language and Revolution: Modern Political Identities.* London: Cass Publishers, 2002.

———*Terror in My Soul: Communist Autobiographies on Trial.* Cambridge, MA: Harvard, 2003.

Halperin, Gilad. "For King and Country: The Palestine Post and Zionist Propaganda in Pre-State Israel, 1932–1950." PhD diss., Haifa University, 2023.

Halperin, Liora R. *Babel in Zion: Jews, Nationalism, and Language Diversity in Palestine, 1920–1948.* New Haven: Yale University Press, 2014.

Harif, Haggai. *Tsiyonut shel sheririm: Tafkidav ha-politi'im shel ha-sport ha-yitsugi ba-Yishuv u-ve-Medinat Yisrael, 1898–1960.* Jerusalem: Yad Izhak Ben-Zvi, 2011.

Harshav, Benjamin. *Language in Time of Revolution.* Berkeley: University of California Press.

Harvey, Adrian. *The Beginnings of a Commercial Sporting Culture in Britain, 1793–1850.* Burlington, VT: Ashgate, 2004.

Hau, Michal. *The Cult of Health and Beauty in Germany: A Social History, 1890–1930*, Chicago: University of Chicago Press, 2003.

———. *Performance Anxiety: Sport and Work in Germany from the Empire to Nazism*. Toronto: University of Toronto Press, 2017.

Hazaz, Haim. *Siporim Nevcharim*. Tel Aviv: Dvir, 1977.

Hellbeck, Jochen. *Revolution on My Mind: Writing a Diary Under Stalin*. Cambridge, MA: Harvard University Press, 2009.

Helman, Anat. "Sport on the Sabbath: Controversy in 1920s and 1930s Jewish Palestine." *International Journal of the History of Sport* 25, no. 1 (2008): 41–64.

———. *Young Tel Aviv: A Tale of Two Cities*. Waltham, MA: Brandeis University Press, 2010.

Hobsbawm, Eric J., and T. O. Ranger, eds. *The Invention of Tradition*. Cambridge: Cambridge University Press, 1992.

———. *The Age of Extremes: The Short Twentieth Century, 1914–1991*. London: Abacus Books, 1995.

Hofmann, Annette R., ed. *Turnen and Sport: Transatlantic Transfers*. New York: Waxmann Publishing, 2004.

Houlihan, Barrie, and Jinming Zheng. "The Olympics and Elite Sport Policy: Where Will It All End?" *International Journal of the History of Sport* 30, no. 4 (2013): 338–355.

Huet, Marie-Heléné. "The Revolutionary Sublime." *Eighteenth-Century Studies* 28, no. 1 (Autumn 1994): 51–64.

Huggins, Mike. *The Victorians and Sport*. New York: Palgrave, 2004.

Hughes, Jon. *Max Schmeling and the Making of a National Hero in Twentieth-Century Germany*. Cham, Switzerland: Palgrave Macmillan, 2018.

Huizinga, Johan. *Homo Ludens: A Study of the Play-Element in Culture*. London: Routledge, 1980.

Hunt, Lynn. "The Experience of Revolution." *French Historical Studies* 32 (2009): 671–678.

Idels, Ofer. "Mis'hakim medumyanim: Sport, ha-Yishuv, ve-ha-Olympiada ha-ahat 'esre, 1931–1963." *Cathedra* 167 (2018): 92–97.

———. "How to Lose Gracefully in an Internationally Selfish World: Gender, the 'New Jew' and the Underestimation of Athletic Performance in Interwar Palestine." *Journal of Modern Jewish Studies* 21, no. 2 (2021): 215–233.

———. "'The Idea of Sports Is Pure and Noble': Internationalism, Zionism and the Formation of a Global Universal Language." *International History Review* (2024): 1–15.

———. *Zionism: Emotions, Language and Experience* Cambridge: Cambridge University Press, 2024.

Inbari, Assaf. "Towards a Hebrew Literature." *Azure* (2000): 99–154.

Ish Shalom, David, "Maccabi Eretz Israel Union 1906–1948." PhD diss., Hebrew University of Jerusalem, 2004.

Jacob, Wilson Chacko. *Working out Egypt: Effendi Masculinity and Subject Formation in Colonial Modernity, 1870–1940*. Durham, NC: Duke University Press, 2011.

Jensen, Erik. *Body by Weimar: Athletes, Gender, and German Modernity*. New York: Oxford University Press, 2010.

———. "Crowd Control: Boxing Spectatorship and Social Order in Weimar Germany," in *Histories of Leisure*, edited by Rudy Koshar (Oxford: Berg, 2002), 79–101.

Kaplan, Ron. *The Jewish Olympics: The History of the Maccabiah Games*. New York: Simon & Schuster, 2015.

Kaufman, Haim. "Ha-zika ha-re'ayonit ben sport ha-po'alim le-ven hitagdut 'Hapoel' bitekufat ha-Mandat." *BiTenu'a* 3 (1995): 56–71.

———. "Agudot ha-sport ha-Tsiyoniut—mi-sport leumi le-sport politi." *Zmanim* 63 (1998): 81–91.

———. "Mas'ot shel kevutsot sport lehul, masa Maccabi Haifa le-artsot ha-berit bi-sh'nat 1927" *Ha-hinukh ha-gufani ve-ha-sport* 4 (2001): 19–21.

———. "Yesoda shel 'Hitagdut ha-Sport Hapoel." *Cathedra* 80 (1996): 122–149.

Kaufman, Haim, and Yair Galili. "Maccabi Versus Hapoel: The Political Divide That Developed in Sports in Eretz Israel, 1926–1935." *Israel Affairs* 13 (2007): 554–565.

———. "The Early Development of Hebrew Football in Eretz Israel, 1910–1928." *Soccer & Society* (2008): 81–95.

Kaufman, Haim, and Hagi Harif, eds. *Tarbut ha-guf Ve-ha-sport*. Jerusalem: Yad-Ben Zvi Press, 2002.

Keys, Barbara J. "Soviet Sport and Transnational Mass Culture in the 1930s." *Journal of Contemporary History* 38 (2003): 413–434.

———. *Globalizing Sport: National Rivalry and International Community in the 1930s*. Cambridge, MA: Harvard University Press, 2006.

———. ed. *The Ideals of Global Sport: From Peace to Human Rights*. Philadelphia: University of Pennsylvania Press, 2019.

Kirk, David, *Schooling Bodies: School Practice and Public Discourse 1880–1950*. Leicester: Leicester University Press, 1998.

Koazma, Liat. "Sexology in the Yishuv: The Rise and Decline of Sexual Consultation in Tel Aviv, 1930–39." *International Journal of Middle East Studies* 42 (2010): 231–249.

Krüger, Arnd, and Riordan James, eds. *The Story of Worker Sport*. Champaign, IL: Human Kinetics, 1996.

Kruger, Michael. "Body Culture and Nation Building: The History of Gymnastics in Germany in the Period of Its Foundation as a Nation-State." *International Journal of the History of Sport* 13, no. 3 (1996): 409–417.

———. "The German Workers' Sport Movement Between Socialism, Workers' Culture, Middle-Class Gymnastics and Sport for All." *International Journal of the History of Sport* 31, no. 9 (2013): 1098–1117.

Kruger, Michael, and Annette R. Hofmann. "The Development of Physical-Education Institutions in Europe: A Short Introduction." *International Journal of the History of Sport* 32 (2015): 737–739.

Kugelmass Jack, ed. *Jews, Sports, and the Rites of Citizenship*, Urbana: University of Illinois Press, 2007.

Large, David Clay. *Nazi Games: The Olympics of 1936*. New York: W. W. Norton, 2007.

Latour, Bruno. "Why Has Critique Run out of Steam? From Matters of Fact to Matters of Concern." *Critical Inquiry* 30 (2004): 225–248.

Leconte, Maxence Pascal Philippe. "Reexamining Violence and Trauma in the French Boxing Literature of the Interwar Period: Henri Decoin Quinze Rounds (1930) and Alfred Menguy Gueules Aplaties (1933)." *International Journal of the History of Sport* 36, nos.1–2 (2019): 207–224.

Levine, Peter. *Ellis Island to Ebbets Field: Sport and the American Jewish Experience*. New York: Oxford University Press, 1992.

Lichtenstein, Tatjana. "'An Athlete like a Soldier Must Not Retreat': Zionists, Sport, and Belonging in Interwar Czechoslovakia." *Shofar: An Interdisciplinary Journal of Jewish Studies* 15 (2015): 1–26.

Llewellyn, Matthew P. "Olympic Games Are an International Farce." *International Journal of the History of Sport* 28, no. 5 (2011): 751–772.

Loeffler, James. *Rooted Cosmopolitans: Jews and Human Rights in the Twentieth Century*. New Haven, CT: Yale University Press, 2018.

Lyons, F.S.L. *Internationalism in Europe, 1815–1914*. Leyden: A. W. Sythoff, 1963.

MacAloon, John J. *This Great Symbol: Pierre de Coubertin and the Origins of the Modern Olympics*. London: Routledge, 2013.

Mackenzie, Michael. "From Athens to Berlin: The 1936 Olympics and Leni Riefenstahl's Olympia." *Critical Inquiry* 29, no. 2 (2003): 302–336.

Magdalinski, Tara. *Sport, Technology and the Body: The Nature of Performance*. London: Routledge, 2009.

Manela, Erez. *The Wilsonian Moment: Self-Determination and the International Origins of Anticolonial Nationalism*. New York: Oxford University Press, 2007.

Mangan. J. A., *Athleticism in the Victorian and Edwardian Public School*. New York: Routledge, 2000.

———. ed. *Superman Supreme: Fascist Body as Political Icon: Global Fascism*. London: Cass Publishers, 2000.

———. ed. *Militarism, Sport, Europe: War Without Weapons*. London: Cass Publishers, 2003.

———. *The Cultural Bond: Sport, Empire, Society*. New York: Routledge, 2011.

Marcus, Nathan. "Zionist Football and Jewish Identity in Weimar Germany." *Judaica* (2005): 147–166.

Marschik, Matthias. "Depicting Hakoah: Images of a Zionist Sports Club in Interwar Vienna." *Historical Social Research* 43, no. 2 (2018): 129–147.

Martínková, Irena, and Jim Parry. *Phenomenological Approaches to Sport*. London: Routledge, 2015.

Meiri, Shmuel. *Nahum Het*. Haifa: Gestlit, 1996.

Meisl, Willy, ed. *Der Sport am Scheidewege*. Heidelberg: Iris, 1928.

Moi, Toril. *Revolution of the Ordinary: Literary Studies After Wittgenstein, Austin, and Cavell*. Chicago: University of Chicago Press, 2017.

Moss, Kenneth. *Jewish Renaissance in the Russian Revolution*. Cambridge, MA: Harvard University Press, 2009.

———. *An Unchosen People Jewish Political Reckoning in Interwar Poland*. Cambridge, MA: Harvard University Press, 2021.

Moss, Kenneth, Benjamin Nathans, and Taro Tsurumi, eds. *From Europe's East to the Middle East: Israel's Russian and Polish Lineages*. Philadelphia: University of Pennsylvania Press, 2021.

Mosse, George L. *The Image of Man: The Creation of Modern Masculinity*. Oxford: Oxford University Press, 1996.

Muller, Norbert, ed. *Olympism: Pierre De Coubertin Selected Writings*. Lausanne: International Olympic Committee, 2000.

Neumann, Boaz. *Land and Desire in Early Zionism*. Waltham, MA: Brandeis University Press, 2011.

Nishri (Orloff), Zvi. *Kadur Regel*. Jaffa: Maccabi Palestine Federation, 1914.

———. *Shi'ure hit'amlut: Le-vate sefer, la-agudot ve-la-bayit*. Jaffa: A. Eitan and S. Shoshani, 1920.

———. *Mi-divre yeme ha-hinukh ha-gufani*. Tel Aviv: National Committee, 1940.

Oriard, Michael. *Reading Football: How the Popular Press Created an American Spectacle*. Chapel Hill: University of North Carolina Press.

Palestine Football Federation. *Sefer shimushi li-shenat 1930/31*. Jerusalem: Palestine Football Federation, 1930.

Paterno, Wolfgang. *Faust und Geist: Literatur und Boxen zwischen den Weltkriegen*. Vienna: Böhlau, 2018.

Penslar, Derek J. *Jews and the Military: A History*. Princeton: Princeton University Press, 2013.

Pfister, Gertrud, ed. *Gymnastics, a Transatlantic Movement: From Europe to America.* New York: Routledge, 2011.

Picard, Jacques, Michael Steinberg, and Idith Zertal. *Makers of Jewish Modernity: Thinkers, Artists, Leaders, and the World They Made.* Princeton: Princeton University Press, 2015.

Plamper, Jan. "Sounds of February, Smells of October: The Russian Revolution as Sensory Experience." *American Historical Review* 126 (2021): 140–165.

Polak, Frank. *Ha-sipur ba-mikra.* Jerusalem: Mosad Bialik, 1999.

Presner, Todd, *Muscular Judaism: The Jewish Body and the Politics of Regeneration.* New York: Routledge, 2007.

Rabinbach, Anson. *The Human Motor: Energy, Fatigue, and the Origins of Modernity.* University of California Press, 1992.

Rabinovitch, Simon. *Jewish Rites, National Rights: Nationalism and Autonomy in Late Imperial and Revolutionary Russia.* Stanford, CA: Stanford University Press, 2014.

Reiche, Danyel, and Tamir Sorek, eds. *Sport, Politics and Society in the Middle East.* Oxford: Oxford University Press, 2019.

Ricoeur, Paul. *Freud and Philosophy: An Essay on Interpretation.* New Haven, CT: Yale University Press, 1970.

Riess, Steven A., ed. *Sports and the American Jew.* New York: Syracuse University Press, 1998.

Roche, Helen, and Demetriou Kyriakos, eds. *Brill's Companion to the Classics: Fascist Italy, and Nazi Germany.* Leiden: Brill, 2018.

Rowe, Sharon. "Modern Sports: Liminal Ritual or Liminoid Leisure." *Journal of Ritual Studies* 12 (1998): 47–60.

Runia, Eelco. *Moved by the Past: Discontinuity and Historical Mutation.* New York: Columbia University Press, 2014.

Rybak, Jan. *Everyday Zionism in East-Central Europe: Nation-Building in War and Revolution, 1914–1920.* Oxford: Oxford University Press, 2021.

Sammons, Jeffrey T. *Beyond the Ring: The Role of Boxing in American Society.* Urbana: University of Illinois Press, 1988.

Saposnik, Arieh Bruce. *Becoming Hebrew: The Creation of a Jewish National Culture in Ottoman Palestine.* Oxford: Oxford University Press, 2008.

Savage, R. W. H. "Effort, Play, and Sport." *Sport, Ethics and Philosophy* 10 (2016): 392–402.

Scott, Joan Wallach. "The Evidence of Experience." *Critical Inquiry* 17 (1991): 773–797.

Sefer huke ha-kaduregel: Lefi ha-hahlatot ha-rishmiyot shel ha-va'ad ha-ben leumi. Jerusalem: Y. Azrieli, 1927–1928.

———. "25 shana la-mis'hak kadur ha-regel be-Tel Aviv: 1911–1936." *Hesegav shel Maccabi Tel Aviv be-25 ha-shanim ha-aharonot.* Jaffa: M. Shoham, 1936.

Shapira, Anita. *Land and Power: The Zionist Resort to Force, 1881–1948.* Oxford: Oxford University Press, 1992.

Shavit, Zohar. "Can It Be That Our Dormant Language Has Been Wholly Revived? Vision, Propaganda, and Linguistic Reality in the Yishuv Under the British Mandate." *Israel Studies* 22, no 1 (Spring 2017): 101–138.

Shoham, Hizky. "Of Other Cinematic Spaces: Urban Zionism in Early Hebrew Cinema." *Israel Studies Review* 26, (2011): 109–131.

Silver, Mike. *Stars in the Ring: Jewish Champions in the Golden Age of Boxing.* Lanham, MD: Rowman & Littlefield, 2016.

Simon, Ernst. *Atletika kala.* Haifa, 1937.

Sluga, Glenda. *Internationalism in the Age of Nationalism.* Philadelphia: University of Pennsylvania Press, 2013.

Sluga, Glenda, and Patricia Clavin, ed. *Internationalisms: A Twentieth-Century History.* Cambridge: Cambridge University Press, 2016.

Snowdon, David. "Hazlitt's Prizefight Revisited: Pierce Egan and Jon Bee's Boxiana-Style Perspective." *Romantic Textualities: Literature and Print Culture* 20 (2011).

Spiegel, Nina S. *Embodying Hebrew Culture: Aesthetics, Athletics, and Dance in the Jewish Community of Mandate Palestine.* Detroit: Wayne State Press, 2013.

Stanislawski, Michael. *Zionism and the Fin de Siècle: Cosmopolitanism and Nationalism from Nordau to Jabotinsky.* Berkeley: University of California Press, 2001.

Steinberg, David. "The Worker's Sport International 1920–1928." *Journal of Contemporary History* 13, no. 2 (1978): 233–251.

Stoddart, Brian. "Sport, Cultural Imperialism, and Colonial Response in the British Empire." *Comparative Studies in Society and History* 40 (1988): 649–667.

Suits, Bernard. "Tricky Triad: Games, Play, and Sport." *Journal of the Philosophy of Sport* 15, no. 1 (2012): 1–9.

Szymanski, Stefan. "A Theory of the Evolution of Modern Sport." *Journal of Sport History* 35, no.1 (2008): 1–64.

Taylor, Matthew. "Round the London Ring: Boxing, Class, and Community in Interwar London." *London Journal* 34, no. 2 (2009): 139–162.

Tomlinson, Alan, and Christopher Young. "Towards a New History of European Sport." *European Review* 19, no. 4 (2011): 487–507.

Tranter, Neil, *Sport, Economy and Society in Britain 1750–1914.* Cambridge: Cambridge University Press, 1998.

Tsuri, Shneor. *Mis'hake sport: Kadur-yad.* Haifa: Hapoel Body-Culture Association, 1928.

Tumblety, Joan. *Remaking the Male Body: Masculinity and the Uses of Physical Culture in Interwar and Vichy France.* Oxford: Oxford University Press, 2012.

———. "Rethinking the Fascist Aesthetic: Mass Gymnastics, Political Spectacle and the Stadium in 1930s France." *European History Quarterly* 43, no. 4 (2013): 707–730.

Turner, Victor. *On the Edge of the Bush: Anthropology as Experience.* Tucson: University of Arizona Press, 1985.

Vamplew, Wray. *Pay up and Play the Game: Professional Sport in Britain 1875–1914.* New York: Cambridge University Press, 2004.

Vertinsky, Patricia A. *The Eternally Wounded Woman: Women, Doctors, and Exercise in the Late Nineteenth Century.* Urbana: University of Illinois Press, 1994.

Wahnich, Sophie. *In Defense of the Terror: Liberty or Death in the French Revolution.* New York: Verso, 2016.

Walvin, James. *The People's Game: A Social History of British Football.* London: Random House, 2014.

Weber, Eugen. "Pierre de Coubertin and the Introduction of Organized Sport in France." *Journal of Contemporary History* 15 (1970): 3–26.

———. "Gymnastics and Sports in Fin-de-Siècle France: Opium of the Classes?" *American Historical Review* 76, no. 1 (1971): 70–98.

Weiss, Yfaat. "The Transfer Agreement and the Boycott Movement: A Jewish Dilemma on the Eve of the Holocaust." *Yad Vashem Studies* 26 (1998): 129–171.

White, Hayden. "The Public Relevance of Historical Studies: A Reply to Dirk Moses." *History and Theory* 44 (October 2005): 333–338.

Wigglesworth, Neil. *The Evolution of English Sport.* London: Frank Cass, 1996.

Wildmann, Daniel. *Der Veranderbare Korper: Judische Turner, Mannlichkeit und das Wiedergewinnen Von Geschichte in Deutschland Um 1900.* Tübingen: Mohr Siebeck, 2009.

Wu, Duncan. *William Hazlitt: The First Modern Man.* Oxford: Oxford University Press, 2010.

Yekutieli-Cohen, Edna. *Ba'al ha-halomot.* Tel Aviv: Akhshav Books, 1995.

Yekutieli, Yosef. *Mi-gola le-ge'ula.* Tel Aviv: self-published, 1971.

Young, David. *The Modern Olympics: A Struggle for Revival.* Baltimore: Johns Hopkins University Press, 1996.

Zilcosky, John, and Marlo A. Burks, eds. *The Allure of Sports in Western Culture.* Toronto: University of Toronto Press, 2019.

Zimbalist Andrew, *Circus Maximus: The Economic Gamble Behind Hosting the Olympics and the World Cup*. Washington, DC: Brookings Institution Press, 2016.

Zimri, Uriel. *Agudot ha-hit'amlut ve-ha-sport be-Eretz Yisrael lifne milhemet ha-'olam ha-rishona.* Netanya: Wingate Institute, 1969.

Zweig, Stefan. *The World of Yesterday*. Lincoln: University of Nebraska Press, 1964.

Zweiniger-Bargielowska, Ina. "Building a British Superman: Physical Culture in Interwar Britain." *Journal of Contemporary History* 41, no. 4 (October 2006): 595–610.

———. *Managing the Body: Beauty, Health, and Fitness in Britain, 1880–1939*. Oxford: Oxford University Press, 2010.

INDEX

Agadati, Baruch, 58
Alexandrovich, Alexander, 36–37, 39, 52, 64, 79, 85–86; on HaBoker Sport, 36–37, 39; on "useful sport," 86
Allenby (football team), 47
Alouf, Yehoshua, vi, 17, 44
Alroey, Gur, 3
amateurism, 2, 45–46, 55, 59, 61, 71, 93; and Hebrew sports, 46, 53, 55, 94; vs. professionalism, 2, 45–48
American Jewish Committee, 75
American Jewish Joint Distribution Committee, 75
antisemitism, 2, 13, 51, 53, 55, 63, 66–67, 69
Arab Revolt (1936–1939), 9, 77, 81–82, 84–88, 91; impact on sports, 85, 87
Arabs: athletes, 7, 63–64, 85, 97; boycott by, 98; in Palestine, 63–64, 85
Arne Borg, 43
artistic gymnastics, 18
athletic body. *See* body, athletic
Atid (sports club), 55–56
Australia, 17, 53, 55, 65
Austria, 51, 53, 80. *See also* Hakoah Vienna
Avineri, Ami'el (Emil Rebelski), 50–51, 58

Baar, Arthur, 90–91
Baer, Max, 30, 43
Balfour Jerusalem (football team), 47
Barcelona, People's Olympiad (1936), 54, 62, 68
Bar Giora (paramilitary organization), 84
Bar-On, Modi, 96–97, 98
Beit Halevy, Avraham, 45
Belkind, Meira, 29, 66
Bell, David A., 3
Ben-Aharon, N., 68–69
Benayahu, Meir, 19, 21, 28, 34, 44, 49, 63, 73
Ben-Gurion, David, 58, 84, 89
Benjamin, Kurt, 38, 57
Benny Leonard Club, 50, 56
Ben-Yehuda, Eliezer, 28
Berlin: Avineri in, 50; Olympics (1936), ix, 61, 66–72, 77, 80
Bernstein, Deborah, 36
Betar (youth movement/sports), 81
Bialik, Chaim Nahman, 19, 28, 34
Biram, Arthur, 21, 89
body, athletic: and aesthetics, 6, 43–45, 57–58; and gender, 7, 20, 45, 64–66; Hebrew, 1, 4–5, 7, 14, 28, 40, 43–46, 48–51, 56, 58–59, 65, 77, 84, 90, 93–94, 97; and meaning, 43–46, 58–59; and professionalism, 45–48; and revolution, ix–x, 3, 5, 7, 43–44, 58–59, 77, 90
Borochov club, 84
boxing, 2, 4, 25–26, 28, 30–33, 35, 38–41, 43, 48–51, 54, 57, 76, 83, 89–90, 93; in Hebrew culture, 26, 48–51, 89–90; international, 30–33, 48; rules of, 28, 50; violence in, 48, 50
Brecht, Bertolt, 19, 25–26
Brinker, Menachem, 96
British Empire, ix, 4, 12–13, 15, 17, 45, 51, 71
Bund, 7, 21

championships, school-level, 21
Champions League (UEFA), 96–97
Cohen, Leo, 14
Cohen, Yaffa, 45, 64
Collins, Tony, 17
colonialism, 3, 6, 7, 17, 54, 95
competition: and children, 20; vs. cooperation, 16; critique of, 4, 15–16, 19–21, 43–45; embrace of, 15, 19, 21–22; and health, 20; international, 5, 7, 17, 21, 29, 31, 33, 38, 40, 53–54, 61–76, 85, 91, 97–98; and language, 19, 27–29; rules of, 4, 12, 16, 19, 62, 74; and women, 7, 20, 64–66
consumerism, 57–58, 96
Coubertin, Pierre de, 71–72, 83
cricket, 12, 17

Davar (newspaper), 25, 30, 34, 36, 38, 40–41, 44, 47, 49, 53–54, 67, 74, 81, 83, 88, 90
Degel Tzion (sports club), 55

degeneration, 3, 14, 20, 49, 87
Demiel, Yitzhak, 75–76
Dempsey, Jack, 31–33
Diaspora, 3, 40, 48, 51, 52, 55, 56, 58, 65, 67, 69. *See also* Europe; Jewish people: in United States
discipline, 12, 15, 20, 49, 58, 81, 83, 87
Do'ar HaYom (newspaper), 30–31, 34, 46, 51–52, 61, 63, 66, 68–70, 78, 85
Dolgopyat, Artem, 98
Dubek (company), 57

Edström, Sigfrid, 64, 70, 76
Egypt, 54, 65, 73, 75, 85; athletes from, 54, 73; Hapoel delegation to, 65; Maccabi delegation to, 73
Elias, Norbert, 26
Eretz Israel (Land of Israel), 2, 14, 26–27, 29, 34, 44–45, 47, 50, 52, 54, 57–59, 62–65, 67–71, 73, 75, 77–78, 80–81, 85, 87, 94, 96, 97; air of, 26, 54, 65, 68; building of, 47, 58, 65, 77, 80, 85; football association of, 64, 73; Olympic committee of, 64, 66–68, 71; soil of, 58, 80–81
Europe, ix, 2, 4, 13, 17, 20, 27, 32, 34, 43, 51–53, 56, 62–63, 67–70, 75, 84, 91, 94, 97
experience: aesthetic, 6, 26, 57, 61, 70, 76, 79, 93; Hebrew, 1–2, 4–9, 23, 25–28, 40, 45, 47, 58, 62, 65, 75–77, 86, 90, 93–95, 97; lived, x, 3, 27, 95; sporting, 4, 6, 8, 16, 25–29, 31–33, 35, 37, 39–41, 44, 46, 48–51, 58, 62, 70, 76–77, 86, 90–91, 93, 98–100

Fédération Internationale de Football Association (FIFA), 8, 61–64, 73, 75, 97–98
Felski, Rita, 5–6, 8
flag, national: Hebrew/Zionist, ix, 64–66, 81, 87, 89, 91, 95, 98; Maccabi, 95; Olympic, 61
football (kaduregel), x, 7, 11, 13, 16–22, 25, 27, 29, 31, 35, 38–40, 46–47, 51–54, 56, 58–59, 61, 64, 73–75, 84, 90–92, 97–99; rules of, 16, 19, 61, 74; violence in, 20–21
Frankel, Walter, 4, 55, 62
French Revolution, 3
Freudenthal, Ernst, 53, 55–56

games: traditional vs. modern, 12. *See also* competition; *specific games*

Gender: and athletic body, 7, 20, 45, 64–66; and boxing, 48; and sports, 2, 7, 20, 45, 61, 64–66, 81, 97. *See also* women
Germany, 1, 13, 19, 21, 30, 35–37, 40, 43, 50, 53, 55–57, 65–67, 69–72, 77, 80, 84, 91, 94
Glickman, Emanuel, 67
globalization, ix, 3, 6, 11, 16–17, 21, 61–62, 75, 93–94, 96, 99
Gordon, A. D., 26–27, 44, 58
Greece, 55, 57, 73–75, 90
Grschebina, Liselotte, 57
Gumbrecht, Hans Ulrich, 6, 26, 79
gymnastics (Turnen), 2, 4, 8, 11–23, 44, 48–49, 58, 78, 81, 83–84, 93–94; decline of, 15, 17–19, 22, 94; equipment for, 13; Hebrew, 14–15, 17, 22, 78; Jewish, 13–14, 22; vs. modern sports, 2, 8, 12, 15–16, 18, 22–23, 78, 93–94; origins of, 12–13; and physical education, 18, 21–22, 34, 37, 81, 83, 90, 94; revival attempts, 17–18; and Zionism, 13–15, 22–23, 44, 78

Haaretz (newspaper), 25, 34, 36–38, 40, 43–45, 48–49, 52, 56, 63, 65–70, 73, 75
HaBoker Sport: on Alexandrovich, 36–37; on boxing, 39, 45, 89–90; on German immigrants, 53, 55, 56, 57; on international sports, 64, 66, 68, 70, 71, 74, 76; on "useful sport," 83, 85, 87, 88; on women athletes, 45
Hagam (Special Physical Education), 89
Haganah (paramilitary organization), 25, 89
Haifa, 4, 14, 17, 20–21, 54, 56, 59, 65, 78, 80, 82, 88–89, 96
Hakoah Vienna, 4, 30, 51–53, 55, 63, 70, 91
HaMaccabi (journal), 77, 78, 79, 80, 81, 82, 86, 87
Hameiri, Avigdor, 19, 58
Hapoel: battalions, 83, 88; boxing, 48–49; Central Committee, 88; football club, 47, 55; founding of, 15; journal, 17, 22; members, 16, 44, 46; Olympic Games and, 67, 68, 72; physical culture organization, 15, 47, 55; physical unfitness in, 88; swimming, 81; Tel Aviv, 47, 54; "useful sport" and, 83, 88, 89
Hashomer, 84
Hazaz, Haim, 25, 41
Hebrew Athletes: Arab Revolt and, 77, 78, 85, 86, 87; athletic body and, 44–45, 48, 58; Central European immigrants and, 55–57; definition of, 4; discipline of, 84;

disillusionment of, 75; emotions of, 27, 29; facilities for, 78; foreignness of, 66; international sports and, 62–63, 64–65, 66, 68, 69, 70–73, 75; journalists as, 34; language of, 27–28, 29, 31, 32, 33, 34, 35, 39, 40, 41; military training and, 83, 84, 85, 86, 87, 88, 89, 90, 91; number of, 4; purpose of, 5, 45, 46, 50, 58; settlement for, 79–80; urban identity of, 78; violence and, 21; water sports and, 81–82
Hebrew culture: athletic body and, 43–44, 50, 51, 53, 59; boxing in, 48–49; foreign influences on, 28; gymnastics and, 14; international sports and, 62, 63, 64, 65, 66, 71, 75; language in, 27–28, 31, 33, 34, 39, 40, 41, 94, 99; militarization and, 83–84, 91–92; modern sports and, 4, 19, 39, 94; physical cultivation in, 13; physical unfitness in, 88; violence in, 20–21
Hebrew Gymnasium, 14, 18, 47, 56
Hebrew language: modernization of, 27–28; proficiency in, 31; revival of, 27; sporting terms in, 27, 28, 31, 39, 41, 99; tense sporting culture and, 99
Hebrew press, 16, 19, 20, 27, 30, 31, 33, 34, 35, 39, 43, 51, 53, 65, 66, 67, 73, 84
Hebrew Revival, 27
Heth, Nahum, 85
Hirschl, Nickolaus "Mickey," 53–54, 55, 57, 59, 98
Histadrut, 15, 47, 84
history: "end of," 3, 93–94; of gymnastics, 12, 13–14; "Jewish return to," 7, 61, 63, 65, 75; of modern sports, 12–13; modern sports and, 11, 12–13; oral, 96; past and present, 99; sporting, 11–23, 25–42, 43–60, 61–76, 77–92, 93–100; of Zionism, 2–5, 7–10, 11–23, 25–42, 43–60, 61–76, 77–92, 93–100
Hitkadmut club, 55, 56
Holocaust, 1, 2, 69, 91, 94
human rights, 3, 75
Hungary, 65, 91

ideology: binary phenomenon, 4; Zionist, 2, 3, 4, 5, 15, 26, 47, 95, 99, 100
immigrants: Central European, 55–57, 79, 94; German, 36, 53, 55, 57, 94; Lithuanian, 35; Polish, 94; Russian, 98
India, 17, 65, 75
individualism, 57, 58
inferiority, feelings of, 66
institutions, 2, 99
International Association Football Federation (FIFA), 61, 62, 64, 75
internationalism, 7, 61–76, 95
International Olympic Committee (IOC), 61, 62, 63, 64, 67, 71, 72, 75
Irgun, 84
Israel Defense Forces, 92
Israeli culture, 13, 97–99
Israeli national team, 53, 97
Istanbul, 13

Jabotinsky, Zeev, 84–85
Jaffa, 14, 84, 95
Jahn, Friedrich Ludwig, 13, 84
Japan, 65, 94
Jerusalem, 14, 15, 44
Jewish Agency, 69, 75
Jewish National Council (Va'ad Le'umi), 89
Jewish National Fund (JNF), 78–79
Jewish people: antisemitism and, 2, 48, 51, 55, 67, 69, 70; in Europe, 2, 4, 13, 14, 48, 51, 52, 53, 68, 69, 70, 75, 79, 91; history of, 25, 63, 69; identity of, 65, 75; minorities, 75; national pride of, 44; national unity of, 23; new, 3, 45, 97; peoplehood of, 69, 70; population of, 53; question, 2; responsibility of, 70; self-defense of, 84; solidarity of, 69; in United States, 4, 48, 51, 63
Jimbo J, 100
journalism, 30, 31, 33, 34, 35, 36, 37, 38, 39, 40, 41, 94, 99
Judaism, Muscular (*Muskeljudentum*), 11, 13, 22, 67
Judo, 94
jujitsu, 83

Kefar Hamaccabi (The Maccabi Village), 79–80, 81, 82
Keisari, Uri, 44, 65
Kisch, Frederick, 67
Kolganov, Michael, 98
Kolnoa, 35–36, 82

language: Arabic, 28, 71, 97; biblical, 29, 81; English, 28, 31, 32, 39; Hebrew, 27–28, 29, 31,

language (*cont.*)
32, 33, 34, 35, 39, 40, 41, 52, 65, 66, 67, 74, 94, 99; of rebirth, 27; Russian, 28; universal, 62, 70–73; Yiddish, 7, 28, 30, 31, 38
Latin America, 17
League of Nations, 63, 75
Lebanon, 85
Lederman, Leah (Fletcher), 66
leisure, 12, 93
Leonard, Benny, 50, 56
Levant Fair, 79
Levitan, Lipa, 36, 65, 66, 74
Lifeguard, Emil the (Emil hamatsil), 51, 56
Lithuania, 35, 55–56
London, 3, 9, 32, 64–66
Los Angeles Olympics (1932), 53

Maccabi: athletics department, 44–45; Central Committee, 81, 83, 85, 86, 87, 88; club, 11, 14; conference, 72; delegation, 29, 36, 65, 66, 75; Federation, 80; founding of, 14; Guard, 83, 89; gymnastics and, 14, 15, 17, 18, 22, 23, 33, 44, 46, 47, 51, 54, 55, 56, 62, 63, 64, 65, 66, 67, 68, 72, 75, 77, 78, 79, 80, 81, 82, 83, 85, 86, 87, 88, 89; health fund, 56; journal, 11, 16, 18, 22, 29, 35, 44, 50, 77, 79, 80, 81, 86, 87; members, 12, 16, 17, 18, 29, 34, 35, 44, 45, 46, 61, 62, 63, 64, 66, 67, 69, 72, 77, 78, 82, 86, 87, 88, 89; North Tel Aviv, 56; Olympic Games and, 67, 68, 72; Palestine Federation for Gymnastics and Sports, 22; political aspirations of, 15; president of, 85; private boxing club and, 50; Rishon Lezion-Jaffa Jewish Gymnastics Association, 14; Tel Aviv, 14, 36, 44–45, 53, 54, 79, 88; World Maccabi Association, 69
Maccabiah Games, 62, 79, 80, 95, 96
Machlis, Ben-Ami, 29, 30
martial arts, 94
masculinity, 13, 43, 48, 50
Matkot, 100
Matusevich, Konstantin, 98
Mayer, Helen, 70
McNamee, Graham, 33
Mediterranean, 81
Meisl, Willy, 109n7
militarism, 7, 77–92, 94, 95
military training, 83, 84, 85, 86, 87, 88, 89, 90, 91, 92
Mishmar VeSport ("Defense and Sports"), 57–58, 90
modernity, 2, 12, 13, 19, 43, 94
Morgenshtern, 7, 21
Mossinson, Benzion, 18
Moustafa, Ibrahim, 54

nationalism, 4, 7, 13, 37, 46, 61, 62, 95
Nazi Germany, 69, 72
Nazi Olympics, 66–68, 69–70, 71–73, 80
Neufeld, Alexander "Nemesh," 55, 57
New York Times, The, 31–33, 39
Nishri, Zvi, 15, 18, 84
Nordau, Max, 11, 14, 22, 84
nudism, 13
Nuremberg Laws, 69, 70
Nurmi, Paavo, 43

Ohana, Eli, 97
Olympic Games, 7, 43, 54, 59, 61, 62, 63, 64, 66–68, 69–70, 71–73, 75, 93, 97, 98
Olympism, 70–73, 91
organizations: antifascist, 68; body-culture, 17, 34, 47, 84; international, 62, 63, 64, 71, 75; Jewish, 69, 75; Maccabi, 11, 14, 15, 17, 18, 22, 23, 33, 44, 46, 47, 51, 54, 55, 56, 62, 63, 64, 65, 66, 67, 68, 72, 75, 77, 78, 79, 80, 81, 82, 83, 85, 86, 87, 88, 89; Socialist Workers' Sport Internationale (SASI), 22, 62, 67, 75; Zionist, 79
Oxford English Dictionary, 12

paddle ball (Matkot), 100
Palestine Football Association, 64, 73
Palestine Olympic Committee, 64, 68, 71, 75
The Palestine Post, 39, 40
penalty kick (fendel), 20
phenomenology, 5, 26, 71
physical education, 18, 22, 37, 94, 99
physical strength, 1, 43, 59, 91, 97
pioneers (halutzim), 3, 15, 27, 58, 96
Poland, 30, 36, 55, 65, 91, 94
Pollak, Egon, 53, 57
postcritique, 5, 6
pre-World War I, 12, 14, 16, 94
professionalism, 14, 28, 45–48, 50, 57, 97
propaganda, 68, 69, 73, 82
Prussia, 13, 83
Purim, 56

Rabinovitch, Dov, 65
radio stations, 32
Reali School, 20, 89
Rehovot, 14, 16
Reisinger, Dan, 95–96
Revolution, Zionist, 3, 4, 5, 7, 9, 15, 26, 27, 28, 45, 47, 58, 59, 62, 65, 75, 77, 78, 80, 86, 87, 91, 94, 95, 96, 99
Ricoeur, Paul, 5, 6
Riefenstahl, Leni, 57
Rieger, Eliezer, 52
Rosecki, Selig, 26, 68, 72, 73, 85, 91
rugby, 13, 17
Runia, Eelco, 26
Ruth, Babe, 43

Sabbath, 15, 18, 20, 45
sacrifice, 16, 87
sailing, 16, 81, 82
Samet, Shimon, 20, 28, 44
Schmidt, Theodor, 66, 71
Scouts movement, 84
sea, 81–82
self-defense, 83, 84, 89
self-respect, 55, 69
The Sermon, 25
settlement, 79–80, 81
Shababo, Shoshana, 25, 28, 29, 30, 31, 40
Sharett, Moshe (Shertok), 58, 75
Shkedi, Meir, 35
Siman, Ernst, 37, 65
Smilanski, Moshe, 19, 52
Socialist Workers' Sport Internationale (SASI), 22, 62, 67, 75
soldier-figure, 9, 83, 90, 91
Spanish civil war, 68
spectacle: cultural, 48; emotional, 26; modern, 3, 26, 30, 36, 37, 39, 49, 57, 58, 59, 61, 71, 93, 99; non-spectacular, 49; sporting, 11, 12, 19, 25, 26, 29, 30, 36, 37, 39, 40, 48, 49, 57, 58, 59, 61, 71, 93, 99
Sport (magazine), 36, 38
sports: amateurism in, 3, 26, 47, 49, 55, 57, 94; as amusement, 16; as art, 26; autotelic nature of, 26, 28, 44, 46, 49, 71, 74, 76, 93, 94, 99, 100; in Britain, 6, 12, 13, 17, 19, 45, 83; cultural assimilation of, 19; decline of, 17–18; economic dimension of, 17; emotional presence of, 27; as entertainment, 37; in Europe, 4, 13, 17, 21, 30, 33, 43, 46, 48, 51, 52, 53, 55, 63, 65, 69, 70, 75, 79, 91, 94, 97; globalization of, 3, 4, 11, 17, 45, 61, 93, 94, 96; golden age of, 4, 48, 91; as an indicator of national readiness, 83; as an industry, 45; international, 61–76; as an international farce, 117n4; in Japan, 94; journalism, 30, 31, 33, 34, 35, 36, 37, 38, 39, 40, 41, 94, 99; lack of tradition in, 19; meaning of, 43–60; in Middle East, 46; and military, 9, 83–92; as national cultural movement, 18; national importance of, 85; as national sport, 81; as a novelty, 19–22; as an object of admiration, 43; Olympic, 61, 62, 63, 64, 66, 67, 68, 69, 70, 71, 72, 73, 75, 93, 97, 98; origins of, 11–13; physical benefits of, 5; and politics, 6, 67, 72, 98; popularity of, 7, 17, 19, 49, 73; professionalism in, 14, 28, 45–48, 50, 57, 97; purity of, 70, 71, 72, 76; rules of, 12, 19, 61; scholarly indexes, 100; social costs of, 93; in Soviet Union, 21; as symbol of strength, 1; terminology in, 12, 27, 28, 31, 39, 41, 99; time in, 32; as a tool for nation-building, 59; training, 83, 84, 85, 86, 87, 88, 89, 90, 91, 92, 99; transformation of, 11; as a unifying force, 91; in United States, 4, 13, 17, 30, 31, 33, 48, 51, 63, 94; universal language of, 62, 70–73; value of, 62, 94; as a vehicle for modernization, 17; violence in, 12, 20–21, 32, 48, 85, 86, 91; as a vocation, 48; war, 91; water, 81–82; and women's, 7, 62, 64, 65, 66
sportscasting, 33
stadium, 79, 95, 96
Stadlaender, Sigge, 39–40
State of Israel, 2, 59, 92, 96, 97
Stelmach, Nahum, 59
sub-subentries, 19
swimming, 43, 81, 82

tabloid press, 30, 35
tachles, 28
Tel Aviv, 14, 16, 25, 26, 36, 44, 47, 50, 51, 52, 54, 56, 73, 79, 82, 83, 88, 95, 100
Tiberias, 82
track and field, 13, 38, 90
training, 15, 48, 49, 54, 83, 84, 85, 86, 87, 88, 89, 90, 91, 92, 99

Treaty of Versailles, 12
Tunney, Gene, 31, 32, 33
Turnen (gymnastics), 11, 12, 13–14, 15, 16, 17, 18, 21, 22, 23, 26, 27, 28, 39, 44, 45, 49, 50, 51, 58, 63, 71, 81, 82, 83, 84, 90, 94, 95, 100
Turner, Victor, 26

"useful sport" (sport shimushi), 9, 83, 85, 86, 87, 88, 89, 90
Uzenu, 33, 67

vegetarianism, 13
violence, 12, 20–21, 32, 48, 85, 86, 91

Wahnich, Sophie, 3
water sports, 81–82
Weisborg, Haim, 65
White, Hayden, 2, 6
Wingate Institute, 92
winning, 15, 16, 17, 45, 49, 74, 75, 93, 98
women: athletes, 7, 45, 57, 62, 64, 65, 66; body of, 20; grace and beauty of, 20; in Tel Aviv, 50
World Athletics Championships, 1
World Cup, 43, 61, 74, 75, 97
World Maccabi Association, 69, 81
World War I, 11, 12, 13, 14, 15, 16, 17, 21, 25, 41, 48, 61, 83, 91, 93, 94
World War II, 9, 55, 76, 88, 91
wrestling, 16, 54, 59, 90

Yekutieli, Yosef, 16, 19, 22, 36, 39, 45, 61, 62, 63, 64, 69, 71, 73, 87, 96
Yellin, Aviezer, 84
Yellin, David, 14
Yellin, Eliezer, 87
Yiddish, 7, 28, 30, 31, 38

Zikhron Ya'akov, 14
Zola, Émile, 72
Zweig, Stefan, 19

ABOUT THE AUTHOR

OFER IDELS is the Jenny Belzberg Fellow at the University of Calgary. He is the author of *Zionism: Emotions, Language and Experience*.